Study Guide

Macroeconomics: Principles and Policy

11ᵗʰ EDITION

BAUMOL

BLINDER

 SOUTH-WESTERN
CENGAGE Learning™

Australia • Brazil • Japan • Korea • Mexico • Singapore • Spain • United Kingdom • United States

SOUTH-WESTERN
CENGAGE Learning

Study Guide to accompany

Macroeconomics: Principles and Practice, 11e

William J. Baumol, Alan S. Blinder

VP/Editorial Director: Jack W. Calhoun

Editor-in-Chief: Alex von Rosenburg

Executive Editor: Mike Worls

Developmental Editor: Katie Yanos

Marketing Manager: John Carey

Marketing Communications Manager: Sarah Greber

Content Project Manager: Corey Geissler

Manager, Editorial Media: John Barans

Technology Project Editor: Deepak Kumar

Senior Buyer—Manufacturing: Sandee Milewski

Production Service: OffCenter Concept House

Compositor: OffCenter Concept House

Senior Art Director: Michelle Kunkler

Cover Design: Lisa Albonetti

Internal Design: Lisa Albonetti

Cover Images: © Getty Images; © First Light Associated Photographers, Inc.

Senior Permissions Rights Acquisitions Account Manager—Images: Deanna Ettinger

For product information and technology assistance, contact us at
Cengage Learning Academic Resource Center, 1-800-423-0563

For permission to use material from this text or product, submit all requests online at **cengage.com/permissions**
Further permissions questions can be emailed to
permissionrequest@cengage.com

ISBN-13: 978-0-324-58624-4
ISBN-10: 0-324-58624-8

South-Western Cengage Learning
5191 Natorp Boulevard
Mason, OH 45040
USA

Cengage Learning products are represented in Canada by Nelson Education, Ltd.

For your course and learning solutions, visit **academic.cengage.com**

Purchase any of our products at your local college store or at our preferred online store **www.ichapters.com**

Printed in the United States
2 3 4 5 6 7 12 11 10 09

Contents

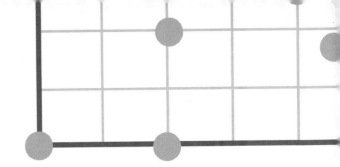

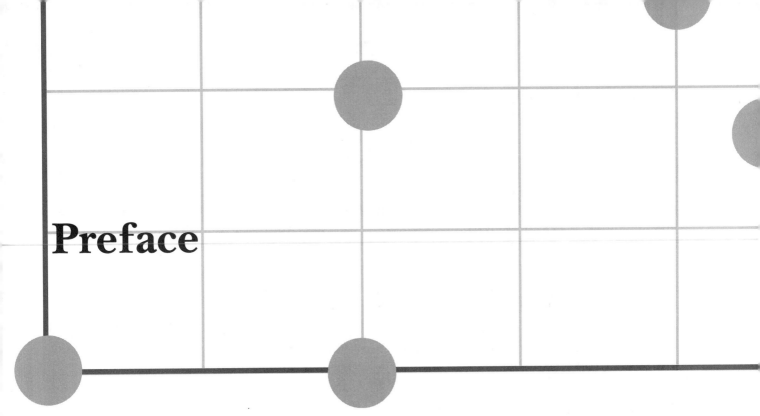

Preface

Introduction

This study guide is designed to be used with *Economics: Principles and Policy,* Eleventh Edition, by William J. Baumol and Alan S. Blinder. This guide is not a substitute for the basic textbook; rather, experience has shown that conscientious use of a supplement such as this guide can lead to greater learning and understanding of the course material. It might also improve your grade.

   The chapters in this book parallel those in *Economics: Principles and Policy,* Eleventh Edition. Each chapter in the study guide is a review of the material covered in the textbook chapters. You should first read and study each chapter in the textbook and then use the corresponding chapter in this book. "Use" is the correct verb, as chapters in this book are designed for your active participation.

   The material with which you will be working is organized into the following elements.

Learning Objectives

Each chapter starts with a set of behavioral learning objectives. These objectives indicate the things you should be able to do upon completing each chapter.

Important Terms and Concepts

As one of the learning objectives for each chapter states, you should be able to define, understand, and use correctly the terms and concepts that are listed in this section. They parallel the important terms and concepts listed at the end of the text chapter. Being able to define these terms is likely to be important for your grade. But to really understand what they mean, rather than to temporarily memorize their definition, is even better. The ultimate test of your understanding will be your ability to use correctly the terms and concepts in real life situations.

● Chapter Review

Each chapter review is a summary discussion of the major points for that chapter. The reviews are designed to be used actively. Frequently, you will need to supply the appropriate missing term or to choose between pairs of alternate words. Some of the missing terms are quite specific and can be found in the list of important terms and concepts. At other times, the answers are less clear-cut, as the following hypothetical example illustrates: "If people expect inflation at higher rates than before, nominal interest rates are likely to _____." Any of the following would be correct answers: increase, rise, go up. In cases like this, do not get concerned if the answer you choose is different from the one in the back of the book.

● Important Terms and Concepts Quiz

Each chapter contains a quiz to help you review important terms and concepts. Match each term with the most appropriate definition.

● Basic Exercises

Most chapters have one or more exercises that are designed for you to use as a check on your understanding of a basic principle discussed in the chapter. Many of the exercises use simple arithmetic or geometry. While getting the correct answers is one measure of understanding, do not mistake the arithmetic manipulations for the economic content of the problems. A hand calculator or spreadsheet program may make the arithmetic less burdensome.

● Self-Test for Understanding

Each chapter has a set of multiple choice and true-false questions for you to use as a further check on your understanding. It is important to know not only the correct answers but also why the other alternatives are wrong. Answers for the Self-Tests are in the back of this guide.

● Appendix

A number of chapters in the text contain an appendix, which generally is designed to supplement the chapter content with material that is either a bit more difficult or offers further exposition of a particular economic concept. In some cases, the review material for the appendix parallels that for the chapter, including learning objectives, important terms and concepts, and so forth. On other cases, the appendix material is reviewed here in the form of an additional exercise designed to illustrate the material discussed in the appendix.

● Supplementary Exercise

Many chapters end with a supplementary exercise, which may be either an additional mathematical exercise or some suggestions that allow you to use what you have learned in real-world situations. Some exercises use more advanced mathematics. Since many of these exercises review Basic Exercise material, they illustrate how economists use mathematics and are included for students with an appropriate background in mathematics. The mathematics are a means to an end and not an end in themselves. It is most important to understand the economic principles that underlie the Basic Exercise, something that does not depend upon advanced mathematics.

● Economics in Action

Most chapters include a brief example, often from recent newspapers or magazines. Each example has been chosen to show how economic concepts and ideas can help one understand real world problems and issues.

● Economics Online

Many chapters include one or more World Wide Web addresses that you can use to access current information or for additional information.

● Study Questions

Each chapter ends with a short list of study questions. Working with friends on these questions is a useful way to review chapter material and should help on examinations.

Being introduced to economics for the first time should be exciting and fun. For many, it is likely to be hard work, but hard work does not have to be dull and uninteresting. Do not look for a pat set of answers with universal applicability. Economics does not offer answers but rather a way of looking at the world and thinking systematically about issues. As the English economist John Maynard Keynes said:

> The theory of economics does not furnish a body of settled conclusions immediately applicable to policy. It is a method rather than a doctrine, an apparatus of the mind, a technique of thinking, which helps its possessor to draw correct conclusions.

Bertrand Russell, the distinguished British philosopher and mathematician, had considered studying economics but decided it was too easy. The Nobel prize-winning physicist, Max Planck, also considered studying economics but decided it was too hard. Whether, like Russell, you find economics easy or, like Planck, you find it hard, I trust that with the use of this guide you will find it relevant and exciting!

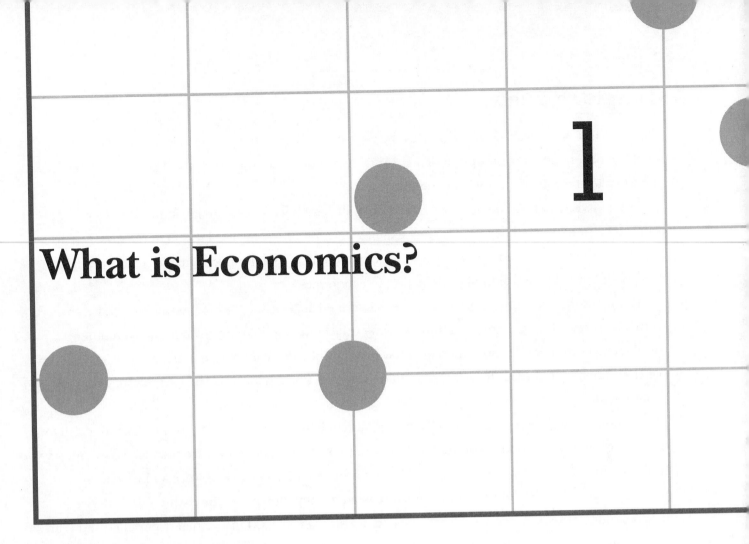

1

What is Economics?

Important Terms and Concepts

Opportunity cost   Theory   Economic model

Abstraction   Correlation

Learning Objectives

After completing this chapter, you should be able to:

- describe each of the ten Ideas for *Beyond the Final Exam.*

- explain the role of abstraction, or simplification, in economic theory.

- explain the role of theory as a guide to understanding real-world phenomena.

- explain why correlation need not imply causation.

- understand what is meant by an economic model.

- explain why imperfect information and value judgments will always mean that economics cannot provide definitive answers to all social problems.

● Chapter Review

Chapter 1 has two objectives: It introduces the types of problems that concern economists, offering a set of important ideas for Beyond the Final Exam, and it discusses the methods of economic analysis, in particular the role of theory in economics.

Problems discussed in the first part of the chapter have been chosen to illustrate basic economic issues to be remembered beyond the final exam. You should not only read this material now, but also reexamine the list at the end of the course. Understanding the economic principles that underlie these basic issues is the real final examination in economics.

The methods of economic inquiry are best described as "eclectic," meaning they are drawn from many sources according to their usefulness to the subject matter. Economists borrow from other social sciences to theorize about human behavior: They borrow from mathematics to express theories concisely and from statistics to make inferences from real-world data about hypotheses suggested by economic theory.

Economists are interested in understanding human behavior not only for its own sake, but also for the policy implications of this knowledge. How can we know what to expect from changes resulting from public policy or business decisions unless we understand how markets work and why people behave the way they do? Consider the ideas discussed in the first part of this chapter. Each derives from economic theory. As you will learn, each idea also offers insight into actual experience and is an important guide to evaluating future changes.

As in other scientific disciplines, theory in economics is an abstraction, or simplification, of innumerable complex relationships in the real world. When thinking about some aspects of behavior, for example, a family's spending decisions or why the price of oil fluctuates so much, economists will develop a model that attempts to explain the behavior under examination. Elements of the model derive from economic theory. Economists study the model to see what hypotheses, or predictions, it suggests. These can then be checked against real-world data. An economist's model will typically be built not with hammer and nails, but with pencil, paper, and computers. The appropriate degree of abstraction for an economic model is determined, to a large extent, by the problem at hand and is not something that can be specified in advance for all problems.

Economists believe they can make an important contribution to resolving many important social issues. It is hoped that by the time you finish this course, you will agree with this belief. At the same time, you should realize that economics offers a way of posing and looking at questions rather than a comprehensive set of predetermined answers to all questions. Economists will always have differences (1) of opinion on final policy recommendations because of incomplete _____ and different _____ judgments.

Important Terms and Concepts Quiz

Choose the best definition for each of the following terms.

1. _____ Opportunity cost

2. _____ Abstraction

3. _____ Theory

4. _____ Correlation

5. _____ Economic model

a. Ignoring many details to focus on essential parts of a problem

b. Two variables change simultaneously, whether or not a causal relationship exists

c. Effects on third parties that are not part of an economic transaction

d. Deliberate simplification of relationships to explain how those relationships work

e. Value of the next best alternative

f. Simplified version of some aspect of the economy

Basic Exercises

Each statement or vignette below illustrates one of the 10 important Ideas for Beyond the Final Exam. Which statement goes with which idea?

_____ 1. Opportunity cost is the correct measure of cost.

_____ 2. Attempts to fight market forces often backfire or have unintended consequences.

_____ 3. Nations can gain from trade by exploiting their comparative advantage.

_____ 4. Both parties gain in a voluntary exchange.

_____ 5. Good decisions typically require marginal analysis.

_____ 6. The adverse impact of externalities can often be repaired by market methods.

_____ 7. There is a trade-off between efficiency and equality. Many policies that promote one damage the other.

_____ 8. The government's tools to even out booms and busts are imperfect.

_____ 9. In the short run, policymakers face a trade-off between inflation and unemployment.

_____ 10. In the long run, productivity is almost the only thing that matters for a society's material well-being.

A. In June 2008, Northwest Airlines offered a last-minute roundtrip cybersaver fare between Los Angeles and New York City for $274. This fare required travelers to fly on Saturday and return the following Monday or Tuesday. At the same time, a regular unrestricted fare was more than $1,422, and the ten-day, advance purchase Saturday stay-over fare was around $315. Economists would argue that, properly counted, Northwest was more than covering costs on the $274 passengers.

B. "We trade because we can get more of the goods and services we value by devoting our energies to what we can do well and using the proceeds to purchase what others are good at making (or doing)." I.M. Destler, "Trade Policy at a Crossroads," *Brookings Review,* Winter 1999.

C. In New York, individuals who need a passport at the last minute have to pay a $35 fee for rush service and often spend most of a day waiting in line. Others pay up to $150 extra for someone else to stand in line for them. "If six hours of your time is worth more than $150, you're going to be prepared to use one of these services," said George Brokaw, a New York investment banker. "Speeding Up a Passport," *The New York Times,* June 6, 1999.

D. Commenting on the economy in July 1998, Alan Greenspan, Chairman of the Board of Governors of the Federal Reserve System, said, ". . . the extent to which strong growth and high labor force utilization have been joined with low inflation over an extended period is . . . exceptional . . . With labor markets very tight and domestic final demand retaining considerable momentum, the risks of a pickup in inflation remain significant . . . [T]he impending constraint from domestic labor markets could bind more abruptly than it has to date, intensifying inflation pressures." Testimony of Alan Greenspan, Chairman of the Federal Reserve Board of Governors Before the Committee on Banking, Housing, and Urban Affairs, U.S. Senate, July 21, 1998.

E. Third–graders Jennifer and Jolene trade sandwiches at lunch because each prefers what the other's mother fixed.

F. Robert Arnold and Robert Dennis argue that the impact of the growth in labor productivity since the beginning of this century has been astounding. Not only has output per worker increased more than sevenfold, but "the typical workday and typical workweek shrank . . . the share of family income required to meet the bare necessities was cut in half . . . and goods that were once considered luxuries came within reach of the middle class." "Perspectives on productivity growth," *Business Economics,* April 1, 1999.

G. A study of 16 American cities found that advertised rents for vacant units were higher in cities with rent control than cities without rent control. In cities without rent control, advertised rents are distributed almost evenly above and below median rents as measured by the U.S. Bureau of the Census. In cities with rent control, "most available units are priced well above the median. In other words, inhabitants in cities without rent control have a far easier time finding moderately priced rental units than do inhabitants in rent-controlled cities." William Tucker, "Rent control drives out affordable housing," *USA Today* (Magazine), July 1998.

H. "There is great comprehension today that ambitious redistribution policies will reduce either economic efficiency or economic growth, or both, because of undesired behavioral adjustment of work, savings, investment, and entrepreneurship." Assar Lindbeck, "How Can Economic Policy Strike a Balance Between Economic Efficiency and Income Equality," in *Income Inequality: Issues and Policy Options,* a symposium sponsored by the Federal Reserve Bank of Kansas City, August 27–28, 1998. Available online at http://www.kc.frb.org/publicat/sympos/1998/sym98prg.htm.

I. Under the EPA's Acid Rain Program, fossil fuel–fired power plants are allotted SO_2 emission allowances that allow them to emit one ton of SO_2. Utilities with surplus allowances may sell them to utilities whose emissions levels exceed their allowances.

J. "If we knew precisely where we were, understood precisely the relationship between our instruments and macroeconomic performance, had a single objective, and could instantly affect the variable or variables associated with our target(s), implementing [monetary] policy would be easy... It is precisely because none of these preconditions hold that monetary policy is so difficult and principles are needed to guide its implementation." Remarks by former Federal Reserve Governor Laurence H. Meyer. The Alan R. Holmes Lecture, Middlebury College, Middlebury, Vermont, March 16, 1998.

● Self-Tests for Understanding

Test A
Circle the most appropriate answer.

1. Economists define opportunity cost as
   a. the money price of goods and services.
   b. the lowest price you can bargain for.
   c. the value of the next best alternative.
   d. retail prices including sales taxes.

2. Most economists believe that attempts to set prices by decree
   a. will work best in the long run.
   b. are likely to create significant new problems.
   c. are the only way to establish fair prices.
   d. have a history of practical effectiveness.

3. With respect to international trade,
   a. a country can gain only if its neighbors lose.
   b. countries should try to be self-sufficient of all goods.
   c. only those countries with the highest productivity levels will gain.
   d. a country can gain by producing those goods in which it has a comparative advantage.

4. Most economists believe that exchange
   a. is likely to be mutually advantageous to both parties when it is voluntary.
   b. only takes place when one side can extract a profit from the other.
   c. usually makes both parties worse off.
   d. is best when strictly regulated by the government.

5. Marginal analysis is concerned with the study of
   a. buying stocks and bonds on credit.
   b. those groups that operate on the margins of the market economy.
   c. changes, such as the increase in cost when output increases.
   d. an engineer's fudge factor for possible errors.

6. When the actions of some economic agents impose cost on others, for example, the polluting smoke of a factory or power plant,
   a. market mechanisms may exist that can help remedy the situation.
   b. the only answer is government regulation.
   c. there is very little one can do; such is the price of progress.
   d. it is always best to close down the offending action.

7. Economic analysis suggests that
   a. policies that promote the highest rate of economic growth unambiguously improve the distribution of income.
   b. policies to increase equality may reduce output.
   c. incentives for work and savings have almost no impact on people's behavior.
   d. there is no trade-off between the size of the economic pie and how the pie is divided.

8. Monetary and fiscal policy
   a. can eliminate booms and busts if used appropriately.
   b. have no power to influence the economy.
   c. are too complicated to be of practical use.
   d. are powerful but imperfect tools to limit the swings of the business cycle.

9. Most economists believe that policies to reduce inflation
   a. have never been successful.
   b. will never be adopted in democracies.
   c. normally require a higher rate of unemployment.
   d. have an immediate and lasting impact.

10. Small differences in the productivity growth rate
    a. make little difference, even over periods as long as a century.
    b. can compound into significant differences.
    c. can be safely ignored by citizens and politicians.
    d. will lead only to small differences in the standard of living between countries.

Test B

Circle T or F for true or false.

T F   1. Economic models are no good unless they include all of the details that characterize the real world.

T F   2. Material in this text will reveal the true answer to many important social problems.

T F   3. Economic theory deliberately simplifies relationships to concentrate on their essential casual elements.

T F   4. Economists' policy prescriptions differ because of incomplete information and different value judgments.

T F   5. Theory and practical policy have nothing to do with each other.

T F   6. If two variables are correlated, we can be certain that one causes the other.

T F   7. The best economic models all use the same degree of abstraction.

T F   8. An economist tests a hypothesis when she deliberately simplifies the nature of relationships in order to explain cause and effect.

T F   9. The dollars one must pay is the best measure of the cost of any decision.

T F 10. We would all be better off if the government regulated more markets.

T F 11. The most productive economies would be better off if they did not trade with other nations and tried to produce everything they need by themselves.

T F 12. In any transaction, one party must always gain at the expense of the other.

T F 13. No business should ever sell its output at a price that does not cover its full cost.

T F 14. Because pollution problems are often seen as a market shortcoming, market methods cannot help correct the problem.

T F 15. There is no trade-off between policies that increase output and those that equalize income.

T F 16. The government has all the tools it needs to keep the economy out of recessions.

T F 17. Policies to lower unemployment usually reduce the rate of inflation at the same time.

T F 18. Over the long run, it makes little difference whether productivity grows at 1 percent or 2 percent per year.

| APPENDIX | *Using Graphs*

Important Terms and Concepts

Variable

Origin (of a graph)

Slope of a straight (or curved) line

Tangent to a curve

Y-intercept

Ray through the origin, or ray

45-degree line

Production indifference map

Learning Objectives

After completing this chapter, you should be able to:

- interpret various graphs.

- use a two-variable graph to determine what combinations of variables go together.

- compute the slope of a straight line and explain what it measures.

- explain how to compute the slope of a curved line.

- explain how a 45-degree line can divide a graph into two regions, one in which the Y variable exceeds the X variable, and another in which the X variable exceeds the Y variable.

- construct two-variable and three-variable graphs.

- use a three-variable graph to determine what combinations of the X and Y variables are consistent with the same value for the Z variable.

● Appendix Review

Economists like to draw pictures, primarily *graphs.* Your textbook and this study guide will make extensive use of graphs. There is nothing very difficult about graphs, but understanding them from the beginning will help you avoid mistakes later on.

All the graphs we will use start with two straight lines, one on the bottom and one on the left side. These edges of the graph will usually have labels to indicate what is being measured in both the vertical and horizontal directions. The line on the bottom is called the [horizontal/vertical] axis, and (1) the line running up the side is called the _____ axis. The point at which the two lines meet is called the _____. The variable measured along the horizontal axis is often called the X variable, whereas the term Y variable is often used to refer to the variable measured along the vertical axis.

Figure 1-1 is a two-variable diagram plotting expenditures on alcoholic beverages and ministers' salaries. Does this graph imply that wealthier clergymen drink more, or does it suggest that more drinking in general is increasing the demand for, and hence the salaries of, clergymen? Most likely neither interpretation is correct; just because you can plot two variables does not mean that one caused the other.

Many two-variable diagrams encountered in introductory economics use straight lines, primarily for simplicity. An important characteristic of a straight line is its *slope*, measured by comparing differences between two points. To calculate the slope of a straight line, divide the
(2) [horizontal/vertical] change by the corresponding _____ change as you move to the right along the line. The change between any two points can be used to compute the slope because the slope of a straight line is _____. If the straight line shows that both the horizontal and vertical variables increase together, then the line is said to have a [positive/negative] slope; that is, as we move to the right, the line slopes [up/down]. If one variable decreases as the other variable increases, the line is said to have a _____ slope. A line with a zero slope shows _____ change in the *Y* variable as the *X* variable changes.

Figure 1-1

Ministers' Salaries and Expenditures on Alcohol

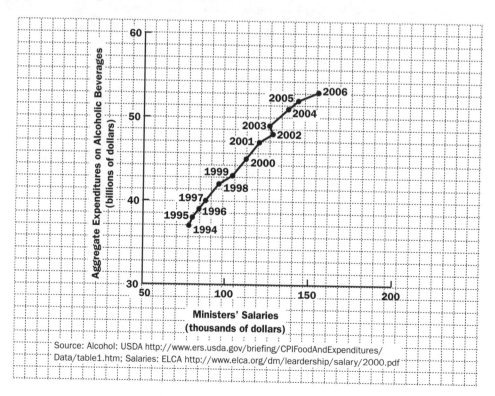

Source: Alcohol: USDA http://www.ers.usda.gov/briefing/CPIFoodAndExpenditures/
Data/table1.htm; Salaries: ELCA http://www.elca.org/dm/leardership/salary/2000.pdf

A special type of straight line passes through the origin of a graph. This is called a _____ (3) through the origin. Its slope is measured the same as the slope of any other straight line. A special type of ray is one that connects all points where the vertical and horizontal variables are equal. If the vertical and horizontal variables are measured in the same units, then this line has a slope of +1 and is called the _____ line.

Like straight lines, curved lines also have slopes, but the slope of a curved line is not constant. We measure the slope of a curved line at any point by the slope of the one straight line that just touches, or is _____ to, the line at that point. (4)

A special type of graph is used by economists as well as cartographers. Such a graph can represent three dimensions on a diagram with only two axes by the use of _____ lines. (5) A traditional application of such a graph in economics is a diagram that measures inputs along the horizontal and vertical axes and then uses contour lines to show what different combinations of inputs can be used to produce the same amount of output. This graph is called a _____ _____ map.

Important Terms and Concepts Quiz

Choose the best definition for each of the following terms.

1. _____ Variable
2. _____ Origin
3. _____ Slope
4. _____ Tangent to a curve
5. _____ *Y*-intercept
6. _____ Ray
7. _____ 45-degree line
8. _____ Production indifference map

a. Graph of how a variable changes over time

b. Straight line, touching a curve at a point without cutting the curve

c. Straight line emanating from the origin

d. Object whose magnitude is measured by a number

e. Straight line through the origin with a slope of +1

f. Point at which a straight line cuts the vertical axis

g. Ratio of vertical change to corresponding horizontal change

h. Point where both axes meet and where both variables are zero

i. A graph showing different combinations of two inputs necessary to produce a given level of output

• Basic Exercises

Reading Graphs

These exercises are designed to give you practice working with two-variable diagrams.

1. **Understanding a Demand Curve**

   The demand curve in **Figure 1-2** represents the demand for new Ph.D. economists.

   a. What quantity would colleges and universities demand if they have to pay a salary of $70,000? _____

   b. What does the graph indicate would happen to the quantity demanded if salaries fall to $50,000? The quantity demanded would [increase/decrease] to _____.

   c. If salaries were $60,000 the quantity demanded would be _____.

   d. What is the slope of the demand curve? _____

Figure 1-2

Demand Curve

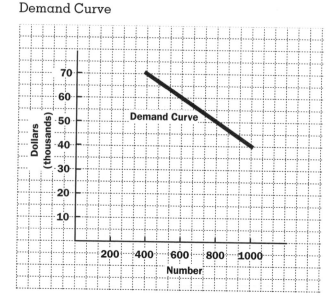

   e. Explain how the slope of the demand curve provides information about the change in the number of new Ph.D. economists demanded as salary changes.

2. **Understanding a 45-degree Line**

   Figure 1-3 shows data on grade point averages (GPA) for Valerie and her friends. Overall averages are measured along the horizontal axis while GPAs for courses in economics are measured along the vertical axis. Figure 1-3 also includes a 45-degree line.

   a. How many individuals have higher overall GPAs than economics GPAs? _____

   b. How many individuals do better in economics courses than in their other courses? _____

   c. If all of Valerie's friends had their best grades in economics courses, all of the points in Figure 1-3 would lie [above/below] the 45-degree line.

   d. If all of the points in Figure 1-3 were below the 45-degree line, we could conclude that Valerie and her friends did better in [economics/non-economics] courses.

Figure 1-3

45-Degree Line

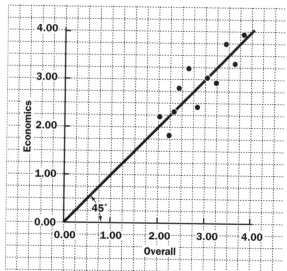

Self-Tests for Understanding

Test A

Circle the most appropriate answer.

1. The vertical line on the left side of a two-variable diagram is called the
   a. ray through the origin.
   b. vertical axis.
   c. X axis.
   d. slope of the graph.

2. A two-variable diagram
   a. can only be drawn when one variable causes another.
   b. is a useful way to show how two variables change simultaneously.
   c. is a useful way of summarizing the influence of all factors that affect the Y variable.
   d. can only be used when relationships between variables can be represented by straight lines.

3. The origin of a two-variable graph is
   a. found in the lower right corner of a graph.
   b. the same as the Y-intercept.
   c. the intersection of the vertical and horizontal axes where both variables are equal to zero.
   d. found by following the slope to the point where it equals zero.

4. The slope of a straight line is found by dividing the
   a. Y variable by the X variable.
   b. vertical axis by the horizontal axis.
   c. largest value of the Y variable by the smallest value of the X variable.
   d. vertical change by the corresponding horizontal change.

5. The slope of a straight line
   a. is the same at all points along the line.
   b. increases moving to the right.
   c. will be zero when the X variable equals zero.
   d. is always positive.

6. If a straight line has a positive slope, then we know that
   a. it runs uphill, moving to the right.
   b. the slope of the line will be greater than that of a 45-degree line.
   c. it must also have a positive Y-intercept.
   d. it will reach its maximum value when its slope is zero.

Figure 1-4

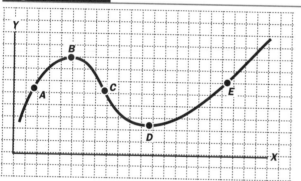

7. Referring to parts (a), (b), (c), and (d) of **Figure 1-4,** determine which line has a(n)

    a. positive slope _____

    b. negative slope _____

    c. zero slope _____

    d. infinite slope _____

Figure 1-5

8. Referring to **Figure 1-5,** determine at which point(s) the curved line has a(n)

    a. positive slope   _____   _____   _____

    b. negative slope   _____   _____   _____

    c. zero slope   _____   _____   _____

    d. infinite slope   _____   _____   _____

9. If when $X = 5$, $Y = 16$ and when $X = 8$, $Y = 10$, then the
    a. line connecting X and Y has a positive slope.
    b. line connecting X and Y is a ray through the origin.
    c. slope of the line connecting X and Y is +6.
    d. slope of the line connecting X and Y is –2.

10. The slope of a curved line is
    a. the same at all points on the line.
    b. found by dividing the *Y* variable by the *X* variable.
    c. found by determining the slope of a straight line tangent to the curved line at the point of interest.
    d. always positive.

11. If a curved line is in the shape of a hill, then the point of zero slope will occur at the
    a. origin of the line.
    b. highest point of the line.
    c. *Y*-intercept of the line.
    d. point where a ray from the origin intercepts the line.

12. The *Y*-intercept is
    a. the same as the origin of a graph.
    b. the point where a line cuts the *Y* axis.
    c. usually equal to the *X*-intercept.
    d. equal to the reciprocal of the slope of a straight line.

13. If the *Y*-intercept of a straight line is equal to zero, then this line is called
    a. the opportunity cost of a graph.
    b. a ray through the origin.
    c. the 45-degree line.
    d. the *X* axis.

14. A ray is
    a. any straight line with a slope of +1.
    b. any line, straight or curved, that passes through the origin of a graph.
    c. a straight line with a positive *Y*-intercept.
    d. a straight line that passes through the origin.

15. If the *X* and *Y* variables are measured in the same units, a 45-degree line will
    a. have a positive *Y*-intercept.
    b. have a negative slope.
    c. show all points where *X* and *Y* are equal.
    d. be steeper than the *Y* axis.

16. If *X* and *Y* are measured in the same units, and we consider a point that lies below a 45-degree line, then we know that for the *X* and *Y* combination associated with this point,
    a. the *X* variable is greater than the *Y* variable.
    b. a line from the origin through this point will be a ray with a slope greater than +1.
    c. the *Y* variable is greater than the *X* variable.
    d. the slope of the point is less than 1.

Figure 1-6

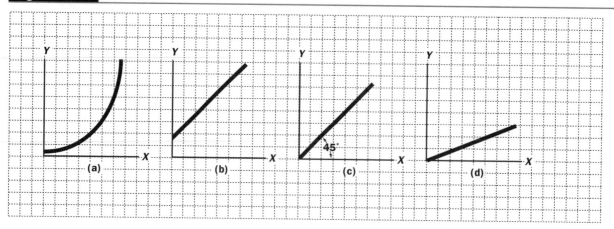

17. Referring to parts (a), (b), (c), and (d) of **Figure 1-6,** which part(s) show a ray through the origin?
    a. (b)
    b. (a) and (c)
    c. (a) and (d)
    d. (c) and (d)

18. If in part (d) of Figure 1-6, the Y variable changes by 2 units when the X variable changes by 5 units, then the slope of the line is
    a. (2/5) = .4.
    b. (5/2) = 2.5.
    c. (2 + 5) = 7.
    d. Insufficient information is available to compute.

19. If two straight lines have the same slope, then they
    a. must also have the same Y-intercept.
    b. will show the same change in Y for similar changes in X.
    c. will both pass through the origin.
    d. are said to be complements.

20. A contour map
    a. is always better than a two-variable diagram.
    b. is a way of collapsing three variables into a two-variable diagram.
    c. shows how the Y variable changes when the X variable is held constant.
    d. is only of relevance to cartographers.

Test B

Circle T or F for true or false.

T F   1. The line along the bottom of a two-variable graph is called the vertical axis.

T F   2. The slope of a line measures the value of the Y variable when the X variable is equal to zero.

T F   3. The slope of a straight line is the same at all points on the line.

T F   4. A negative slope means that the Y variable decreases when the X variable increases.

T F   5. The slope of a curved line cannot be measured.

T F   6. A straight line that has a *Y*-intercept of zero is also called a ray through the origin.

T F   7. All rays through the origin have the same slope.

T F   8. If *X* and *Y* are measured in the same units, then a 45-degree line is a ray through the origin with a slope of +1.

T F   9. If *X* and *Y* are measured in the same units, then any point above a 45-degree line is a point at which the *Y* variable is greater than the *X* variable.

T F   10. A contour map is a way to show the relationship between two variables in three dimensions.

Supplementary Exercise

The following suggested readings offer an excellent introduction to the ideas and lives of economists past and present:

1. *The Worldly Philosophers: The Lives, Times & Ideas of the Great Economic Thinkers,* 7th ed., by Robert L. Heilbroner (Touchstone Books, 1999).

2. *Lives of the Laureates,* 4th edition, edited by William Breit and Barry Hirsch (MIT Press, 2004). This is a collection of recollections by 18 winners of the Nobel Prize in Economics.

Economics in Action

Play Ball

Are baseball players overpaid? Does it make sense to pay someone more than $10 million to play what is, after all, just a game? Does it seem like baseball salaries have gotten out of hand? Even after adjusting for inflation, Babe Ruth's highest salary is estimated to have been slightly more than $700,000. Why are players today paid so much, and does it make economic sense?

Writing in *Scientific American,* Paul Wallich and Elizabeth Corcoran explain the difference in salaries using the concepts of opportunity cost and marginal analysis, ideas used extensively by economists. Under the reserve clause, in effect from 1903 until the mid-1970s, a baseball player who did not like his contract had little choice other than retiring from baseball. Players were not free to bargain with other teams. After the introduction of free agency, baseball players could sell their services to the team with the best offer.

Gerald Scully, in his book *The Business of Major League Baseball,* used statistical techniques to see how hitting and pitching help determine a team's winning percentage and how a team's revenue relates to its record and the size of the market in which it plays. He then estimated how adding a particular player might add to a team's performance and hence its revenue.

Using data from the late 1980s, Scully found that the performance of selected superstars increased team revenues by $2 million to $3 million, numbers consistent with the highest salaries at the time. Using data from the late 1960s, he estimates that superstars increased team revenues by $600,000 to $1 million and noted that the highest salaries were only $100,000 to $125,000.

1. How would marginal analysis help a team determine how much it should offer a free agent?

2. How does the concept of opportunity cost help explain baseball salaries? What was the opportunity cost of a baseball player's time under the reserve clause? How did free agency change the opportunity cost for a player deciding whether to stay with a team or move to a new team?

Sources: Paul Wallich and Elizabeth Corcoran, "The MBAs of Summer," *Scientific American* (June 1992): p. 120. Gerald W. Scully, *The Business of Major League Baseball* (Chicago: University of Chicago Press, 1989).

Study Questions

1. Explain the relationships among theories, models, and hypotheses.

2. Why are theories necessary for understanding the causal links between economic variables? Why can't the facts speak for themselves?

3. Many trace the establishment of economics as a formal field of study to the publication of Adam Smith's *Wealth of Nations* in 1776. Why, after more than 200 years, do so many questions remain?

Economics Online

Find out about the current and former Nobel Prize winners in Economics at this site maintained by the Nobel Prize committee. There are easy links to the Nobel Prize in Economics from this site:

http://nobelprize.org

The Minneapolis Federal Reserve Bank regularly publishes interviews with economists in its quarterly publication, *The Region*. The December 1994 interview is with Alan Blinder. You can read these interviews online at:

http://minneapolisfed.org/pubs/region/int.cfm

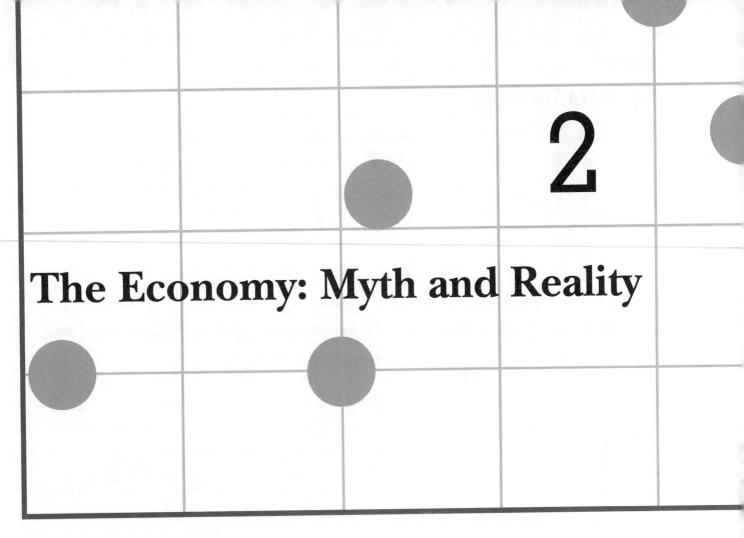

The Economy: Myth and Reality

Important Terms and Concepts

Factors of production, or Inputs	Gross domestic product (GDP)	Closed economy	Progressive tax
Outputs	Open economy	Recession	Mixed economy
		Transfer payments	

Learning Objectives

After completing this chapter, you should be able to:

- explain the difference between inputs and outputs.

- explain why total output of the American economy is larger than that of other nations.

- explain the difference between a closed and an open economy.

- describe the broad changes in American work experience: Who goes to work outside the home? What sorts of jobs do they hold? What sorts of goods and services do they produce?

- describe who gets what proportion of national income.

- describe the central role of business firms.

- describe the role of government in the American economy.

Chapter Review

This chapter offers an introduction to and overview of the American economy. The money value of total output of the American economy is usually measured by something called gross

(1) _____ _____ or _____ for short. American GDP is so large because of the size of the work force and the _____ of American workers. Other countries, for example China and India, have larger populations, but the productivity of their workers does not compare with that of American workers.

Why is the American economy so productive? It is useful to view an economic system as a social

(2) mechanism that organizes [inputs/outputs] to produce _____. Many believe that the productivity of the American economy is a reflection of business competition fostered by the extensive use of _____ markets and _____ enterprise.

No economy is self-sufficient. All economies trade with each other, although their reliance on trade varies. The average of exports and imports as a percentage of GDP is often used as a measure

(3) of the degree to which an economy can be called _____ or _____. Compared to other industrialized countries, the United States would look like a(n) [closed/open] economy. Both exports and imports have increased substantially since World War II and are now about 14 percent of American GDP.

The term *real GDP* is used to refer to measures of GDP that have been corrected for inflation. Although the time series graph of real GDP for the United States shows significant growth since World War II, it has not been continual growth. There have been periods when total output declined.

(4) These periods are called _____. How the government should respond during or in anticipation of a period of recession continues to spark controversy.

(5) Organizing inputs, also called _____ of production, is a central issue that any economy must address. For the most part, output in the United States is produced by private firms that compete in free markets. Most economists believe that having to meet the competition is an important reason why the American economy is so productive. Inputs include labor, capital (e.g., machinery and buildings), and natural resources. It is the revenue from selling output that creates income for these factors of production.

In the United States, the largest share of income accrues to which factor of production?

(6) _____. The income earned by those who put up the money to buy buildings and machinery comes in the form of interest and profits. Profits account for about _____ cents of each sales dollar. Most Americans work in [manufacturing/service] industries.

The discussion in the text lists five roles for government:

1) To enforce the rules of business and society, including property rights
2) To regulate business

3) To provide certain goods and services, e.g., national defense

4) To raise taxes to finance its operations

5) To redistribute income.

The size of government in the United States relative to GDP is [small/large] compared to most (7) other industrialized countries. This comparison and any others listed do not say whether particular actions are best done by the government or by the private economy. Are there legitimate unmet needs that should be addressed by government, or is government already too big? Much of the material in subsequent chapters is designed to help you understand what markets do well and what they do poorly. It is hoped that a better understanding of the insights from economic analysis will help you decide where you would draw the line between markets and government.

Important Terms and Concepts Quiz

Choose the best definition for each of the following terms.

1. _____ Factors of production or Inputs

2. _____ Outputs

3. _____ Gross domestic product (GDP)

4. _____ Open economy

5. _____ Closed economy

6. _____ Recession

7. _____ Transfer payments

8. _____ Progressive tax

9. _____ Mixed economy

a. Money value of final goods and services produced in a year

b. Economy with public influence over the workings of free markets

c. A sustained increase in the average level of prices

d. Money that individuals receive from the government as grants

e. Economy in which exports and imports are small relative to GDP

f. International trade is a large proportion of GDP

g. A period when real GDP declines

h. Labor, machinery, buildings, and natural resources used in production

i. Goods and services desired by consumers

j. The proportion of income paid as taxes increase as income increases

Basic Exercises

The More Things Change, the More They Are the Same—or Not?

Chapter 2 is a quick introduction to the structure of the American economy. These questions ask you to consider how some things may have changed since 1960.

1. What do Americans buy? Complete the missing columns in **Table 2-1** to see how consumption spending has changed. Do these changes surprise you? What do you think explains them? You can find more detail about consumption spending at http://www.bea.doc.gov/National/Index. htm.

Table 2-1

Composition of Consumption Spending

	1960 Spending ($ billions)	Proportion	2007 Spending ($ billions)	Proportion
Durables[a]	42.7	_____	1,078.4	_____
Non-Durables[b]	148.5	_____	2,833.2	_____
Services[c]	126.5	_____	5,822.8	_____
Total	317.7		9,734.2	

[a] e.g., automobiles, furniture

[b] e.g., food, clothing, gasoline

[c] e.g., housing, medical care, entertainment, education

2. How has the spending of the federal government changed? Complete the missing columns in **Table 2-2** to see. Do these changes surprise you? What do you think explains them?

Table 2-2

Composition of Federal Government Spending

	1960[a] Spending ($ billions)	Proportion	2007[a] Spending ($ billions)	Proportion
National Defense	48.1	_____	560.1	_____
Health	0.8	_____	641.7	_____
Pensions and Income Security	19.0	_____	953.5	_____
Interest	6.9	_____	237.9	_____
All Other	17.4	_____	575.2	_____
Total	92.2		2,968.4	

[a] Fiscal Year

3. Who is going to work outside the home now? The labor force participation rate is an important measure of labor markets. It is computed by looking at the number of people working or looking for work as a proportion of total population. This measure excludes those who are retired and those who are not looking for paid work. **Figure 2-1** shows labor force participation by men and women of various ages in 1950. Complete the missing column in **Table 2-3** to compute labor force participation rates for 2007 and then plot your results in Figure 2-1 to see how labor force participation has changed since 1950. Are you surprised by the differences for men and women? Do the changes over time surprise you? What do you think explains these differences?

Figure 2-1

Labor Force Participation Rate: 1950 and 2007

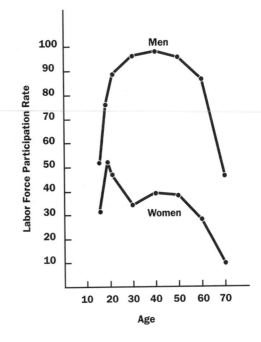

Table 2-3

Labor Force Participation: 2007

Age	Men Labor Force[a] (Numbers in thousands)	Population (Numbers in thousands)	Rate[b] Participation	Women Labor Force[a] (Numbers in thousands)	Population (Numbers in thousands)	Participation Rate[b]
16–17	1,354	4,658	_____	1,417	4,564	_____
18–19	2,187	3,960	_____	2,055	3,800	_____
20–24	8,095	10,291	_____	7,110	10,137	_____
25–34	18,308	19,858	_____	14,822	19,893	_____
35–44	19,299	20,910	_____	16,277	21,491	_____
45–54	18,801	21,313	_____	16,896	22,231	_____
55–64	10,904	15,658	_____	9,846	16,876	_____
65 & over	3,188	15,525	_____	2,615	20,703	_____

[a]Labor Force = people working plus those looking for work

[b]Labor Force Participation Rate = Labor Force/Population

Source: Bureau of Labor Statistics, *Employment and Earnings*, January 2008, http://www.bls.gov/data

Self-Tests for Understanding

Test A

Circle the most appropriate answer.

1. Which of the following helps to explain why the output of the American economy is as high as it is? (There may be more than one correct answer to this question.)
   a. The size of the labor force
   b. The amount of money provided by the government
   c. Business regulation
   d. The productivity of American workers

2. Total output of the U.S. economy
   a. is slightly less than that of Japan.
   b. is comparable to that of other industrialized countries.
   c. exceeds that of other national economies.
   d. is among the lowest for industrialized countries.

3. Many economists believe that the success of the American economy reflects, in part, our reliance on (There may be more than one correct answer.)
   a. regulation.
   b. private enterprise.
   c. free markets.
   d. nationalization.

4. Gross domestic product measures
   a. consumer spending.
   b. the vulgarity of many consumer goods.
   c. unpaid economic activity that takes place inside households.
   d. the money value of all the goods and services produced in an economy in a year.

5. American reliance on foreign trade—exports and imports—is _____ most other industrialized countries.
   a. less than
   b. about the same as
   c. greater than

6. Since 1950, the proportion of women employed in the market place has
   a. declined.
   b. shown little change.
   c. more than doubled.

7. Since the mid-1970s, the proportion of the labor force accounted for by teenagers has
   a. declined.
   b. stayed about the same.
   c. increased.

8. Compared to high school graduates, college graduates earn about
   a. the same.
   b. 25 percent more.
   c. 50 percent more.
   d. 75 to 80 percent more.

9. The term *recession* refers to
   a. a period of inflation.
   b. a period of above-average economic growth.
   c. reductions in government spending designed to reduce the deficit.
   d. a period when real GDP declines.

10. When referring to inputs, the term *capital* refers to
    a. money business firms need to borrow.
    b. the importance of a firm's head office.
    c. machines and buildings used to produce output.
    d. all of a firm's factors of production.

11. Which of the following would not be classified as an input?
    a. A farmer's time to grow wheat
    b. The farmer's tractor
    c. The farmer's land
    d. The bread that is made from the wheat

12. The majority of American workers work for
    a. manufacturing companies.
    b. the federal government.
    c. state and local governments.
    d. firms that produce a variety of services, including retail and wholesale trade.

13. When businesses pay for factors of production, which of the following gets the largest share of income?
    a. Profits
    b. Labor
    c. Interest
    d. The government (taxes)

14. In the United States there are about
    a. 250,000 business firms or one for every 1,200 people.
    b. 1.5 million business firms or one for every 200 people.
    c. 5 million business firms or one for every 60 people.
    d. 25 million business firms or one for every 12 people.

15. When Americans buy goods produced abroad, _____ increase.
    a. exports
    b. taxes
    c. transfer payments
    d. imports

16. When Americans are able to sell goods to foreigners, this adds to
    a. exports.
    b. taxes.
    c. transfer payments.
    d. imports.

17. Consumer spending accounts for _____ of American GDP.
    a. about 33 percent
    b. about 50 percent
    c. about 70 percent
    d. about 90 percent

18. The largest share of federal government spending is for
    a. national defense.
    b. interest.
    c. health.
    d. pensions and social security.

19. For the most part, the United States has chosen to let markets determine distribution of before-tax incomes, and then use taxes and _____ to reduce income inequalities.
    a. tariffs
    b. inflation
    c. transfer payments
    d. government production

20. Compared to other industrialized countries, taxes as a percent of GDP in the United States are
    a. among the lowest.
    b. about the same as most other industrialized countries.
    c. among the highest.

Test B

Circle T or F for true or false.

T F   1. An economic system is a social mechanism that organizes inputs to produce outputs.

T F   2. Since World War II, American real GDP has increased every year without interruption.

T F   3. The American economy is a more open economy than other industrialized economies.

T F   4. The American economy relies on free markets and private enterprise to a greater extent than most other industrialized economies.

T F   5. During a recession, unemployment usually increases.

T F   6. Government production accounts for more than one-half of American GDP.

T F   7. Interest on the national debt is now the largest category of federal government spending.

T F   8. Women hold more than one-half of the jobs outside the home.

T F   9. Most American workers still produce goods rather than services.

T F 10. Labor gets most of the income generated in the United States.

● Economics in Action

The Proper Role for Government

How far should the government go when regulating business? If the government is to provide some goods and services, what principles determine which goods and services? How far should the government go in redistributing income?

Noted economist Milton Friedman consistently argued for a limited role for government. In a widely publicized Public Broadcasting Service series, Friedman and his wife Rose advocated four principles as tests of the appropriate business of government. National defense, domestic police and justice, the provision of goods and services in the limited cases where markets do not work well, and protection for citizens who cannot protect themselves (e.g., children) define the Friedmans' four principles. These principles, especially the third, could be seen as justifying a wide range of government action. The Friedmans are as concerned with government failures as with market failures. They note that once started, government initiatives are rarely stopped. In their view, the burden of proof should be on the proponents of government action.

The Friedmans argued that government should be organized to maximize individual "freedom to choose as individuals, as families, as members of voluntary groups." They endorsed the view of Adam Smith that as long as individuals do not violate the laws of justice, they should be free to pursue their own interests and that competitive markets rather than government regulation are usually the most effective forms of social organization. "We can shape our institutions. Physical and human characteristics limit the alternatives available to us. But none prevents us, if we will, from building a society that relies primarily on voluntary cooperation to organize both economic and other activity, a society that preserves and expands human freedom, that keeps government in its place, keeping it our servant and not letting it become our master."[1]

The equally renowned John Kenneth Galbraith, on the other hand, argued that increasing affluence led to an imbalance between private and public goods. Goods and services that are marketable to individuals allow private producers to accumulate the financial resources that give them control of labor, capital, and raw materials. Sophisticated advertising creates and sustains demand for private goods, generating more income and profits. This affluence of the private sector is in marked contrast to the poverty of the public sector. Galbraith argues that society needs a balance between private and public goods but that the pernicious effects of advertising that creates the demand that sustains the production of private goods gives rise to a serious imbalance. One result is an increasing demand for private goods and services to protect individuals from the poverty of public goods and services, such as elaborate alarm systems and private guards to counteract the lack of police.

How much increase in public spending is necessary to redress the balance? Galbraith will only say that the distance is considerable. "When we arrive, the opulence of our private consumption will no longer be in contrast with the poverty of our schools, the unloveliness and congestion of our cities, our inability to get to work without a struggle, and the social disorder that is associated with imbalance . . . the precise point of balance will never be defined. This will be of comfort only to those who believe that any failure of definition can be made to score decisively against the larger idea."[2]

1. How would you define the proper role of government? Where would you draw the line between those activities best left to individual initiative and markets and those that are the appropriate business of government?

Study Questions

1. What is the difference between inputs and outputs? Is steel an input or an output? What about the steel used to build factories compared to the steel used in home appliances?

---

[1]Milton and Rose Friedman, *Free to Choose: A Personal Statement*, Harcourt Brace Jovanovich, 1980.
[2]John Kenneth Galbraith, *The Affluent Society*, Houghton Mifflin, 1958.

2. How can output of the American economy be greater than that of countries like China and India with larger populations?

3. What does the historical record show regarding the growth in real GDP and real GDP per capita in the United States?

4. What is meant by a closed or an open economy? How would you characterize the United States?

5. In the United States, who works outside the home for wages and salary and what types of jobs do they hold?

6. How is income in the United States distributed among factors of production?

7. How does the role of government in the American economy compare with that of other industrialized countries?

8. What is meant by the term "mixed economy"?

● Economics Online

The *Statistical Abstract of the United States* is a good place to begin a statistical profile of the United States.

    http://www.census.gov/compendia/statab/.

It is often useful to compare the United States to other countries. Information about the major industrialized countries can be found from the homepage for the Organization for Economic Cooperation and Development (OECD).

    http://www.oecd.org

The *CIA World Factbook* is a useful summary of information about many countries. It is available online.

    http://www.odci.gov/cia/publications/factbook

The Fundamental Economic Problem: Scarcity and Choice

3

Important Terms and Concepts

Resources	Outputs	Principle of increasing costs	Division of labor
Opportunity cost	Inputs		Comparative advantage
Optimal decision	Production possibilities frontier	Efficiency	Market system
		Allocation of resources	

Learning Objectives

After completing this chapter, you should be able to:

- After completing this chapter, you should be able to:

- explain why the true cost of any decision is its opportunity cost.

- explain the link between market prices and opportunity costs.

- explain why the scarcity of goods and services (outputs) must be attributed to a scarcity of resources (inputs) used in production processes.

- draw a production possibilities frontier for a firm or for the economy.

- explain how the production possibilities frontier contains information about the opportunity cost of changing output combinations.

- explain why specialized resources mean that a firm's or an economy's production possibilities frontier is likely to bow outward.

- explain how the shape of the production possibilities frontier illustrates the principle of increasing costs.

- explain why production efficiency requires that an economy produce on, rather than inside, its production possibilities frontier.

- describe the three coordination tasks that every economy must confront.

- explain why specialization and division of labor are likely to require the use of markets.

- describe how the allocation of tasks by the principle of comparative advantage increases the total output of all parties.

- explain how both parties gain from voluntary exchange even if no new goods are produced.

- describe how a market economy solves the three coordination tasks.

● Chapter Review

"You can't always get what you want"—Mick Jagger

Even rock stars whose income and wealth are beyond comprehension understand that scarcity and the resulting necessity to make choices are fundamental concerns of economics.[1] This chapter is an introduction to these issues.

The importance of *choice* starts with the fact that virtually all resources are _____.

(1) Most people's desires exceed their incomes, and, thus, everyone makes buying choices all the time. Similarly, firms, educational institutions, and government agencies make choices between what kinds of outputs to produce and what combination of inputs to use.

What is a good way to make choices? The obvious answer is to consider the alternatives. Economists

(2) call these forgone alternatives the _____ _____ of a decision. Imagine it is the night before the first midterm in Introductory Economics, which will cover Chapters 1–6, and here you are only on Chapter 3. A friend suggests a night at the movies and even offers to buy your ticket so "it won't cost you anything." Do you agree? What will you be giving up?

At first, the idea of choices for the economy may sound strange. It may be easiest to imagine such choices being made by bureaucrats in a centrally planned economy. Even though there is no central planning bureau for the U.S. economy, it is useful to think of opportunities available to the American economy. The opportunities selected result from the combined spending and production decisions of all citizens, firms, and governmental units, decisions coordinated by our reliance on markets.

The *production possibilities frontier* is a useful diagram for representing the choices available to a firm or an economy. The frontier will tend to slope downward to the right because resources are

(3) [scarce/specialized]. The frontier will tend to bow out because most resources are _____. Opportunity cost is the best measure of the true cost of any decision. For a single firm or an economy as a whole, with choices represented by a production possibilities frontier, the opportunity cost of changing the composition of output can be measured by the _____ of the production possibilities frontier.

As an economy produces more and more of one good, say automobiles, the opportunity cost

(4) of further increases is likely to [increase/decrease]. This change in opportunity cost illustrates the principle of _____ cost and is a result of the fact that most resources are [scarce/specialized].

For given amounts of all but one good, the production possibilities frontier for an economy measures the maximum amount of the remaining good that can be produced. Thus, the production possibilities frontier defines maximum outputs or efficient production. Note that all points on the production possibilities frontier represent efficiency in production. There is, of course, no guarantee

---

[1]Before he was a rock star, Mick Jagger studied economics at the London School of Economics.

that the economy will operate on its frontier. If there is unemployment, then the economy is operating [on/inside] the frontier. If a firm or economy operates inside its production possibilities frontier, it is said to be _____; that is, with the same resources the firm or the economy could have produced more of some commodities. Assigning inputs to the wrong or inappropriate tasks because market prices are sending the wrong signals or discrimination that limits opportunities for individuals will also result in production inefficiency. Assigning tasks according to the principle of comparative advantage helps to achieve economic efficiency. (5)

All economies must answer three questions:

1. How can we use resources efficiently to operate on the production possibilities frontier?

2. What combinations of output shall we produce: that is, where on the frontier shall we produce?

3. To whom shall we distribute what is produced?

The American economy answers these questions through the use of markets and prices. If markets are functioning well, then money prices [will/will not] be a reliable guide to opportunity costs. Problems arise when markets do not function well and when items do not have explicit price tags. (6)

Important Terms and Concepts Quiz
Choose the best definition for each of the following terms.

1. _____ Resources
2. _____ Opportunity cost
3. _____ Optimal decision
4. _____ Outputs
5. _____ Inputs
6. _____ Production possibilities frontier
7. _____ Principle of increasing costs
8. _____ Efficiency
9. _____ Allocation of resources
10. _____ Division of labor
11. _____ Comparative advantage
12. _____ Market system

a. Resources used to produce goods and services

b. System in which allocation decisions are made in accordance with centralized direction

c. Breaking tasks into smaller jobs

d. Ability to produce goods less inefficiently than other producers

e. Decision on how to divide scarce resources among different uses

f. Instruments used to create the goods and services people desire

g. Graph of combinations of goods that can be produced with available inputs and existing technology

h. Goods and services that firms produce

i. System in which decisions on resource allocation come from independent decisions of consumers and producers

j. Absence of waste

k. Forgone value of the next best alternative

l. Tendency for the opportunity cost of an additional unit of output to rise as production increases

m. A decision that best serves the decision maker's objectives

Basic Exercises

Figure 3-1 shows the production possibilities frontier (PPF) for the economy of Adirondack, which produces bread and computers.

Figure 3-1

Production Possibilities Frontier

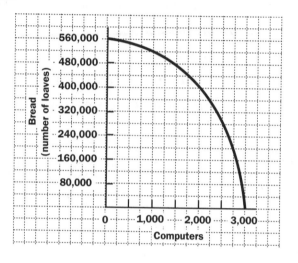

1. If all resources are devoted to the production of bread, Adirondack can produce _____ loaves of bread. In order to produce 1,000 computers, the opportunity cost in terms of bread is _____ loaves. To produce another 1,000 computers, the opportunity cost [rises/falls] to _____ loaves. As long as the PPF continues to curve downward, the opportunity costs of increased computer output will [continue to rise/start to fall]. These changes are the result, not of scarce resources per se, but of _____ resources. (You might try drawing a PPF on the assumption that all resources are equally productive in the production of both outputs. Can you convince yourself that it should be a straight line?)

2. Find the output combination of 2,500 computers and 320,000 loaves on **Figure 3-1.** Label this point A. Is it an attainable combination for Adirondack? Label the output combination 1,500 computers and 400,000 loaves as point B. Is this combination attainable? Finally, label the output combination 1,000 computers and 520,000 loaves as point C. Is this combination attainable? We can conclude that the attainable output combinations for Adirondack are [on/inside/outside] the production possibilities frontier. Among the obtainable output combinations, efficient points of production are located [on/inside/outside] the production possibilities frontier.

3. An output combination is inefficient if it is possible to produce more of one or both goods. Which, if any, of the output combinations identified in question 2 is an inefficient

combination? _____ Show that this point is inefficient by shading in all attainable points indicating more of one or both goods.

4. Consider point C in question 2, 1,000 computers and 520,000 loaves of bread, and point D, 2,000 computers and 400,000 loaves of bread. Which point is best for Adirondack and why?

● Self-Tests for Understanding

Test A
Circle the most appropriate answer.
1. Economists define opportunity cost as the
   a. dollar price of goods and services.
   b. hidden cost imposed by inflation.
   c. value of the next best alternative use that is not chosen.
   d. time spent shopping.

2. The position of an economy's production possibilities frontier is determined by all but which one of the following?
   a. the size of the labor force
   b. labor skills and training
   c. the amount of consumption goods the economy can produce
   d. current technology

3. A firm's production possibilities frontier shows
   a. the best combination of output for a firm to produce.
   b. its plans for increasing production over time.
   c. the architectural drawings of its most productive plant.
   d. the different combinations of goods it can produce with available resources and technology.

4. An efficient economy utilizes all available resources and produces the _____ output its technology permits.
   a. minimum amount of
   b. best combination of
   c. one combination of
   d. maximum amount of

5. The fact that resources are scarce implies that the production possibilities frontier will
   a. have a negative slope.
   b. be a straight line.
   c. shift out over time.
   d. bow out from the origin.

6. Which of the following statements implies that production possibilities frontiers are likely to be curved rather than straight lines?
   a. Ultimately all resources are scarce.
   b. Most resources are more productive in certain uses than in others.
   c. Unemployment is a more serious problem for some social groups than for others.
   d. Economists are notoriously poor at drawing straight lines.

7. The set of attainable points for a firm that produces two goods is given by
   a. all points on the production possibilities frontier.
   b. all points inside the production possibilities frontier.
   c. all points on or inside the production possibilities frontier.
   d. none of the above.

8. If an economy is operating efficiently, it will be producing
   a. inside its production possibilities frontier.
   b. on its production possibilities frontier.
   c. outside its production possibilities frontier.
   d. the maximum amount of necessities and the minimum amount of luxuries.

9. The principle of increasing cost is consistent with a _____ production possibilities frontier.
   a. straight-line
   b. bowed-in
   c. shifting
   d. bowed-out

10. The inability of the economy to produce as much as everyone would like is ultimately a reflection of
    a. a lack of money in the economy.
    b. congressional gridlock.
    c. the inability of a market economy to perform the necessary coordination tasks.
    d. a limited amount of productive resources.

11. When, in Figure 3-1, the production of bread is increased from 280,000 loaves to 400,000 loaves, the opportunity cost in terms of reduced output of computers is
    a. 0.
    b. 500.
    c. 2,000.
    d. 2,500.

12. When the output of bread increases by another 120,000 loaves to 520,000, the opportunity cost in terms of reduced output of computers is
    a. 0.
    b. 500.
    c. 1,000.
    d. 2,000.

13. Comparing answers to questions 11 and 12, we can conclude that the production possibilities frontier for Adirondack
    a. is a straight line.
    b. shows a decline in the opportunity cost of more bread.
    c. illustrates the principle of increasing cost.
    d. has a positive slope.

14. Consider a production possibilities frontier showing alternative combinations of corn and computers that can be produced in Cimonoce, a small island in the South Pacific. The opportunity cost of more computers can be measured by the
    a. slope of the production possibilities frontier.
    b. X-intercept of the production possibilities frontier.
    c. Y-intercept of the production possibilities frontier.
    d. area under the production possibilities frontier.

15. Which of the following implies a shift in the production possiblities frontier for a shoe firm?
    a. raising prices by 10 percent
    b. borrowing money to hire more workers and buying more machines
    c. changing the composition output toward more women's shoes and fewer men's shoes
    d. expanding the advertising budget

16. Which of the following would not shift an economy's production possibilities frontier?
    a. a doubling of the labor force
    b. a doubling of the number of machines
    c. a doubling of the money supply
    d. more advanced technology

17. An optimal decision is one that
    a. will win a majority if put to a vote.
    b. is supported unanimously.
    c. best serves the objectives of the decision maker.
    d. is supported by *The New York Times.*

18. If exchange is voluntary,
    a. there can be mutual gain even if no new goods are produced.
    b. one party will always get the better of the other.
    c. there can be mutual gain only if new goods are produced as a result of the trade.
    d. there can be mutual gain only if the government regulates retail trade.

19. All but which one of the following are examples of waste and inefficiency?
    a. Employment discrimination against women and people of color
    b. Operating on an economy's production possibilities frontier
    c. High levels of unemployment
    d. Quotas that limit the educational opportunities of particular ethnic groups

20. The three coordination tasks that all economies must perform can
    a. only be done by a central planning bureau.
    b. only be done by markets.
    c. only be done inefficiently.
    d. be done by planning bureaus or markets.

Test B

Circle T or F for true or false.

T F 1. There can never be any real scarcity of manufactured goods because we can always produce more.

T F 2. Market prices are always the best measure of opportunity cost.

T F 3. The principle of increasing costs is a reflection of the fact that most productive resources tend to be best at producing a limited number of things.

T F 4. Markets are incapable of solving the three coordination tasks that all economies must address.

T F 5. Because they have the power to tax, governments do not need to make choices.

T F 6. The existence of specialized resources means that a firm's production possibilities frontier will be a straight line.

T F 7. The existence of widespread unemployment means that an economy is operating inside its production possibilities frontier.

T F 8. An economy using its resources efficiently is operating on its production possibilities frontier.

T F 9. Because they are nonprofit organizations, colleges and universities do not have to make choices.

T F 10. A sudden increase in the number of dollar bills will shift the economy's production possibilities frontier.

Supplementary Exercises

1. The Cost of College

Those of you paying your way through college may not need to be reminded that the opportunity cost of lost wages is an important part of the cost of education. You can estimate the cost of your education as follows: Estimate what you could earn if instead of attending classes and studying, you used those hours to work. Add in the direct outlays on tuition, books, and any differential living expenses incurred because you go to school. (Why only differential and not your total living expenses?)

2. Production Possibilities Frontier

Consider an economy with a production possibilities frontier between cars (C) and tanks (T) given by

$$C = 6L^5K^5 - 0.3T^2$$

where L is the size of the labor force (50,000 people) and K is the number of machines, also 50,000.

a. What is the maximum number of cars that can be produced? Call this number of cars C^*. The maximum number of tanks? Call this number of tanks T^*.
b. Draw the PPF graph for this economy.
c. Is this frontier consistent with the principle of increasing costs?
d. Is the output combination $(1/2C^*, 1/2T^*)$ attainable? Is the output combination $(1/2C^*, 1/2T^*)$ efficient? Why or why not?
e. What is the opportunity cost of more tanks when 10 tanks are produced? 50 tanks? 200 tanks?
f. Find a mathematical expression for the opportunity cost of tanks in terms of cars. Is this mathematical expression consistent with the principle of increasing cost?

Economics in Action

Free Theater?

In the summer of 2001, New York City's Public Theater presented Chekhov's *Seagull* at the Delacorte Theater in Central Park. The director was Mike Nichols, and the production starred Meryl Streep, Kevin Kline, and Marcia Gay Harden. The tickets were free, or were they?

Tickets were given away each day at 1 p.m. on a first-come, first-served basis. As Joyce Purnick reported, arriving at 6 a.m. and waiting seven hours would not necessarily get you a ticket. The day she reported on, the first person in line arrived at 12:30 a.m., more than twleve hours before the tickets were distributed. Ms. Purnick concluded that "[t]he scene . . . strongly suggested that free tickets were for the retired, the unemployed, and the vacationing only."

If you were not up for spending the night in Central Park, you could call Peter London. Mr. London would hire students and underemployed actors to stand in line for you. He charged up to $200 for this service.

When there were objections, Mr. London responded that he was not doing anything illegal. "Only unemployed people should see this? I don't see this as being fair," he said.

Were the tickets free? How do you value your time? Would you pay $200 for someone to stand in line for you? Would you be willing to stand in line for someone else for $200? Who was likely to use Mr. London's service: those who felt the opportunity cost of their time was high or low? Who was likely to be interested in working for Mr. London? What is fair?

Source: Joyce Purnick, "Free Theater, but the Lines Unspeakable," *The New York Times*, July 30, 2001.

● Study Questions

1. How do markets help an economy address the three coordination tasks of deciding "how," "what," and "to whom"?

2. What do economists mean by opportunity cost and why do they say it is the true measure of the cost of any decision?

3. Explain when market prices are likely to be a good measure of opportunity cost and when they are not.

4. What are the factors that determine the location of a country's production possibilities frontier?

5. What is the difference between resources being scarce and resources being specialized? What are the implications of scarcity and specialization for the production possibilities frontier?

6. How do specialization and the division of labor enhance economic efficiency? Why do they require a system of exchange?

7. What is the difference between attainable points of production and efficient points of production? (It may be easiest to illustrate your answer using a diagram of a production possibilities frontier. Be sure that you can define and identify those points that are attainable and those points that are efficient.)

8. What is meant by the principle of comparative advantage? What does it imply for individuals and economies?

Supply and Demand: An Initial Look

4

Important Terms and Concepts

Invisible hand	Shift in a demand curve	Supply-demand diagram	Law of supply and demand
Quantity demanded	Quantity supplied	Shortage	
Demand schedule	Supply schedule	Surplus	Price ceiling
Demand curve	Supply curve	Equilibrium	Price floor

Learning Objectives

After completing this chapter, you should be able to:

- explain why the quantity demanded and the quantity supplied are not fixed numbers but rather depend upon a number of factors including price.

- draw a demand curve, given appropriate information from a demand schedule of possible prices and the associated quantity demanded.

- draw a supply curve, given appropriate information from a supply schedule of possible prices and the associated quantity supplied.

- explain why demand curves usually slope downward and supply curves usually slope upward.

- determine the equilibrium price and quantity, given a demand curve and a supply curve.

- explain what forces tend to move market prices and quantities toward their equilibrium values.

- list major factors that will affect the quantity demanded by shifting the demand curve.

- list major factors that will affect the quantity supplied by shifting the supply curve.

- distinguish between a shift in and a movement along either the demand or supply curve.

- analyze the impact on prices and quantities of shifts in the demand curve, supply curve, or both.

- explain why sellers are unlikely to be able to pass on the full increase in excise or sales taxes.

- distinguish between price ceilings and price floors.

- explain the likely consequences of government interference with market-determined prices.

Chapter Review

Along with scarcity and the need for choice, demand and supply analysis is a fundamental idea that pervades all of economics. After studying this chapter, look back at the Ideas for Beyond the Final Exam in Chapter 1 and see how many concern the "law" of supply and demand.

Economists use a demand curve as a summary of the factors influencing people's demand for different commodities. A demand curve shows how, during a specified period, the quantity
(1) demanded of some good changes as the _____ of that good changes, holding all other determinants of demand constant. A demand curve usually has a (negative/positive) slope, indicating that as the price of a good declines, people will demand (more/less) of it. A particular quantity demanded is represented by a point on the demand curve. The change in the quantity demanded as price changes is a (shift in/movement along) the demand curve. Quantity demanded is also influenced by other factors, such as consumer incomes and tastes, population, and the prices of related goods. Changes in any of these factors will result in a (shift in/movement along) the demand curve.

Economists use a supply curve to summarize the factors influencing producers' decisions. Like
(2) the demand curve, the supply curve is a relationship between quantity and _____. Supply curves usually have a (negative/positive) slope, indicating that at higher prices producers will be willing to supply (more/less) of the good in question. Like quantity demanded, quantity supplied is also influenced by factors other than price. The size of the industry, the state of technology, the prices of inputs, and the price of related outputs are important determinants. Changes in any of these factors will change the quantity supplied and can be represented by a (shift in/movement along) the supply curve.

Demand and supply curves are hypothetical constructs that answer what-if questions. For example, the supply curve answers the question, "What quantity of milk would be supplied if its price were $10 a gallon?" At this point it is not fair to ask whether anyone would buy milk at that price. Information
(3) about the quantity demanded is given by the _____ curve, which answers the question, "What quantity would be demanded if its price were $10 a gallon?" The viability of a price of $10 will be determined when we consider both curves simultaneously.

Figure 4-1 shows a demand and supply curve for stereo sets. The market outcome will be a price
(4) of $_____ and a quantity of _____. If the price is $400, then the quantity demanded will be (less/more) than the quantity supplied. In particular, from Figure 4-1 we can see that at a price of $400, producers would supply _____ sets while consumers would demand _____ sets. This imbalance is a (shortage/surplus) and will lead to a(n) (increase/reduction) in price as inventories start piling up and suppliers compete for sales. If, instead, the price of stereo sets is only $200, there will be a (shortage/surplus) as the quantity (demanded/supplied) exceeds the quantity

Figure 4-1

Demand and Supply: Stereos

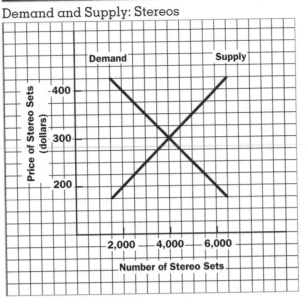

_____. Price is apt to (<u>decrease/increase</u>) as consumers scramble for a limited number of stereos at what appear to be bargain prices.

These forces working to raise or lower prices will continue until price and quantity settle down at values given by the _____ of the demand and supply curves. At this point,   (5) barring outside changes that would shift either curve, there will be no further tendency for change. Market-determined price and quantity are then said to be in _____. This price and quantity combination is the only one in which consumers demand exactly what producers supply. There are no frustrated consumers or producers. However, equilibrium price and quantity will change if anything happens to shift either the demand or supply curves. The Basic Exercise in this chapter asks you to examine a number of shifts in demand and supply curves.

Often factors affect demand but not supply, and vice versa. For example, changes in consumer incomes and tastes will shift the (<u>demand/supply</u>) curve but not the _____ curve.   (6) Following a shift in the demand curve, price must change to reestablish equilibrium. The change in price will lead to a (<u>shift in/movement along</u>) the supply curve until equilibrium is reestablished at the intersection of the new demand curve and the original supply curve.[1] Similarly, a change in technology or the price of inputs will shift the _____ curve but not the _____ curve. Equilibrium will be reestablished as the price change induced by the shift in the supply curve leads to a movement along the _____ curve to the new intersection.

_____

[1]If following an increase in consumer income the increase in price were sufficiently large to induce an increase in the size of the industry, the supply curve would shift. However such a change would take some time. The analysis here focuses on immediate or short-run impacts. Questions of long-run industry equilibrium are addressed in Chapters 8, 9, and 10.

In many cases governments intervene in the market mechanism in an attempt to control prices. Some price controls dictate a particular price; other controls set maximum or minimum prices.

(7) A price ceiling is a (<u>maximum/minimum</u>) legal price, typically below the market-determined equilibrium price. Examples of price ceilings include rent controls and usury laws. A price floor sets a(n) _____ legal price. To be effective, the price floor would have to be (<u>above/below</u>) the market equilibrium price. Price floors are often used in agricultural programs.

In general, economists argue that interferences with the market mechanism are likely to have a number of undesirable features. Price controls will almost surely lead to a misallocation of resources, as it is unlikely legislated prices will equal opportunity cost. If there are a large number of suppliers,

(8) price controls will be (<u>hard/easy</u>) to monitor and evasion will be hard to police. In order to prevent the breakdown of price controls, governments quite likely find it necessary to introduce a large number of _____ _____. The enforcement of price controls can provide opportunities for favoritism and corruption. If all of this is not enough, price controls are almost certain to produce groups with a monetary stake in preserving controls. Another form of inefficiency involves the use of time and resources to evade effective controls.

(9) Price ceilings have a history of persistent (<u>shortages/surpluses</u>) and the development of black markets. Prices in the illegal market are likely to be greater than those that would have prevailed in a free market, with substantial income going to those whose only business is circumventing the controls. Over a longer period of time, new investment is likely to (<u>decrease/increase</u>) as controlled prices reduce the profitability of investment in the industry.

Firms try to get around effective price floors by offering nonprice inducements for consumers to buy from them rather than from someone else. (Remember that effective price floors result in excess supply.) These nonprice inducements are apt to be less preferred by consumers than would a general reduction in prices. Price floors will also result in inefficiencies as high-cost firms are protected from

(10) failing by artificially (<u>high/low</u>) prices.

Important Terms and Concepts Quiz

Choose the best definition for each of the following terms.

1. _____ Invisible hand

2. _____ Quantity demanded

3. _____ Demand schedule

4. _____ Demand curve

5. _____ Shift in a demand curve

6. _____ Quantity supplied

7. _____ Supply schedule

8. _____ Supply curve

9. _____ Supply-demand diagram

10. _____ Shortage

11. _____ Surplus

12. _____ Equilibrium

13. _____ Law of supply and demand

14. _____ Price ceiling

15. _____ Price floor

a. Observation that in a free market, price tends to a level where quantity supplied equals quantity demanded

b. Legal minimum price that may be charged

c. Graph depicting how quantity demanded changes as price changes

d. Change in price causing a change in quantity supplied or demanded

e. Number of units consumers want to buy at a given price

f. Individual actions to pursue self-interest in a market system promote societal well-being

g. Table depicting how the quantity demanded changes as price changes

h. Situation in which there are no inherent forces producing change

i. Table depicting how quantity supplied changes as price changes

j. Legal maximum price that may be charged

k. Number of units producers want to sell at a given price

l. Table depicting the changes in both quantity demanded and quantity supplied as price changes

m. Change in a variable other than price that affects quantity demanded

n. Excess of quantity supplied over quantity demanded

o. Graph depicting the changes in both quantity supplied and quantity demanded as price changes

p. Excess of quantity demanded over quantity supplied

q. Graph depicting how quantity supplied changes as price changes

• Basic Exercises

These exercises ask you to analyze the impact of changes in factors that affect demand and supply.

1. a. Table 4-1 has data on the quantity of candy bars that would be demanded and supplied at various prices. Use the data to draw the demand curve and the supply curve for candy bars in Figure 4-2.

    b. From the information given in Table 4-1 and represented in Figure 4-2, the equilibrium price is _____ cents and the equilibrium quantity is _____ million candy bars.

Table 4-1

Demand and Supply Schedules for Candy Bars

Quantity Demanded	Price per Bar	Quantity Supplied
1,200	55	1,050
1,100	60	1,100
900	70	1,200
800	75	1,250
700	80	1,300

Figure 4-2

Demand and Supply: Candy Bars

Price of Candy Bars (cents)

100
95
90
85
80
75
70
65
60
55

700 — 800 — 900 —1,000 —1,100 —1,200 —1,300 —1,400 —1,500 —

Number of Candy Bars (millions)

c. Now assume that increases in income and population mean the demand curve has shifted. Assume the shift is such that, at each price, the quantity demanded has increased by 300 candy bars. Draw the new demand curve. At the new equilibrium, price has (increased/decreased) to _____ cents, and quantity has (increased/decreased) to _____ million candy bars. Note that the change in the equilibrium quantity is (less/more) than the shift in the demand curve. Can you explain why?

d. Next assume that Congress imposes a tax of 15 cents on every candy bar sold. As sellers must now pay the government 15 cents for each candy bar sold, the tax can be modeled as a 15 cent upward shift in the supply curve. This tax-induced shift in the supply curve will (increase/decrease) the equilibrium price and _____ the equilibrium quantity. Draw this new supply curve in Figure 4-2. Using the demand curve you drew in part c, the new equilibrium price following the imposition of the candy tax will be _____ cents and the equilibrium quantity will be _____ million candy bars. Compared to the equilibrium price you identified in part c, the increase in the market price of candy bars is (less than/equal to/more than) the new tax.

2. Figure 4-3 shows the demand and supply of chicken. Use Figure 4-3 while you fill in Table 4-2 to trace the effects of various events on the equilibrium price and quantity.

Figure 4-3

Demand and Supply: Chicken

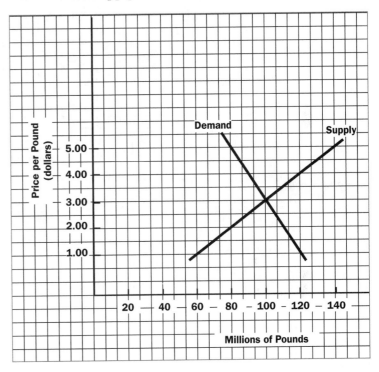

Table 4-2

Event	Which curve shifts?	Is the direction left or right?	Does the equilibrium price rise or fall?	Does the equilibrium quantity rise or fall?
a. A sharp increase in the price of beef leads many consumers to switch from beef to chicken.				
b. A bumper grain crop cuts the cost of chicken feed in half.				
c. Extraordinarily cold weather destroys a significant number of chickens.				
d. A sudden interest in Eastern religions converts many chicken eaters to vegetarians.				

43

3. Figure 4-4 shows the demand and supply of DVDs. Complete Table 4-3 to examine the impact of alternative price ceilings and price floors on the quantity demanded and the quantity supplied. What conclusion can you draw about when ceilings and floors will affect market outcomes?

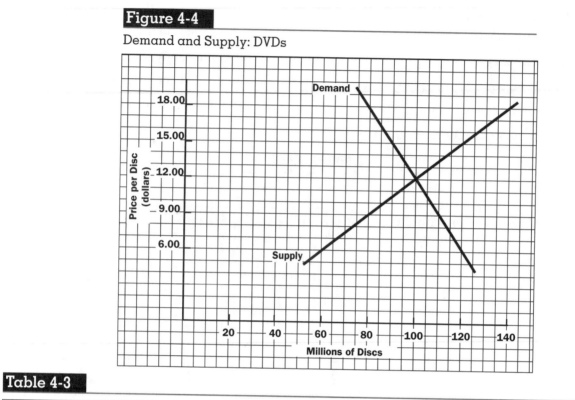

Figure 4-4

Demand and Supply: DVDs

Table 4-3

	Quantity Demanded	Quantity Supplied	Shortage or Surplus
a. Price ceiling = $18			
b. Price ceiling = $9			
c. Price floor = $15			
d. Price floor = $6			

Self-Tests for Understanding

Test A

Circle the most appropriate answer.

1. A demand curve is a graph showing how the quantity demanded changes when _____ changes.
   a. consumer income
   b. population
   c. price
   d. the price of closely related goods

2. The slope of a demand curve is usually _____, indicating that as price declines the quantity demanded increases.
   a. negative
   b. positive
   c. infinite
   d. zero

3. Quantity demanded is likely to depend upon all but which one of the following?
   a. consumer tastes
   b. consumer income
   c. price
   d. the size of the industry producing the good in question

4. A supply curve is a graphical representation of information in a(n)
   a. demand schedule.
   b. equilibrium.
   c. supply schedule.
   d. balance sheet.

5. If price decreases, the quantity supplied usually
   a. increases.
   b. is unchanged.
   c. decreases.
   d. goes to zero.

6. The entire supply curve is likely to shift when all but which one of the following change?
   a. the size of the industry
   b. price
   c. the price of important inputs
   d. technology that reduces production costs

7. There will likely be a movement along a fixed supply curve if which one of the following changes?
   a. price
   b. technology that reduces production costs
   c. the price of important inputs
   d. the size of the industry

8. There will be a movement along a fixed demand curve when which one of the following changes?
   a. price
   b. population
   c. consumer incomes
   d. consumer preferences

9. Graphically, the equilibrium price and quantity in a free market will be given by the
   a. Y-axis intercept of the demand curve.
   b. X-axis intercept of the supply curve.
   c. point of maximum vertical difference between the demand and supply curves.
   d. intersection of the demand and supply curves.

10. When the demand curve shifts to the right, which of the following is likely to occur?
    a. Equilibrium price rises and equilibrium quantity declines.
    b. Both equilibrium price and quantity rise.
    c. Equilibrium price declines and equilibrium quantity rises.
    d. Both equilibrium price and quantity decline.

11. If equilibrium price and quantity both decrease, it is likely that the
    a. supply curve has shifted to the right.
    b. demand curve has shifted to the right.
    c. demand curve has shifted to the left.
    d. supply curve has shifted to the left.

12. A shift in the demand curve for sailboats resulting from a general increase in incomes will lead to
    a. higher prices.
    b. lower prices.
    c. a shift in the supply curve.
    d. lower output.

13. Which of the following is likely to result in a shift in the supply curve for dresses? (There may be more than one correct answer.)
    a. an increase in consumer incomes
    b. an increase in tariffs that forces manufacturers to import cotton cloth at higher prices
    c. an increase in dress prices
    d. higher prices for skirts, pants, and blouses

14. From an initial equilibrium, which of the following changes will lead to a shift in the supply curve for Chevrolets?
    a. import restrictions on Japanese cars
    b. new environmental protection measures that raise the cost of producing steel
    c. a decrease in the price of Fords
    d. increases in the price of gasoline

15. If the price of oil (a close substitute for coal) increases, then the
    a. supply curve for coal will shift to the right.
    b. demand curve for coal will shift to the right.
    c. equilibrium price and quantity of coal will not change.
    d. quantity of coal demanded will decline.

16. If the price of shoes is initially above the equilibrium value, which of the following is likely to occur?
    a. Stores' inventories will decrease as consumers buy more shoes than shoe companies produce.
    b. The demand curve for shoes will shift in response to higher prices.
    c. Shoe stores and companies will reduce prices in order to increase sales, leading to a lower equilibrium price.
    d. Equilibrium will be reestablished at the original price as the supply curve shifts to the left.

17. A new tax on backpacks that shifts the supply curve should increase the market price of backpacks
    a. not at all.
    b. by less than the increase in the tax.
    c. by an amount equal to the increase in the tax.
    d. by more than the increase in the tax.

18. Binding price floors are likely to
    a. lead to a reduction in the volume of transactions, as we move along the demand curve, above the equilibrium price to the higher price floor.
    b. result in increased sales as suppliers react to higher prices.
    c. lead to shortages.
    d. be effective only if they are set at levels below the market equilibrium level.

19. Effective price ceilings are likely to
    a. result in surpluses.
    b. increase the volume of transactions as we move along the demand curve.
    c. increase production as producers respond to higher consumer demand at the low ceiling price.
    d. result in the development of black markets.

20. A surplus results when
    a. the quantity demanded exceeds the quantity supplied.
    b. the quantity supplied exceeds the quantity demanded.
    c. the demand curve shifts to the right.
    d. effective price ceilings are imposed.

Test B

Circle T or F for true or false.

T   F   1. The Law of Supply and Demand was passed by Congress in 1776.

T   F   2. The demand curve for hamburgers is a graph showing the quantity of hamburgers that would be demanded during a specified period at each possible price.

T   F   3. The slope of the supply curve indicates the increase in price necessary to get producers to increase output.

T   F   4. An increase in consumer income will shift both the supply and demand curves.

T   F   5. Both demand and supply curves usually have positive slopes.

T   F   6. If at a particular price the quantity supplied exceeds the quantity demanded, then price is likely to fall as suppliers compete for sales.

T   F   7. Equilibrium price and quantity are determined by the intersection of the demand and supply curves.

T   F   8. Because equilibrium is defined as a situation with no inherent forces producing change, the equilibrium price and quantity will not change following an increase in consumer income.

T   F   9. A change in the price of important inputs will change the quantity supplied but will not shift the supply curve.

T F 10. Increases in commodity specific taxes typically lead to equal increases in market prices.

T F 11. When binding, price ceilings are likely to result in the development of black markets.

T F 12. Price controls, whether floors or ceilings, likely will increase the volume of transactions from what it would be without controls.

T F 13. An effective price ceiling is normally accompanied by shortages.

T F 14. An effective price floor is also normally accompanied by shortages.

T F 15. An increase in both the market price and quantity of beef following an increase in consumer incomes proves that demand curves do not always have a negative slope.

● Supplementary Exercise

Imagine that the demand curve for tomatoes can be represented as:

$$Q = 1,000 - 250P.$$

The supply curve is a bit trickier. Farmers must make planting decisions on what they anticipate prices to be. Once they have made these decisions, there is little room for increases or decreases in the quantity supplied. Except for disastrously low prices, it will almost certainly pay a farmer to harvest and market his tomatoes. Assuming that farmers forecast price on the basis of the price last period, we can represent the supply curve for tomatoes as:

$$Q = 200 + 150P_{-1},$$

where P_{-1}, refers to price in the previous period. Initial equilibrium price and quantity of tomatoes are $2 and 500, respectively. Verify that at this price the quantity supplied is equal to the quantity demanded. (Equilibrium implies the same price in each period.)

Now assume that an increase in income has shifted the demand curve to:

$$Q = 1,400 - 250P.$$

Starting with the initial equilibrium price, trace the evolution of price and quantity over time. Do prices and quantities seem to be approaching some sort of equilibrium? If so, what? You might try programming this example on a computer or simulating it with a spreadsheet program. What happens if the slope of the demand and/or supply curve changes?

Ask your instructor about cobweb models. Do you think looking at last period's price is a good way to forecast prices?

● Economics in Action

Hey, Buddy . . .

Scalping tickets—selling tickets at whatever the market will bear rather than at face value—is illegal in a number of states, including New York City. In 1992 the high demand for tickets to a retrospective exhibition of Henri Matisse at the Museum of Modern Art prompted renewed interest in the economic effects of scalping. Admission to the exhibition was by special ticket. By the time the exhibit opened, all advance sale tickets had been sold. A limited number of tickets were available each day. Art lovers had to wait in line for up to two hours early in the morning to purchase these tickets at $12.50 each. Tickets also were available without the wait at $20 to $50 from scalpers who evaded the police.

The Monet retrospective exhibit at the Art Institute in Chicago in 1995 attracted such interest that scalpers were reported to be getting $100 for tickets with a face value of $10. Scalpers also do a lively business at the Super Bowl, the Final Four of the NCAA basketball playoffs, and other major sporting and entertainment events.

Why don't museums, the National Football League, and the NCAA simply raise the price of tickets? Some argue that these organizations, along with other businesses, are concerned with "goodwill." Even if higher profits could be earned from higher ticket prices, it might come by sacrificing profits over the long run as goodwill is replaced by ill will and a growing lack of consumer interest.

Some economists view scalpers as providing a service to those who have not planned ahead or do not wish to stand in line. They point out that other businesses, such as airlines, charge a hefty price for last-minute purchases.

It is often argued that scalping should be illegal, as it makes events unaffordable for the average person. Others wonder whether the average person ever gets tickets to such events and, if she does, whether she might not prefer the option of selling her tickets at a handsome profit.

The following two-tier price system has been proposed by some economists. First, a limited number of tickets would be sold at lower prices to those willing to stand in line or enter a lottery. Then the remaining tickets would be sold at whatever price the market will bear.

In fall 2001, the producers of the hit Broadway show "The Producers" announced just such a plan. Their top ticket price had been $100, and it was rumored that scalpers were getting up to $1,000 a ticket. The producers announced a plan under which 50 seats for each performance would be available at $480 a piece.

1. Who is harmed when scalping is illegal? Who would be harmed if scalping were legal?

2. Would you expect legalizing scalping to affect the price of tickets from scalpers? Why?

3. Evaluate the pros and cons of the two-tier price system.

Source: "Tickets: Supply Meets Demand on Sidewalk," *The New York Times*, December 26, 1992; "For the Asking, a $480 Seat," *The New York Times*, October 26, 2001.

Study Questions

1. Why do economists argue that neither quantity demanded nor quantity supplied is likely to be a fixed number?

2. What adjustment mechanisms are likely to ensure that free-market prices move toward their equilibrium values given by the intersection of the demand and supply curves?

3. What important factors help to determine the quantity demanded? The quantity supplied?

4. Why are changes in all of the supply determinants, except price, said to shift the entire supply curve while changes in price are said to give rise to a movement along a fixed supply curve?

5. How do factors that shift the supply curve give rise to movements along a given demand curve?

6. Why do economists expect that an increase in a tax on a specific commodity will not lead to an equal increase in market prices?

7. If price cannot adjust, say due to an effective price ceiling, what factors will likely allocate the quantity supplied among consumers?

8. Consider the demand for a necessity (for example, food), and the demand for a luxury (for example, home hot tubs). For which good would you expect the quantity demanded to show a greater response to changes in price? Why? For which good would you expect the demand curve to be steeper? Why? For which good would you expect the demand curve to show a greater shift in response to changes in consumer income? Why?

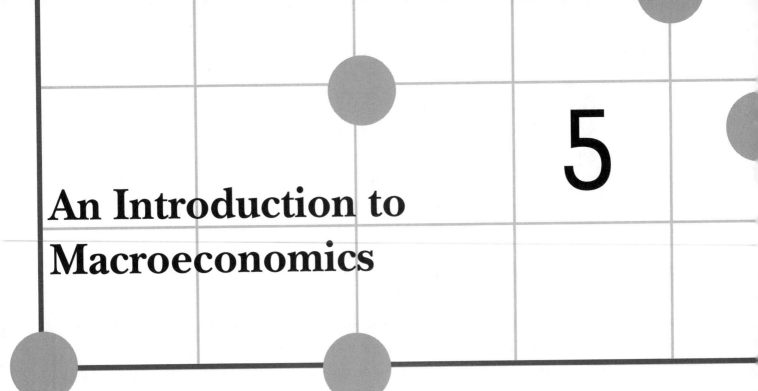

An Introduction to Macroeconomics

5

Important Terms and Concepts

Aggregation	Nominal GDP	Fiscal policy
Aggregate demand curve	Real GDP	Stagflation
Aggregate supply curve	Final goods and services	Monetary policy
Inflation	Intermediate goods	Stabilization policy
Recession	Real GDP per capita	
Gross domestic product (GDP)	Deflation	

Learning Objectives

After completing this chapter, you should be able to:

- explain the difference between microeconomics and macroeconomics.

- determine whether particular problems are within the realm of microeconomics or macroeconomics.

- describe the role of economic aggregates in macroeconomics.

- explain how supply-demand analysis can be used to study inflation, recessions, and stabilization policy.

- distinguish between real and nominal GDP.

- explain how GDP is a measure of economic production, not economic well-being.

- characterize, in general terms, the movement in prices and output over the last 130 years.

- use aggregate demand and supply curves to explain how stabilization policy addresses problems of unemployment and inflation.

• Chapter Review

(1) Economic theory is traditionally split into two parts, microeconomics and macroeconomics. If one studies the behavior of individual decision-making units, one is studying _____. If one studies the behavior of entire economies, one is studying _____. This chapter is an introduction to macroeconomics.

The American economy is made up of millions of firms, hundreds of millions of individuals, and innumerable different goods and services. Since it would be impossible to list each of these firms, individuals, and commodities, economists have found it useful to use certain overall averages or aggregates. The concept of domestic product is an example. If we concentrate on macroeconomic aggregates, we ignore much of the micro detail; whereas by concentrating on the micro detail, we may miss the big picture. The two forms of analysis are not substitutes; rather, they can be usefully employed together. (Remember the map analogy in Chapter 1 of the text.) It has been argued that only successful macroeconomic policy leads to a situation in which the study of microeconomics is important, and vice versa.

Supply and demand analysis is a fundamental tool of both micro and macro theory. In microeconomics one looks at the supply and demand for individual commodities, while in macroeconomics one studies aggregate supply and aggregate demand. The intersection of the

(2) demand and supply curves in microeconomics determines equilibrium _____ and _____. In macroeconomics the intersection of the aggregate demand and supply curves determines the price level and aggregate output, or the gross _____ _____.

(3) A sustained increase in the price level would be called _____, whereas a sustained decrease would be called _____. Because of long-term growth factors, domestic product in the U.S. economy usually increases every year. Periods when real domestic product declines are referred to as _____. With an unchanged aggregate supply curve, an outward (rightward) shift of the aggregate demand curve would lead to (higher/lower) prices and (higher/lower) output. Higher prices would also result if the aggregate supply curve shifted to the (left/right), but, this time, higher prices would be associated with a(n) (increase/decrease) in output. Such a combination of rising prices and declining output is called _____. If both curves shift to the right at the same rate, then it is possible to have increased output without inflation.

(4) Gross domestic product is defined as the sum of the _____ values of all _____ goods and services produced in the domestic economy and sold on organized markets during a year. Because GDP counts only production in the domestic economy it (excludes/includes) the foreign operations of American firms and _____ the activities of foreign firms and

workers operating in the United States. For the most part GDP includes only those newly produced goods and services that are traded in markets. Illegal activities, the underground economy, and unpaid housework (and childcare) are all examples of economic activities that (<u>are/are not</u>) included in GDP.

To measure GDP, economists and national income statisticians use prices to add up the different kinds of output. If one uses today's prices, the result is (<u>nominal/real</u>) GDP. If one values output using prices from some base period, one gets _____ GDP. Which is the better measure of changes in output? (<u>Nominal/Real</u>) GDP. If all prices rise and all outputs are unchanged, (<u>nominal/real</u>) GDP will increase while _____ GDP will not.   (5)

It is important to remember that GDP is a measure of production; it (<u>is/is not</u>) a measure of economic well-being. The economic activity necessary to recover from a natural disaster such as an earthquake or hurricane is likely to (<u>decrease/increase</u>) GDP while _____ people's sense of well-being. Similarly, goods and services used to clean up the environment mean a (<u>larger/smaller</u>) GDP but are likely to reflect a (<u>higher/lower</u>) sense of well-being.   (6)

If you look at a long period of American history, you will see that there have been periods when both output and prices have risen and fallen. The long-term trend for output is (<u>up/down</u>). The overall trend for prices (<u>depends/does not depend</u>) upon the period you are reviewing. Up until World War II, prices rose and fell whereas since 1945, prices seem only to have _____.   (7)

The government would like to keep output growing, thus avoiding recession; at the same time, it would like to keep prices from rising, thus avoiding (<u>inflation/deflation</u>). Attempts to do just this are called _____ policy. The American government has been formally committed to such policies only since the end of World War II. A look at Figures 5-5 and 5-6 in the text suggests that since 1950, stabilization policy has done a good job of avoiding _____ but not of avoiding _____. Chapter 16 discusses why this result is not surprising; that is, why, if one concentrates on maintaining high levels of employment and output, the result is likely to be higher prices.   (8)

Important Terms and Concepts Quiz

Choose the best definition for each of the following terms.

1. _____ Microeconomics
2. _____ Macroeconomics
3. _____ Aggregation
4. _____ Aggregate demand curve
5. _____ Aggregate supply curve
6. _____ Inflation
7. _____ Deflation
8. _____ Recession
9. _____ Gross domestic product (GDP)
10. _____ Nominal GDP
11. _____ Real GDP
12. _____ Final goods and services
13. _____ Intermediate goods
14. _____ GDP per capita
15. _____ Stagflation
16. _____ Fiscal policy
17. _____ Monetary policy
18. _____ Stabilization policy

a. Period of expansion in an economy's total output
b. Period of decline in an economy's total output
c. Inflation occurring while the economy is growing slowly or in a recession
d. Gross domestic product calculated at current price levels
e. Actions by the Federal Reserve that affect interest rates and/or the money supply
f. Government programs designed to prevent or shorten recessions and to counteract inflation
g. Products purchased by their ultimate users
h. Study of behavior of an entire economy
i. Combining individual markets into a single, overall market
j. Gross domestic product calculated using prices from some agreed-upon base year
k. Products purchased for resale or for their use in producing other products
l. Sustained decrease in general price level
m. Graph of quantity of domestic product demanded at each possible price level
n. Sum of money values of all final goods and services produced in the domestic economy and sold on organized markets within the year
o. Graph of quantity of domestic product produced at each possible price level
p. Study of individual decision-making units
q. Sustained increase in general price level
r. Output divided by populations
s. The government's plan for spending and taxes

● Basic Exercises

These exercises use the aggregate demand-aggregate supply diagram to review a few basic concepts.

1. **Figure 5-1** has four panels. The solid lines indicate the initial situation, and the dashed lines indicate a shift in one or both curves.

   a. Which panel(s) suggest(s) a period, or periods, of inflation? _____

   b. Which panel(s) suggest(s) a period, or periods, of deflation? _____

   (Did prices in the U.S. economy ever decline in the 20th century? If so, when? _____)

Figure 5-1

Aggregate Demand and Aggregate Supply

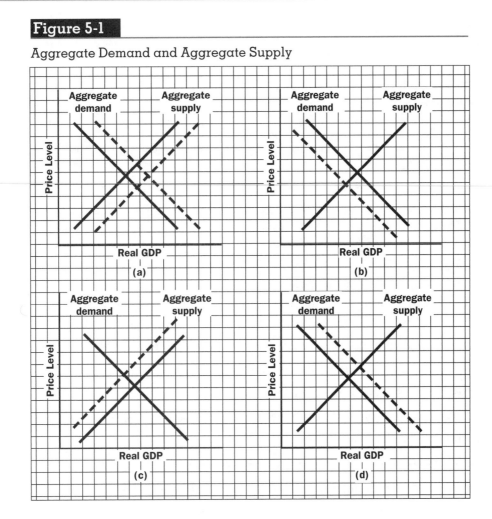

c. Which panel(s) illustrate(s) growth in real output with stable prices? _____

d. Which panel(s) illustrate(s) stagflation? _____

2. Stabilization policy involves changes in government policies designed to shorten recessions and stabilize prices. For reasons examined in later chapters, stabilization policies have their initial and primary effect on the aggregate demand curve. For the cases listed below, explain how stabilization policy can reestablish the initial levels of output and prices. Do this by indicating the appropriate shift in the aggregate demand curve. (The exact policies that will achieve these shifts will be described in detail in later chapters.)

a. Inflation [panel (d)]

b. Recession [panel (b)]

c. Consider panel (c), the case of stagnation. If the government is restricted to policies that shift the aggregate demand curve, what will happen to output if the government adopts policies to combat inflation and restore the original price level? What happens to prices if the government is committed to maintaining the original level of output?

3.   **Table 5-1** contains data on output and prices in a hypothetical economy that produces only fast food.

Table 5-1

Prices and Quantities

| | 2004 | | | 2005 | | |
	Price (1)	Quantity (2)	Nominal Value (3)	Price (4)	Quantity (5)	Nominal Value (6)
Hamburgers	$2.00	300	_____	$2.80	310	_____
Shakes	1.00	300	_____	1.30	320	_____
Fries	0.75	300	_____	0.90	330	_____
		Nominal GDP	_____		Nominal GDP	_____

a. Calculate the money value of the production of hamburgers, shakes, and fries by multiplying price and quantity. Sum these results to calculate nominal gross domestic product (GDP) for each year.

b. What is the percentage increase in nominal GDP from 2004 to 2005? _____

c. Use 2004 prices to compute real GDP for 2005.

  Value of 2005 hamburger production using 2004 prices _____

  Value of 2005 shake production using 2004 prices _____

  Value of 2005 fries production using 2004 prices _____

  Real GDP for 2005 (expressed in terms of 2004 prices) _____

d. Calculate the percentage increase in real GDP from 2004 to 2005. _____

e. How does this figure compare to the increase in nominal GDP calculated in question b? Which is the better measure of the increase in production?

● Self-Tests for Understanding

Test A

Circle the most appropriate answer.

1. Microeconomics is concerned with
   a. economic aggregates.
   b. the actions of individual economic decision-making units.
   c. small people.
   d. small countries.

2. The study of macroeconomics focuses on
   a. the economic actions of large people.
   b. decisions by the largest 500 industrial companies.
   c. the prices and output of all firms in an industry.
   d. the behavior of entire economies.

3. Which of the following is an example of a macroeconomic aggregate?
   a. the national output of Haiti
   b. the total output of General Motors
   c. employment at Wal-Mart
   d. the price of unleaded gas

4. The aggregate demand curve shows
   a. the history of real GDP over the recent past.
   b. alternative levels of domestic output that policymakers might choose.
   c. how the quantity of domestic product demanded changes with changes in the price level.
   d. the demand for goods and services by the federal government.

5. The graph showing how the quantity of output produced by all firms depends upon the price level is called the
   a. aggregate supply curve.
   b. Phillips curve.
   c. production possibilities frontier.
   d. economy's aggregate indifference curve.

6. GDP measures the sum of money values of
   a. all goods sold in the domestic economy during the past year.
   b. all final goods and services produced in the domestic economy during the past year.
   c. attendance at all the worst movies during the past year.
   d. all payments to household domestic help during the past year.

7. GDP is designed to be a measure of
   a. economic activity conducted through organized markets.
   b. national well-being.
   c. all economic activity during the preceding year.
   d. all economic transactions involving cash.

8. Using current prices to aggregate all final output in the economy will yield
   a. nominal GDP.
   b. real GDP.
   c. the cost of living.
   d. GDP in constant dollars.

9. Real GDP is computed by valuing output at
   a. manufacturers' costs.
   b. current prices.
   c. prices from an agreed-upon base year.
   d. last year's rate of inflation.

10. Which of the following would not be included in GDP for 2005?
   a. the production of refrigerators in 2005
   b. the government's purchase of paper clips produced in 2005
   c. consumer expenditures on haircuts in 2005
   d. General Motors' expenditures on steel for producing Cadillacs in 2005

11. Which of the following would not be part of GDP for 2005?
    a. Stacey's purchase of a 2005 Chevrolet
    b. Tanya's purchase of the latest iMac
    c. Ramon's expenditures on new furniture for his apartment
    d. Jamal's purchase of a guitar originally used by John Lennon in 1965

12. Which of the following is counted by the GDP statisticians?
    a. Jerita's purchase of Boeing stock from Walter
    b. your spending on tuition and fees for this year
    c. Durwood's winnings from his bookie
    d. the value of Yvonne's volunteer time at her daughter's school

13. Which of the following will be measured as an increase in GDP but need not reflect an increase in economic well-being?
    a. expenditures to clean up a major oil spill in Prince William Sound
    b. the value of the time Roland spends painting his own house
    c. the cost of new medical care that reduces infant mortality
    d. earnings of numbers runners in Chicago

14. In 1990, nominal GDP was $5.803 trillion. In 1991, nominal GDP increased to $5.986 trillion. On the basis of just this information, which of the following statements is true?
    a. Total output of the American economy was greater in 1991 than in 1990.
    b. The whole increase in nominal GDP was the result of inflation.
    c. Actual output increased by 3.15 percent. [(5.986 ñ 5.803) ÷ 5.803] = .0315
    d. It is impossible to determine what happened to prices and output from data on nominal GDP alone.

15. A recession is likely to occur if
    a. unemployment is falling.
    b. the aggregate supply curve shifts to the right.
    c. the increase in nominal GDP exceeds the increase in real GDP.
    d. the aggregate demand curve shifts to the left.

16. Inflation is defined as a period of
    a. rising nominal GDP.
    b. generally rising prices.
    c. falling real GDP.
    d. falling unemployment.

17. Which of the following conditions will result in stagflation?
    a. The aggregate demand curve shifts to the right.
    b. The aggregate demand curve shifts to the left.
    c. The aggregate supply curve shifts to the right.
    d. The aggregate supply curve shifts to the left.

18. Stabilization policy refers to actions by the government to
    a. keep real GDP from rising.
    b. minimize changes in government regulation.
    c. prevent recessions and fight inflation.
    d. equalize the rate of unemployment and inflation.

19. Successful stabilization policy to reduce inflation would shift
    a. the aggregate supply curve to the left.
    b. the burden of taxes from individuals to corporations.
    c. the aggregate demand curve to the left.
    d. decision making about monetary policy to the Congress.

20. In the period following World War II, the historical record shows
    a. more frequent and severe recessionary dips in real output than before World War II.
    b. an economy that appears to be more inflation prone.
    c. little if any increase in real GDP.
    d. little increase in the price level.

Test B

Circle T or F for true or false.

T F   1. A study of the economy of Luxembourg would be an example of microeconomics.

T F   2. GDP is an example of a macroeconomic aggregate.

T F   3. An increase in nominal GDP necessarily implies an increase in real GDP.

T F   4. Changes in real GDP are a better measure of changes in national output than changes in nominal GDP.

T F   5. Deflation can occur only as a result of shifts in the aggregate supply curve.

T F   6. On the eve of World War II, national output, or real GDP, was not much greater than at the end of the Civil War.

T F   7. Stagflation refers to the simultaneous occurrence of rising prices and little if any increase in output.

T F   8. A reduction in taxes that is meant to spur consumer spending would be an example of fiscal policy.

T F   9. Federal Reserve's policies designed to increase interest rates would be an example of monetary policy.

T F   10. Stabilization policy refers to attempts by the government to influence both prices and output by shifting the aggregate demand curve.

Economics in Action

Leading Indicators and Turning Points

The text describes recessions as a period when real GDP declines. This is also the definition that is used by many media commentators. However, the timing of business cycle expansions and recessions has traditionally been determined by a group of economists associated with the National Bureau of Economic Research (NBER). For a number of reasons, the NBER Business Cycle Dating Committee has concentrated its attention on monthly data. GDP data are only available quarterly, i.e., for three-month periods; data on quarterly GDP is not immediately available as it takes some time to gather all of the relevant data to construct accurate estimates of GDP, and data on GDP are often revised years later. As a result, the NBER committee has traditionally focused on four monthly measures of economic activity: total civilian employment, industrial production, personal income less transfer payments adjusted for inflation, and manufacturing and trade sales adjusted for inflation.

During the summer of 2001 there was much commentary in the press about whether the economic expansion of the 1990s had ended and the United States had slipped into a recession. These concerns were only heightened by the terrorist attacks of September 11.

Using **Figure 5-2**, how would you have dated the end of the expansion and the beginning of the 2001 recession? How would you have dated the end of the recession?

The committee's decision is reported in the answers section of the Study Guide, but make your own determination before looking at their decision. As should be clear from Figure 5-2, measures of economic activity do not go up and down in lockstep. Your determination, like that of the NBER committee, is likely to require some weighting and averaging of these series.

Economist James Tobin has argued that the traditional approach to dating business cycles is misguided in that it assumes that any increase in economic activity would

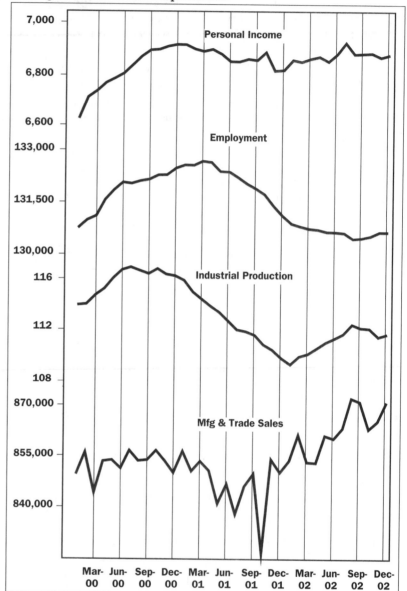

Figure 5-2

Dating Recessions and Expansions

forestall the beginning of a recession or signal the end of a recession. Tobin notes that in a growing economy, output and employment have to increase simply to keep pace with a growing population and more productive workforce. He prefers growth-oriented dating and definitions of business cycles. Any period where the growth of output and employment failed to match the growth in the potential output would be called a recession or growth-recession.

1. How would you date the end of the 1990s expansion? Why?

2. How would date the end of the recession? Why?

3. Do you think the definition of recessions should be growth-oriented as advocated by Tobin? Why?

4. Just who are the members of the NBER Business Cycle Dating Committee? Read about them in "Six economists play the dating game," *Fortune,* October 29, 2001.

Information on the timing of business cycles back to 1854 can be found on the NBER Web site at http://www.nber.org/cycles/cyclesmain.html.

Study Questions

1. Why is GDP, a measure of domestic production, not a good measure of national well-being?

2. Why does GDP exclude the sales of existing goods and assets such as used college textbooks and existing homes?

3. Why does GDP include only final goods and exclude intermediate goods?

4. Which is the better measure of the change in domestic output, nominal GDP or real GDP? Why?

5. Should measures of GDP include estimates of nonmarket economic activity? Why?

6. How can stabilization policy help to reduce unemployment? Inflation?

7. If stabilization policy has the strongest and most immediate impact on aggregate demand, what are the implications for prices when the government wants to reduce unemployment? What are the implications for unemployment when the government wants to reduce prices?

8. What might account for the differences in the U.S. economy's record of economic growth and inflation after 1950 as compared with the period before World War II?

Economics Online

You can get current information on a number of economic indicators from the following government Web sites:

White House Economic Statistics Briefing Room

http://www.whitehouse.gov/fsbr/esbr.html

Bureau of Economic Analysis (U.S. Department of Commerce)

http://www.bea.gov/

Bureau of Labor Statistics (U.S. Department of Labor)

http://www.bls.gov/eag/eag.us.htm

U.S. Census Economic Briefing Room

http://www.census.gov/cgi-bin/briefroom/BriefRm

Statistical Abstract of the United States

Http://www.census.gov/compendia/statab

Economic Indicators, a monthly publication prepared by the Council of Economic Advisers for the Joint Economic Committee

http://www.gpoaccess.gov/indicators/browse.html

The Goals of Macroeconomic Policy

6

Important Terms and Concepts

Inputs	Production function	Cyclical unemployment	Redistribution by inflation
Outputs	Unemployment rate	Full employment	Real rate of interest
Growth policy	Discouraged workers	Unemployment insurance	Nominal rate of interest
Economic growth	Frictional unemployment	Purchasing power	Expected rate of inflation
Labor productivity	Structural unemployment	Real wage rate	Capital gain
Potential GDP		Relative prices	
Labor force			

Learning Objectives
After completing this chapter, you should be able to:

- summarize arguments in favor of and opposed to higher rates of economic growth.

- explain how potential GDP is estimated and how growth in potential GDP is related to an economy's growth potential.

- explain why growth in labor productivity is the major determinant of the growth in living standards.

- explain how economists use the concept of potential GDP to measure the economic cost of unemployment.

- describe how the Bureau of Labor Statistics measures the number of unemployed and in what ways this number may overestimate or underestimate the unemployment level.

- explain the differences between frictional, structural, and cyclical unemployment.

- summarize the debate over how much unemployment is consistent with full employment.

- explain why unemployment insurance only spreads the financial burden of unemployment that individuals would otherwise face, but does not eliminate the economic cost of unemployment.

- distinguish between real and mythical costs of inflation.

- explain how the concept of real wages suggests that inflation has not systematically eroded the purchasing power of wages.

- distinguish between changes in prices that reflect a change in relative prices and changes that reflect general inflation.
- distinguish between real and nominal rates of interest.
- describe how the difference between real and nominal rates of interest is related to expectations about the rate of inflation.
- explain how the taxation of nominal magnitudes can mean that, during a period of inflation, savers and investors will receive a reduced real return after taxes.
- explain why the variability of inflation is important to an understanding of the cost of inflation.

Chapter Review

This chapter is an introduction to three important issues at the heart of the formulation of macroeconomic policy: economic growth, unemployment, and inflation.

Economic Growth

The tools of economics cannot help you determine whether an economy should grow faster or slower; they can, however, identify the sources of growth and the consequences of more or less growth. In particular, a number of economists oppose zero economic growth on the grounds that a move in this direction would require extensive government controls and may seriously hamper efforts to eliminate poverty and to protect the environment. Solutions to these last two problems are likely to require more rather than fewer resources. Many feel that it is easier to reach a political agreement to devote resources to problems of poverty and the environment if total output is expanding rather than if it is not growing.

(1)   Over long periods of time the major determinant of material well-being or living standards is the growth in labor _____. Growth in labor productivity explains why, on the average, during the last 150 years each generation has been wealthier than its parents. Continued growth in labor productivity will mean that your children and their children will be wealthier than you are.

    For a firm producing a single output, measuring labor productivity per hour is a simple matter of dividing output by total labor hours. For the American economy as a whole, labor productivity is measured as real GDP divided by total labor hours. An increase in labor productivity means that

(2) (more/less) output can be produced with the same number of labor hours. If aggregate output were unchanged, an increase in labor productivity would mean (more/less) unemployment. But remember that total output and the unemployment rate are determined by the intersection of the aggregate _____ and aggregate _____ curves. An increase in productivity means that the economy's capacity to produce has increased; that is, the aggregate supply curve has shifted to the (left/right) and there has been a(n) (increase/decrease) in potential GDP. It is macroeconomic policy that helps to determine whether we take advantage of new possibilities.

What makes labor more or less productive? While there are many factors, certainly the intensity of work, the quality of training, the availability of more and better equipment, and the level of technology are important factors. Sustained growth in labor productivity (is/is not) a relatively new phenomenon, (3) tracing back about (2,000/200) years. The following word equations show why growth in labor productivity is the basic determinant of living standards or output per capita:

We can express total output as the product of labor productivity and total hours worked:

$$\text{Output} = \text{Output/Total hours worked} \times \text{Total hours worked}$$

If we want to examine output per capita, the following expression will be helpful:

$$\frac{\text{Output}}{\text{Population}} = \frac{\text{Output}}{\text{Hours worked}} \times \frac{\text{Hours worked}}{\text{Employment}} \times \frac{\text{Employment}}{\text{Population}}$$

The expression on the left of the equal sign in the second equation is output per capita. The first expression on the right side of the equal sign is labor productivity. The second and third expressions measure the number of hours a typical worker works and the proportion of the population that works. Notice that two of the numerators and denominators on the right-hand side of the equal sign can be canceled, establishing the equality of the expression. If the number of hours per worker does not change and the proportion of the population that works is constant—that is, if the second and third terms on the right-hand side do not change—then the only way that output or GDP per capita can increase is if labor productivity increases. During the 20th century, it was the growth in labor productivity that dominated the other two terms.

Unemployment

Unemployment has two sorts of costs. The personal costs include not only the lost income for individuals out of work, but also the loss of work experience and the psychic costs of involuntary idleness. The economic costs for the nation as a whole can be measured by the output of goods and services that might have been produced by those who are unemployed.

Economists have attempted to measure the economic cost of unemployment by estimating what output would have been at full employment. These figures are estimates of (potential/actual) (4) real GDP. The economic cost of unemployment is the difference between potential real GDP and _____ real GDP.

Unemployment statistics come from a monthly survey by the Bureau of Labor Statistics. People are asked if they have a job. If they answer no, they are asked if they are laid off from a job they expect to return to, are actively looking for work, or are not looking for work. From these answers government statisticians derive estimates of employment, unemployment, and the labor force. These numbers are not above criticism. When unemployment rates are high or rising, some people give up looking for work because they believe that looking for work is not worth the effort. These people are called_____ workers. An increase in the number of people (5) who have given up looking for work means a(n) (<u>increase/decrease</u>) in the amount of statistical unemployment and is an important reason why some observers feel that the official unemployment statistics (<u>understate/overstate</u>) the problem of unemployment. All part-time workers are counted as employed. If part-time work is involuntary and these individuals would prefer full-time work, official unemployment statistics will (<u>understate/overstate</u>) the problem of unemployment. If liberal unemployment compensation induces people to call themselves unemployed even if they have no intention of looking for work then official statistics will (<u>overstate/understate</u>) unemployment.

(6) Some unemployment occurs naturally from the normal workings of labor markets, as people join the labor force and look for their first job, look for better jobs, move to new locations, and so forth. Such unemployment is called _____ unemployment and involves people who are temporarily without a job more or less voluntarily. Full employment would not eliminate this kind of unemployment. Full employment would eliminate unemployment that is due to a decline in the economy's total production; that is, at full employment there would be no _____ unemployment. Unemployment may also occur because people's skills are no longer in demand due to automation or massive changes in production. This type of unemployment is called _____ unemployment.

How do we determine how much unemployment is consistent with full employment or, more succinctly, what is the full employment rate of unemployment? In the early 1960s, President Kennedy argued that the United States should aim for an employment rate of 4 percent. During the 1970s it was argued that the increasing number of young workers in the labor force meant a higher percentage of (7) (<u>cyclical/frictional/structural</u>) unemployment and (<u>decreased/increased</u>) the full employment rate of unemployment. Some argued that more generous unemployment compensation had increased the incentive for people to say they were looking for work when they really were not, a change that would increase the full employment rate of unemployment. Finally, many economists base their estimate of the full employment rate of unemployment on their evaluation of the links between unemployment and inflation. Experience in recent years suggests that the full employment rate of unemployment is (<u>higher/lower</u>) than estimates from the 1970s and 1980s but there is considerable uncertainty about its precise value.

(8) Unemployment insurance can help ease the burden of unemployment for individual families, but it (<u>can/cannot</u>) protect society against the lost output that the unemployed might have produced. Employing these people in the future does not bring back the hours of employment that have already been missed. Unemployment compensation provides (<u>complete/partial</u>) protection for (<u>all/some</u>) unemployed workers.

Inflation

There are important and valid reasons why people are concerned about continuing inflation. Nevertheless, quite a few popular arguments against inflation turn out to be based on misunderstandings. Many people worry that a high rate of inflation reduces their standard of living, or their (real/nominal) income. But the facts show that periods of high inflation are often accompanied (9) by equally large if not larger increases in wages. For many workers, their real standard of living, or the change in their wages adjusted for the change in prices, continues to increase, even during periods of rapid inflation. A worker whose wages double when prices double is able to consume (more/less/the same) goods and services (than/as) before the rise in prices and wages. In this case one would say that real wages (increased/were unchanged/decreased).

During inflationary periods most prices increase at (the same/different) rates. As a result, goods (10) and services with smaller than average price increases become relatively (more/less) expensive than they were before. Analogously, goods and services with larger than average price increases become relatively _____ expensive. Relative prices change all the time, during both inflationary and noninflationary periods. Changes in relative prices usually reflect shifts in demand and/or supply curves or various forms of government interventions. It is inaccurate to blame inflation for a change in relative prices.

But inflation does have real effects. One important effect is the redistribution of wealth between borrowers and lenders in inflationary periods. If lenders expect higher prices in the future they will demand (higher/lower) interest rates to compensate them for the loss of purchasing power of (11) the future dollars used to repay loans. Economists have thus found it useful to distinguish between nominal and real interest rates. If one looks at interest rates only in terms of the dollars that borrowers pay and lenders receive, one is looking at _____ interest rates. If one looks at interest rates in terms of the purchasing power the borrower will pay the lender, one is looking at _____ interest rates. During periods of inflation it is usual for nominal interest rates to incorporate expectations of inflation. There need be no unexpected redistribution of income between borrowers and lenders if actual inflation matches the expectations of inflation embodied in nominal interest rates.

If a change in the rate of inflation is accurately foreseen, and if nominal interest rates are correctly adjusted to reflect the change in expected inflation, then nominal interest rates (will/will not) change (12) while real interest rates will (also change/be unchanged). More typically, expectations of inflation are incorrect, in which case inflation will result in a redistribution of wealth between borrowers and lenders. Who gains and who loses will depend on whether the adjustment of nominal interest rates is too large or too small. Lenders lose when the adjustment of nominal interest rates is too (large/small) and borrowers lose when the adjustment is too _____. The tax treatment of interest payments and capital gains can have a substantial impact on the real after-tax rate of return. Problems here reflect the fact that the tax system, originally designed for a world of no inflation, focuses on (nominal/real) interest rates.

Over the long run, small unexpected differences in the rate of inflation can compound to create large differences in profits and losses. Since most business investments depend on long-term contracts, this area of economic activity may suffer during periods of high inflation. The difficulty of making long-term contracts is a real cost of inflation.

Inflation that proceeds at a fairly moderate and steady pace may pose few problems for an economy, but inflation that progresses at high, sometimes accelerating, and often variable rates imposes significant social and economic costs. There is no simple borderline between the two. In different countries or in different periods of time, the dividing line will vary considerably.

Important Terms and Concepts Quiz

Choose the best definition for each of the following terms.

1. _____ Inputs
2. _____ Outputs
3. _____ Economic growth
4. _____ Growth policy
5. _____ Labor productivity
6. _____ Potential GDP
7. _____ Labor force
8. _____ Production function
9. _____ Unemployment rate
10. _____ Discouraged workers
11. _____ Frictional unemployment
12. _____ Structural unemployment
13. _____ Cyclical unemployment
14. _____ Unemployment insurance
15. _____ Purchasing power
16. _____ Real wage
17. _____ Relative prices
18. _____ Real rate of interest
19. _____ Nominal rate of interest
20. _____ Capital gain

a. Labor, machinery, buildings, and other resources used to produce output
b. Number of people holding or seeking jobs
c. Output per hour of labor input
d. Government transfer payments to eligible workers if unemployed
e. Percentage of labor force unemployed
f. Interest payments, in percentage terms, measured in dollars
g. Total output divided by population
h. Unemployed people who cease looking for work, believing that no jobs are available
i. Unemployment attributable to decline in economy's total production
j. Unemployment due to normal workings of the labor market
k. Government policies to promote economic growth
l. Interest payment, in percentage terms, measured in terms of purchasing power
m. Volume of goods and services that money wage will buy
n. Unemployment due to changes in nature of economy
o. Price of an item in terms of some other item
p. Volume of goods and services that a sum of money will buy
q. Level of real output attainable if all resources were fully employed
r. Increase in total output
s. Difference between an asset's selling price and its original cost
t. Goods and services that firms produce
u. Legal maximum interest rate
v. Relationship between inputs and outputs

• Basic Exercises

1. **Who Gains and Loses from an Adjustment of Nominal Interest Rates?**

This problem is designed to illustrate how the adjustment of nominal interest rates, when it is an accurate reflection of future inflation, can leave the real costs and returns to borrowers and lenders unchanged. For simplicity this problem ignores taxes.

Angela Abbott has a manufacturing firm. After paying other costs she expects a cash flow of $10 million, out of which she must pay the principal and interest on a $5 million loan. If prices are unchanged and if the interest rate is 5 percent, Angela expects a nominal and real profit of $4,750,000. This result is shown in the first column of **Table 6-1.**

Table 6-1				
Angela's Cash Flow				
	(1)	**(2)**	**(3)**	**(4)**
1. Price level	1.00	1.10	1.10	1.10
2. Sales revenue minus labor and materials costs*	10,000,000	11,000,000	11,000,000	11,000,000
3. Principal repayment	5,000,000	5,000,000	5,000,000	5,000,000
4. Interest rate	0.05	0.05	0.155	0.20
5. Interest payment [(4) × (3)]	250,000	_____	_____	_____
6. Total nominal payment to lender [(3) + (5)]	5,250,000	_____	_____	_____
7. Real payment to lender [(6) ÷ (1)]	5,250,000	_____	_____	_____
8. Nominal profits [(2) − (6)]	4,750,000	_____	_____	_____
9. Real profits [(8) ÷ (1)]	4,750,000	_____	_____	_____

*Inflation of 10 percent is assumed to increase sales revenue, labor costs, and materials costs by 10 percent each. As a result, the difference between sales revenue and labor plus material costs also increases by 10 percent in columns 2, 3, and 4.

The next three columns reflect three possible alternatives. The second column shows the consequences of unexpected inflation of 10 percent. In the third column, nominal interest rates have adjusted in expectation of an inflation of 10 percent, which actually occurs. And in the last column, nominal interest rates reflect the consequences of expecting a higher rate of inflation than actually occurs.

a. Fill in the missing figures in the second column. Compare the real returns to both Angela and her lender with those of the noninflationary situation in column 1. Who gains and who loses when there is unexpected inflation?

b. Fill in the missing figures in the third column. This is the case in which nominal interest rates have adjusted appropriately. (The approximation is to add the rate of inflation, 10 percent, to the rate of interest in the noninflationary situation, 5 percent. The extra 0.5 percent comes from a more complex and complete adjustment.) Compare the real returns in rows 7 and 9 with the comparable figures in column 1. Who gains and who loses now?

c. Fill in the missing figures in column 4, where interest rates have adjusted in anticipation of a rate of inflation higher than the rate that actually occurs. Who gains and who loses when inflation turns out to be less than expected?

2. **When Were High Interest Rates Really Low?**

Let R = nominal interest rate,
π = actual rate of inflation, and
r = real rate of interest.

Economists expect expectations of inflation to influence nominal interest rates. When borrowers repay lenders, the real interest rate that borrowers pay and lenders receive will depend upon the actual rate of inflation. One can measure real interest rates after the fact as $r = R - \pi$. Consider the data in **Table 6-2**. Column 1 shows data on nominal interest rates on one-year government securities issued in December of each year from 1975 through

Table 6-2

Nominal and Real Interest Rates

	Nominal Interest Rate on 1-Year Government Securities (December)	Rate of Inflation (December to December)	Real Interest Rate
1975	6.60%	4.9%	_____ %
1976	4.89%	6.7%	_____ %
1977	6.96%	9.0%	_____ %
1978	10.30%	13.3%	_____ %
1979	11.98%	12.5%	_____ %
1980	14.88%	8.9%	_____ %
1981	12.85%	3.8%	_____ %
1982	8.91%	3.8%	_____ %
1983	10.11%	3.9%	_____ %
1984	9.33%	3.8%	_____ %
1985	7.67%	1.1%	_____ %
1986	5.87%	4.4%	_____ %
1987	7.17%	4.4%	_____ %
1988	8.99%	4.6%	_____ %
1989	7.72%	6.1%	_____ %
1990	7.05%	3.1%	_____ %
1991	4.38%	2.9%	_____ %
1992	3.71%	2.7%	_____ %
1993	3.61%	2.7%	_____ %
1994	7.14%	2.5%	_____ %
1995	5.31%	3.3%	_____ %
1996	5.47%	1.7%	_____ %
1997	5.53%	1.6%	_____ %
1998	4.52%	2.7%	_____ %
1999	5.84%	3.4%	_____ %
2000	5.60%	1.6%	_____ %
2001	2.22%	2.4%	_____ %
2002	1.45%	1.9%	_____ %
2003	1.31%	3.3%	_____ %

SOURCES: Federal Reserve, Bureau of Labor Statistics.

2003. Column 2 shows the rate of inflation over the same period, December to December, as measured by the consumer price index. (For example, the rate of inflation reported for 1975 is from December 1975 to December 1976, the same period for which a holder of the government security earned interest.)

a. Complete column 3 by subtracting the rate of inflation from the nominal rate of interest to compute the real rate of interest.

b. The nominal interest rates from column 1 are plotted in **Figure 6-1**. Plot the real interest rates you calculated in column 3 in Figure 6-1.

Figure 6-1

Nominal and Real Interest Rates

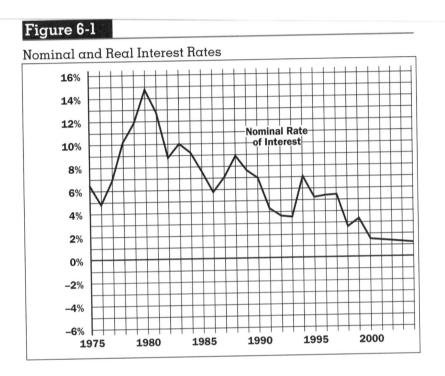

c. Were actual real rates ever negative? If so, how can this be?

d. When were interest rates highest? Is the answer different depending upon whether one is looking at nominal or real interest rates? Which do you think is the best measure of when interest rates were highest?

This exercise has made use of data on actual inflation to calculate after-the-fact real interest rates. Remember that when individuals decide to borrow or lend they typically know the nominal interest rate they will receive or have to pay, but they cannot know what the real interest rate will turn out to be, as that will depend upon future inflation. Thus decisions to borrow and lend will be strongly influenced by expectations of inflation and the corresponding expectations for real interest rates.

3. **When Was Gasoline Most Expensive?**

Table 6-3 has data on the average retail price of a gallon of unleaded gasoline since 1976. Use the data on the CPI for each year to adjust the price of gasoline to see when gasoline was most expensive relative to the price of other goods as measured by the CPI. As explained in the Appendix to Chapter 6, for each year you will need to divide the price of gasoline by the CPI and then multiply by 100.

While 2003 and 2004 show some of the highest nominal prices, when was the relative price of gasoline highest? Was it 2003 or 2004?

Table 6-3

Price of Gasoline

Year	Retail Price of Unleaded gasoline	CPI (82-84 = 100)	Price of gasoline adjusted for inflation
1976	$ 0.61	56.9	$ _____
1977	0.66	60.6	_____
1978	0.67	65.2	_____
1979	0.90	72.6	_____
1980	1.25	82.4	_____
1981	1.38	90.9	_____
1982	1.30	96.5	_____
1983	1.24	99.6	_____
1984	1.21	103.9	_____
1985	1.20	107.6	_____
1986	0.93	109.6	_____
1987	0.95	113.6	_____
1988	0.95	118.3	_____
1989	1.02	124.0	_____
1990	1.16	130.7	_____
1991	1.14	136.2	_____
1992	1.13	140.3	_____
1993	1.11	144.5	_____
1994	1.11	148.2	_____
1995	1.15	152.4	_____
1996	1.23	156.9	_____
1997	1.23	160.5	_____
1998	1.06	163.0	_____
1999	1.17	166.6	_____
2000	1.51	172.2	_____
2001	1.46	177.1	_____
2002	1.36	179.9	_____
2003	1.59	184.0	_____
2004	1.88	188.9	_____

Source: Bureau of Labor Statistics

• Self-Tests for Understanding

Test A

Circle the most appropriate answer.

1. Labor productivity is defined as
   a. output per capita.
   b. GDP divided by population.
   c. the growth in output per worker.
   d. output per hour of labor input.

2. A country's standard of living is usually measured as
   a. GDP per capita.
   b. output per worker.
   c. the growth in GDP.
   d. output per unit of labor input.

3. Which of the following would not explain differences in labor productivity between countries?
   a. the amount of capital per worker
   b. the level of technology
   c. the size of the labor force
   d. the amount of training received by workers

4. The production function tells us how much the economy can produce using all but which one of the following?
   a. labor
   b. capital
   c. outputs
   d. the state of technology

5. Indicate which examples go with which concepts.
   a. an older, unemployed telephone operator replaced by new, computerized switching machines
   b. an unemployed college senior looking for her first job
   c. a former construction worker who has given up looking for work because he believes no one is hiring
   d. an unemployed retail clerk who was laid off because of declining sales associated with a general business recession

   frictional unemployment _____

   structural unemployment _____

   cyclical unemployment _____

   discouraged worker _____

6. Which of the following factors implies that official statistics may understate the magnitude of the problem of unemployment? (There may be more than one correct answer.)
   a. discouraged workers
   b. the loss of expected overtime work
   c. generous unemployment benefits
   d. involuntary part-time work

7. Which of the following people are eligible for unemployment compensation?
   a. a mechanic for Ford Motor Company laid off because of declining auto sales
   b. a housewife seeking paid work after six years spent at home with two small children
   c. a college senior looking for his first job
   d. an engineer who quits to find a better job

8. Which one of the following groups experiences the highest rate of unemployment?
   a. married men
   b. college graduates
   c. teenage workers
   d. adult nonwhite workers

9. The measure of output that the economy could produce with the full employment of all people and factories is called
   a. real GDP.
   b. potential GDP.
   c. nominal GDP.
   d. expected GDP.

10. The difference between potential GDP and actual GDP is a reflection of
    a. frictional unemployment.
    b. cyclical unemployment.
    c. usury laws.
    d. nominal interest rates.

11. The growth of GDP can be expressed as the sum of which of the following?
    a. the growth rate of the labor input
    b. the rate of inflation
    c. the real rate of interest
    d. the growth rate of labor productivity

12. Unemployment insurance
    a. eliminates the cost of unemployment to the economy as a whole.
    b. means that no unemployed worker need suffer a decline in his or her standard of living.
    c. helps to protect insured individuals by spreading the cost.
    d. must be paid back by the unemployed once they find a new job.

13. The real rate of interest relevant for a lender about to lend money is measured as the
    a. nominal interest rate divided by the rate of inflation.
    b. nominal interest rate minus the expected rate of inflation.
    c. rate of inflation minus the nominal interest rate.
    d. the increase in nominal GDP divided by the rate of increase in prices.

14. A nominal interest rate of 10 percent and inflationary expectations of 4 percent imply a real interest rate of _____ percent.
    a. 4
    b. 6
    c. 10
    d. 14

15. If suddenly everyone expects a higher rate of inflation, economists would expect nominal interest rates to
    a. fall.
    b. stay unchanged.
    c. rise.

16. If inflation is unexpected, there is apt to be a redistribution of wealth from
    a. borrowers to lenders.
    b. lenders to borrowers.
    c. rich to poor.
    d. poor to rich.

17. With overall inflation at 5 percent, if the price of jeans increases by 7 percent and the price of calculators declines by 3 percent, we would say that the relative price of
    a. jeans and calculators has increased.
    b. jeans has increased and the relative price of calculators has decreased.
    c. jeans and calculators has decreased.
    d. jeans has decreased and the relative price of calculators has increased.

18. Assume that in a world without inflation, interest rates are 4 percent and 25 percent of interest income must be paid to the government in taxes. (That is, the after-tax real return to lenders is 3 percent.) Assume now that inflation is expected to be and turns out to be 4 percent. Assume further that nominal interest rates increase to 8 percent in line with expectations of inflation at 4 percent. With taxes based on nominal income, what is the after-tax real return when nominal interest rates increase to 8 percent?
    a. Less than 3 percent.
    b. Unchanged at 3 percent.
    c. More than 3 percent.

19. If your wages go up by 10 percent when prices go up by 7 percent, the increase in your real wage is about _____ percent.
    a. 3
    b. 7
    c. 10
    d. 17

20. The historical evidence suggests that in periods with high rates of inflation, nominal wages
    a. increase at about the same rate as before.
    b. increase at much lower rates than inflation.
    c. also increase at high rates.
    d. remain unchanged.

Test B

Circle T or F for true or false.

T   F   1. Long term, it makes little difference whether productivity grows at 1 percent per year or at 3 percent per year.

T   F   2. If the growth in real GDP is less than the growth in potential GDP, there will be an increase in unemployment.

T   F   3. In periods of high unemployment, the only people whose incomes are reduced are those who are out of work.

T   F   4. The official unemployment statistics are adjusted to include those people with part-time jobs who are looking for full-time work.

T F 5. Unemployment insurance protects society against lost output from unemployment.

T F 6. Potential GDP is an estimate of the maximum possible output our economy could produce under conditions similar to wartime.

T F 7. Most economists agree that full employment should be defined as an unemployment rate of zero.

T F 8. Inflation does not redistribute wealth between borrowers and lenders because nominal interest rates are automatically adjusted to reflect actual inflation.

T F 9. The historical record shows that low inflation will always lead to high inflation.

T F 10. Predictable inflation is likely to impose less cost than unpredictable inflation.

| Appendix | *How Statisticians Measure Inflation*

Learning Objectives

After completing this appendix, you should be able to:

- construct a price index from data on prices and the composition of the market basket in the base year.

- use a price index to compute real measures of economic activity by deflating the corresponding nominal measures.

- use a price index to compute the rate of inflation from one period to the next.

- explain how the market baskets differ for the Consumer Price Index and the GDP deflator.

Important Terms and Concepts

Index number	Consumer price index	GDP deflator
Index number problem	Deflating	

Important Terms and Concepts Quiz

Choose the best definition for each of the following terms.

1. _____ Index number

2. _____ Index number problem

3. _____ Consumer Price Index

4. _____ Deflating

5. _____ GDP deflator

a. Dividing a nominal magnitude by a price index to express the magnitude in constant purchasing power

b. Magnitude of some variable relative to its magnitude in the base period

c. Price index obtained by dividing nominal GDP by real GDP

d. Measure of price level based on the spending of urban households

e. Average change in consumer prices

f. Differences between consumption patterns of actual families and the market basket used for a price index

Basic Exercises

The following exercise should help you review the material on price indexes presented in the appendix to Chapter 6.

Table 6-4 presents data on expenditures and prices for a hypothetical family that buys only food and clothing. We see that in 2004 this family spent $5,000 on food at $2 per unit of food, and $10,000 on clothing at $25 per unit. Note that between 2004 and 2005, dollar expenditures by this family increased by 15.65 percent, rising from $15,000 to $17,348. Is this family able to consume 15.65 percent more of everything? Clearly not, since prices have risen. How much inflation has there been on average? What is the increase in real income for this family? These are the sorts of questions that a good price index can help you answer.

Table 6-4

Prices and Expenditures

Year	Food Price	Food Expenditures	Clothing Price	Clothing Expenditures	Total Expenditures
2004	$2.00	$5,000	$25.00	$10,000	$15,000
2005	$2.36	$5,900	$26.50	$11,448	$17,348

1. Use the data in Table 6-4 to construct a family price index (FPI) using 2004 as the base year.

   a. Divide expenditures by price to find the quantities of each good purchased in 2004. This is the base-period market basket.

   Quantity of food _____

   Quantity of clothing _____

   b. Use 2005 prices to find out how much the base-period market basket would cost in 2005.

   2005 cost of 2004 market basket _____

   c. Divide the 2005 cost of the base-period market basket by the 2004 cost of the same market basket and multiply by 100 to compute the value of the FPI for 2005.

   FPI for 2005 _____

   d. Convince yourself that if you repeat steps b and c using 2004 prices you will get an answer of 100 for the value of the FPI for 2004.

   e. Estimate inflation by computing the percentage change in your price index from 2004 to 2005.

   Inflation between 2004 and 2005 _____

   f. Divide total dollar expenditures in 2005 by the 2005 FPI and multiply by 100 to deflate 2005 nominal expenditures.

   Real expenditures in 2005 (2004 prices) _____

   Percentage change in real expenditures 2004 to 2005 _____

   Remember the following points about price indexes:
   - Most price indexes, like the Consumer Price Index, are computed by pricing a standard market basket of goods in subsequent periods.
   - A price index can be used to measure inflation and to deflate nominal values to adjust for inflation.

- Different price indexes, such as the Consumer Price Index and the GDP deflator, will show slightly different measures of inflation because they use different market baskets.

2. (Optional) Compute a new FPI using 2005 as the base period rather than 2004. Now the value of your price index for 2005 will be 100 and the price index for 2004 will be something less than 100. Does this index give the same measure of inflation as the index with 2004 as the base period? Do not be surprised if it does not. Can you explain why they differ?

Supplementary Exercises

1. **Table 6-5** contains data on consumer prices for seven countries. Try to answer each of the following questions or explain why the information in Table 6-5 is insufficient to answer the question.
   a. In 1970, which country had the lowest prices?
   b. In 2004, which country had the highest prices?

Table 6-5

Consumer Prices (1982-84 = 100)

	Canada	France	Germany	Italy	Japan	United Kingdom	United States
1970	35.1	28.8	52.8	17.1	38.5	21.8	38.8
1980	76.1	72.3	86.7	63.2	90.9	78.5	82.4
1990	135.5	133.0	112.2	159.6	111.4	148.2	130.7
2000	164.9	157.6	142.6	231.9	121.0	200.1	172.2
2004	181.0	170.3	150.8	256.3	118.7	219.4	188.9

SOURCE: *Economic Report of the President, 2000 and 2005,* Table B-108.

c. During the period 1970 to 2004, which country experienced the most inflation as measured by the percentage change in the consumer price index? Which country experienced the least inflation?

2. **How Much Difference Can Small Differences Really Make?**

The text argues that although the differences in the growth rate of GDP per capita over the period 1870 to 1979 for the United States, Japan, and the United Kingdom seem quite small when compounded over 100-plus years, the differences can be quite large. Can such small differences really make much of a difference?

Fill in the last column in **Table 6-6** to find out. It compares the experience of three countries, all assumed to start with the same level of GDP per capita.

Table 6-6

The Cumulative Impact of Small Differences in Growth Rates

Country	Annual growth rate of GDP per capita	Initial level GDP per capita	GDP per capita after 109 years
A	1.8%	10,000	_____
B	2.3%	10,000	_____
C	3.0%	10,000	_____

3. **How Accurate Are Consumer Expectations of Inflation?**

You can check for yourself. The Federal Reserve Bank of St. Louis posts data on inflation expectations from the University of Michigan survey of consumers. Try comparing this data to the actual change in consumer prices that you can compute using data on the CPI from the same Web site.

   Data on inflation expectations are found under the "Business/Fiscal" heading at

http://research.stlouisfed.org/fred2

It may be easiest to use the search option. Search for "University of Michigan Inflation Expectations." Data on the CPI is found at the same Web site under the heading "Consumer Price Indexes." You will need to compute the actual rate of inflation from the data on the CPI.

• Economics in Action

How to Measure Inflation

Does the Consumer Price Index (CPI) overstate inflation? If so, by how much? In the late 1990s these questions were of more than academic interest. They became an important part of discussions about how to balance the federal budget. A number of federal programs, most notably Social Security payments and income tax brackets, are adjusted annually in step with increases in the CPI. If the CPI overstates inflation, these adjustments have been too generous in the sense that federal government spending would be larger and revenues would be smaller than they should be to account for inflation. If inflation has been overstated, then the apparent stagnation in real wages that one finds when using the CPI to adjust nominal wages has given a misleading picture of real income.

   In 1995, while looking for ways to eliminate the deficit, the Senate Finance Committee asked a panel of prominent economists, headed by Michael Boskin, an economist at Stanford University and former Chairman of the Council of Economic Advisers, to study this issue and make a recommendation to the Committee.

   The panel issued its final report in December 1996. It concluded that the CPI has overstated inflation by about 1.1 percent per year for four reasons: Substitution bias—as the CPI prices a fixed market basket, it ignores the response of consumers to change their market basket in favor of goods and services with smaller price increases; outlet bias—CPI sampling procedures have tended to ignore the shift of consumers to large discount stores like Wal-Mart and Costco; quality bias—CPI procedures are not always able to identify when an increase in price reflects improved quality; new product bias—because the CPI market basket is changed so infrequently, it often misses the large declines in price that usually accompany the introduction of new products.

   In late 2001, the Bureau of Labor Statistics (BLS) announced that it will adjust the consumer market basket every two years instead of every six to eight years. It also announced that it will adjust its sample of stores more frequently.

   Others are not so sure that the Boskin Commission's criticisms were all on target. These critics question BLS procedures to measure quality changes and are also skeptical of how the Boskin Commission proposed to handle new products. A more fundamental difference has to do with the role of price index like the CPI. The Boskin Commission argued in favor of a consumer price index that measures the cost of living. Critics acknowledge that, while in principle quality improvements reduce the cost of maintaining the previous standard of living, a real focus on the cost of living should include many other factors that may have increased the cost of living, e.g., increase in congestion, environment degradation, and commodities where quality has decreased rather than increase.

1. Do you think that the CPI has overstated inflation? If so by how much?

2. What would you recommend that the Bureau of Labor Statistics do?

Sources: The Boskin Committee Report is available online at http://www.ssa.gov/history/reports/boskinrpt.html. For a contrary view see Dean Baker, "The Inflated Case Against the CPI," *The American Prospect*, December 1, 1996. Baker's article is available online at http://www.prospect.org/print/V7/24/baker-d.html. See also Jolie Solomon, "An economic speedometer gets an overhaul," *The New York Times*, December 23, 2001; Jeff Madrick, "A new study questions how much anyone really knows about the real rate of inflation in the U.S.," *The New York Times*, December 27, 2001.

Study Questions

1. What is the difference between measures of labor productivity and output per capita?

2. Why is the growth of labor productivity so important for the growth in standards of living?

3. What factors are important for growth in labor productivity?

4. Is it possible for the growth in a country's standard of living to exceed the growth in labor productivity? If so, how, and is it likely that such a difference could be sustained over a long period of time?

5. Why doesn't unemployment insurance eliminate the cost of unemployment for the economy as a whole?

6. Do you believe the official rate of unemployment overstates or understates the seriousness of unemployment? Why?

7. Which concepts of unemployment—frictional, structural, and cyclical—are relevant when considering the full-employment rate of unemployment? Why?

8. What rate of unemployment is an appropriate target for macroeconomic policy?

9. When does an increase in the price of textbooks reflect a change in relative prices and when does it reflect inflation?

10. During a period of inflation, which is likely to be higher, nominal or real interest rates? Why?

11. Will inflation always redistribute income from lenders to borrowers?

12. Do you agree or disagree with the argument that the taxation of interest and capital gains should be based on real returns rather than nominal returns? Why?

13. Which is likely to have more adverse effects, steady or variable inflation? Why?

● Economics Online

The Bureau of Labor Statistics keeps tabs on employment, unemployment, and consumer prices. You can access current and historical data online at the following Web sites:

Employment: http://www.bls.gov/bls/employment.htm

Consumer prices: http://www.bls.gov/cpi

7

Economic Growth: Theory and Policy

Important Terms and Concepts

Human capital

Convergence hypothesis

Capital

Investment

Capital formation

Property rights

On-the-job training

Invention

Innovation

Research and development (R&D)

Cost disease of the personal services

Development assistance

Foreign direct investment

Multinational corporations

Learning Objectives

After completing this chapter, you should be able to:

- Explain why growth policies concentrate on efforts to increase

  ○ the rate of capital formation

  ○ the rate of improvement in workforce quality

  ○ the rate of technical progress.

- Describe policies that are meant to address each of these three pillars of economic growth.

- Explain why countries with initial low levels of productivity might be expected to see higher growth in productivity than countries with high levels of productivity.

- Describe the convergence hypothesis and explain whether all countries are participating.

- Describe American productivity growth experience and evaluate the arguments that have been advanced to explain this experience.

- Describe the cost disease of personal services and explain why the production of manufacturing goods would not be expected to suffer the same problem.

- Describe the growth experience of low-income countries and explain why it often differs from that of high-income countries.

• Chapter Review

Macroeconomic policymakers have two major tasks. One task focuses on the long run and is con-
(1) cerned with the rate of growth of potential GDP. This task is called _____ policy. The other
task is concerned with keeping the economy close to its potential and is called _____ policy.
This chapter is concerned with the first task.

We saw in the last chapter that the growth in labor productivity is the major factor in determining
the growth in output per capita or standards of living in the long run. As such it should not be
surprising that growth policy focuses on the growth in labor productivity. The three pillars of
productivity growth are the rate at which an economy adds to its stock of factories, machines, and
(2) software through _____; the rate at which technology improves through _____ and
_____; and the rate at which the quality of the workforce or the stock of _____
capital improves. While the level of output depends upon the size of the capital stock, the current state
of technology, and the quality of the work force, the growth in output depends upon the growth in
these same factors.

Comparing the growth experience across countries suggests that many countries with low levels of
productivity are able to grow more quickly than countries that start with higher levels of productivity.
(3) This differential experience has been called the _____ hypothesis and arises because low
productivity countries are able to learn from high productivity countries. It is the high productivity
countries that need to (imitate/innovate) while the low productivity countries can _____.
While a number of countries have been able to grow in this fashion, not all countries belong to the
"convergence club." Political instability and weak property _____ often plague those that
do not.

A country that wants to improve its growth prospects will want to focus policy actions on the three
pillars of productivity growth. That is, it will want to adopt and promote policies that support capital
formation, improvements in the quality of the work force, and invention and innovation. Policies
(4) that support capital formation are likely to include (high/low) real-interest rates, growth-oriented
tax policies, and levels of aggregate demand close to potential output so that demand presses against
productive capacity. The success of these policies is enhanced when there is a strong rule of law with
secure property rights. It is also important to remember that higher levels of investments (are/are not)
costless. For a country operating on its production possibilities frontier the opportunity cost of more
investment will be a(n) (decrease/increase) in the output of consumption goods.

Policies that support improvements in the quality of the work force are those that support
education and on-the-job training. Data on the earnings of college graduates suggest that in the
United States the returns on higher education are quite substantial. Policies to support invention and

innovation are likely to include government support for research and development through tax policy, public/private partnerships, and direct support of basic research.

It is not always possible to neatly assign growth policies to one of the three pillars. For example, policies that support scientific, technical, and business education are likely to be an important part of policies to enhance research and development. Policies that support invention and innovation will also support high levels of capital formation as firms seek to take advantage of new opportunities.

The record of productivity growth in the United States over the last half century shows some marked differences. For 25 years, from 1948 to 1973, productivity grew at about 2.9 percent per year. Productivity growth then slowed dramatically and averaged only 1.4 percent per year for the next 22 years. Experience from 1995 until the beginning of the recession in 2001 has been more optimistic with productivity growth averaging 3.0 percent per year.

Exactly why productivity growth slowed down so dramatically in the 1970s is not fully understood. Possible explanations include lagging investment, higher energy prices, a decline in work force quality, and a slowdown in the pace of innovation, although not all of these explanations seem as compelling on close examination. The growth in productivity since 1995 seems more closely related to advances in information technology and a surge in _____ spending.   (5)

It is important to remember that not all sectors of the economy participate equally in the process of economic growth. In particular, much of the growth in labor productivity is concentrated in parts of the economy that produce (goods/services) rather than _____. In parts of the economy (6) where labor input and direct personal contact are important, e.g., medical care, education, the arts, police protection, it is harder to find ways to increase productivity that do not degrade the quality of services. While one person using a synthesizer might try playing a Beethoven quartet, many are likely to conclude that it is not the same as four string players.

Because labor is mobile across sectors of the economy, wages and salaries in personal service sectors of the economy need to keep pace with other sectors of the economy where high rates of growth in productivity can support wage increases without implying price increases. The result is higher relative prices for the personal service sectors of the economy, a phenomenon known as the _____ _____ of personal services.   (7)

Growth policies in developing countries will also focus on the three pillars of growth but are likely to be more difficult to implement. Low levels of income make it harder to find the resources for investment in capital, education, and technology. Rich countries can help by providing development assistance. Technology may be imported by encouraging multinational corporations to make direct investments, but there is often resistance to such actions. Adverse geographical conditions and government corruption are additional challenges facing many developing countries.

Important Terms and Concepts Quiz

Choose the most appropriate definition for each of the following terms.

1. _____ Human capital
2. _____ Convergence hypothesis
3. _____ Capital
4. _____ Investment (or capital formation)
5. _____ Property rights
6. _____ On-the-job training
7. _____ Invention
8. _____ Innovation
9. _____ Research and development (R&D)
10. _____ Cost disease of the personal services
11. _____ Development assistance
12. _____ Foreign direct investment
13. _____ Multinational corporation

a. Low productivity countries experience higher growth in productivity

b. Stock of factories, office buildings, and machines

c. Purchase or construction of real business assets in a foreign country

d. Discovering new products or new production methods

e. Devoting resources to the production of new plants, more equipment, and software

f. Reduced output of consumption goods when output of investment goods increases

g. Grants and low interest loans to developing countries

h. Amount of education and training embodied in a nation's labor force

i. Increasing relative prices for services that require direct personal contact

j. Business or government activity that is purposely designed to stimulate invention and innovation

k. Laws and conventions that assign ownership rights

l. Skills workers acquire while working

m. Putting new ideas into practice

n. Corporation that operates in many countries

● Basic Exercises

1. This exercise illustrates the difference between the level of labor productivity and the growth of labor productivity. In particular, we will see whether a decline in the growth of labor productivity results in a decline in the level of productivity. Assume that labor productivity is originally $12 per hour, and that it grows at an annual rate of 2.9 percent for 25 years, and 1.4 percent for the next 22 years.

   a. What is labor productivity at the end of the first 25 years? $ _____

   b. What is labor productivity at the end of the next 22 years? $ _____

   c. Did the decline in the rate of growth of productivity lead to a decline in the level of productivity?

2. Can small differences in growth rates make all that much difference for productivity? Assume that we can index American productivity in 2000 at a value of 100. Fill in the blanks below to show what our productivity index would show in 2050 and 2100 at different rates of growth.

Growth Rate of Productivity	Productivity Index 2050	Productivity Index 2100
1.4 percent	_____	_____
2.5 percent	_____	_____
3.0 percent	_____	_____

Self-Tests for Understanding

Test A

Circle the most appropriate answer.

1. Stabilization policy is concerned with
   a. an economy's growth prospects.
   b. maintaining competitive conditions in industries that might otherwise become monopolized.
   c. seeing that an economy is plagued by neither high unemployment nor high inflation.
   d. maintaining stable exchange rates vis-à-vis other currencies.

2. Growth policy is concerned with
   a. an economy's growth prospects.
   b. maintaining competitive conditions in industries that might otherwise become monopolized.
   c. seeing that an economy is plagued by neither high unemployment nor high inflation.
   d. maintaining stable exchange rates visà-vis other currencies.

3. The growth in potential GDP is equal to the sum of which of the following?
   a. growth in population
   b. growth in labor hours
   c. growth in labor productivity
   d. growth in capital stock

4. The three pillars of productivity growth include which of the following?
   a. growth in the capital stock
   b. growth in technology
   c. growth in unemployment
   d. growth in human capital

5. Increases in which of the following would not be expected to increase labor productivity?
   a. capital stock
   b. technology
   c. labor force
   d. human capital

6. If the growth in labor productivity declines from 3 percent per year to 1.5 percent per year, then
   a. labor productivity will continue to increase although at a slower rate than before.
   b. standards of living will increase only if there is an expansion in average hours per worker.
   c. labor will become less productive over time.
   d. the result will be a declining standard of living.

7. The convergence hypothesis suggests that the growth of labor productivity in the most advanced country
   a. will exceed that of all other countries.
   b. will be less than that of many other countries.
   c. must decline.

8. A major factor leading to the convergence of growth rates across countries is probably the
   a. use of the dollar as the international currency of commerce.
   b. increased levels of GDP devoted to military spending in many countries.
   c. adoption of the euro.
   d. quick pace by which new technologies are spread among countries.

9. The essence of the convergence hypothesis can be summarized by noting that countries with the most advanced technology must _____ while less advanced countries can _____.
   a. import; export
   b. invest; save
   c. innovate; imitate
   d. educate; train

10. A low productivity country that is part of the convergence club will find that the growth in its productivity
    a. lags behind that of more advanced countries.
    b. is about the same as that of more advanced countries.
    c. is greater than that of more advanced countries.

11. Capital formation is another term for
    a. innovation.
    b. investment expenditures.
    c. invention.
    d. capital gains.

12. Which of the following is not conducive to a high level of investment expenditures?
    a. high real interest rates
    b. expectations of rapid economic growth
    c. new technologies that have created new markets
    d. political stability and clearly defined property rights

13. A country's stock of human capital can be increased by which of the following? (There may be more than one correct answer.)
    a. high real interest rates
    b. on-the-job training
    c. higher high school graduation rates
    d. lower taxes on capital gains

14. Since 1980 the income of college graduates has grown _____ the income of high school graduates.
    a. more slowly than
    b. about the same as
    c. much faster than

15. Which of the following is not a policy tool to stimulate research and development?
    a. reductions in taxes when businesses spend money on R&D
    b. monetary policy
    c. public/private research collaborations like the human genome project
    d. direct government expenditures through agencies like the National Science Foundation

16. When compared to the previous 25 years, the growth in productivity over the period 1973 to 1995 was
    a. lower.
    b. about the same.
    c. higher.

17. When compared to the previous 22 years, the growth in productivity over the period 1995 to 2007 was
    a. lower.
    b. about the same.
    c. higher.

18. When trying to understand the recent increase in the growth of productivity, most analysts cite which two of the following factors?
    a. high levels of private investment spending
    b. advances in information technology
    c. increasing energy prices
    d. declining high school graduation rates

19. Which of the following is least likely to suffer from the cost disease of personal services?
    a. manufacturing
    b. health care
    c. education
    d. the arts

20. The cost disease of personal services reflects which of the following? (There may be more than one correct answer.)
    a. Increases in labor productivity will lead to increase in real wages.
    b. Increases in labor productivity are likely to be slow where personal contact is an important part of quality of service provided.
    c. In the long run, real wages in different occupations need to rise at similar rates if different occupations are to continue to be attractive to young people.

Test B

Circle T or F for true or false.

T F 1. Productivity growth in the United States is higher than in most other industrialized countries.

T F 2. Since 1970 the growth in productivity in the United States has been about three times as high as it was right after World War II.

T F 3. A decline in the rate of growth of American labor productivity means a decline in the productivity of American workers.

T F 4. Increased investment spending leading to more capital formation is likely to increase the rate of economic growth.

T F 5. The growth in potential GDP is equal to the growth rate in hours worked plus the growth rate of labor productivity.

T F 6. In recent years workers with a college degree have earned over 40 percent more than workers with just a high school degree.

T F 7. All countries are now participating in the process of convergence of labor productivity.

T F 8. According to the convergence hypothesis, low productivity countries will experience lower rates of growth of labor productivity than high productivity countries.

T F 9. Investment is more likely when firms have excess capacity than when sales mean that firms must operate at full capacity.

T F 10. Labor productivity in services industries should grow more rapidly than in the manufacturing sector of the economy.

● Supplementary Exercise

Assume that growth policies were successful in raising income per capita in China to equal that of the United States. Because of the initial higher level of incomes in the United States, $37,800 vs. $5,000, it would take a number of years for Chinese incomes to reach parity with those in the United States. When answering the questions below assume that the growth rate of income per capita in the United States is 2 percent per year.

How fast would income per capita in China have to grow to match that of the United States in 50 years? In 100 years?

Income per capita in China has been growing at close to 8 percent per year. If it continued to grow at this rate, how long would it take to match that of the United States if income per capita in the United States continues to grow at 2 percent per year?

What does the convergence hypothesis say about China's ability to sustain a higher rate of economic growth as its income approaches that of the United States?

• Economics in Action

How to Improve World Economic Growth

While there is widespread agreement about the importance of increasing economic growth in developing countries, there is as yet no agreement about what are the best ways to achieve this aim or even where to begin. The latter disagreement reflects in part the significant number of challenges that low-income countries face.

In September 2000, the United Nations adopted eight aggressive goals for worldwide economic development. Called the Millennium Development Goals, they include

- Eradicate extreme poverty and hunger by reducing by half the proportion of people living on less than a dollar a day and reducing by half the proportion of people who suffer from hunger

- Ensure that all boys and girls complete a full course of primary schooling

- Eliminate gender disparity in primary and secondary education preferably by 2005, and at all levels by 2015

- Reduce by two-thirds the mortality rate among children under five

- Reduce by three-quarters the maternal mortality ratio

- Combat HIV/AIDS, malaria, and other diseases by halting and beginning to reverse the spread of HIV/AIDS, the incidence of malaria, and other major diseases

- Ensure environmental sustainability

- Develop a global partnership for development.

Regardless of one's ranking of these goals, there is less agreement on what steps will be most effective to achieve them. Some, like economist Jeffrey Sachs, Director of the Earth Institute at Columbia University, argue for massive infusions of foreign aid from developed countries. Sachs estimates that achieving the Millennium goals will require an investment of $150 billion a year of development assistance.

How does $150 billion compare to current aid flows? In 2007 aid flows from developed countries were $103 billion, about 0. 28 percent of the GDP of donor countries. Sachs notes that development aid of $150 billion would raise contributions to a little more than 0.50 percent of GDP, still short of the goal of 0.70 percent endorsed by donor countries in 2002.

Before arguing for massive increases in foreign aid, some economists and others point to the importance of free trade, low taxes, deregulation, privatization, and the critical nature of the rule of law and reductions in government corruption. In March 2005, the Commission for Africa, sponsored by the British government, issued a document, "Our Common Interest" that called for a "radical change in the way donors behave and deliver assistance" to African nations. The report argued that corruption and misgovernment in Africa have been an impediment to economic growth, but goes on to argue for increased foreign aid and adjustments to trade policies in developing countries that have been a significant obstacle to African export growth.

The Copenhagen Consensus, a project organized by Bjorn Lomborg, head of the Environment Assessment Institute in Denmark, pulled together a panel of distinguished economists in May 2004 to evaluate a number of proposals to increase economic development, especially in low-income countries. The development challenges reviewed by the panel included civil conflicts, climate change, communicable diseases, education, financial stability, governance, hunger and malnutrition, migration, trade reform, and water and sanitation.

At the top of the panel's list for action was controlling HIV/AIDS, followed by fighting malnutrition. Third on their list was reducing trade barriers and eliminating agricultural subsidies. Using cost-benefit analysis the panel did not support proposals to mitigate climate change and implement the Kyoto protocol on greenhouse-gas emissions. Although subsequently some members of the panel argued that they were evaluating the specific proposal they had been asked to review and not the importance of the issues per se.

How much progress has been made in increasing GDP per capita in developing countries? How much progress has been made with regard to the specific UN Millennium Development Goals? How important is foreign aid to achieving these goals? How would you evaluate the importance of the issues reviewed by the Copenhagen Consensus?

Sources: "Spend $150 billion Per Year to Cure World Poverty," Daphne Eviatar, *New York Times*, November 7, 2004; "Putting the world to rights—Copenhagen Consensus," *The Economist*, June 5, 2004; "The Debate over Global Warming is getting rancorous," *The Economist*, February 5, 2005. David White, "Top-Level call for radical change in Africa aid," *Financial Times* (London), March 11, 2005.

You might be interested in the following Web sites:

- UN Millennium Goals: http://www.un.org/millenniumgoals

- This website tracks 48 indicators to measure progress towards the Millennium Development goals: http://millenniumindicators.un.org/unsd/mi/mi_goals.asp

- The Copenhagen Consensus: http://www.copenhagenconsensus.com

- The Earth Institute: http://www.earthinstitute.columbia.edu

Study Questions

1. Why is labor productivity so much higher in some countries than others?

2. What are the three pillars of increased productivity?

3. If a country wants to increase its capital stock, what policies might it follow?

4. If a country wants to increase the quality of its work force, what policies might it follow?

5. If a country wants to improve its technology, what policies might it follow?

6. How are a country's options in regard to increasing productivity different depending upon whether the country is a high or low productivity country?

7. What explains the apparent convergence of labor productivity and standards of living among the world's leading industrial countries?

8. What does the convergence hypothesis suggest about the growth of labor productivity in the United States compared to that of other industrialized countries?

9. What do you think explains the American experience with productivity growth over the last half-century?

10. What is the cost disease of personal services?

11. Do you think that the United States should pursue policies that work to increase the rate of American economic growth? Why or why not?

12. Why are successful growth policies so difficult to achieve in many developing countries?

● Economics Online

The World Bank works with developing countries to help them improve their growth prospects. The Bank tracks data for developing and developed countries. Data is available by country and topic at the following Web site.

http://www.worldbank.org/data

For example, to compare data on schooling in different countries, click on Data by Topic and then on Education.

Aggregate Demand and the Powerful Consumer

8

Important Terms and Concepts

Aggregate demand

Consumer expenditure (C)

Investment spending (I)

Government purchases (G)

Net exports ($X - IM$)

$C + I + G + (X - IM)$

National income

Disposable income (DI)

Circular flow diagram

Transfer payments

Scatter diagram

Consumption function

Marginal propensity to consume (MPC)

Movements along versus shifts of the consumption function

Money fixed assets

Temporary versus permanent tax changes

Learning Objectives
After completing this chapter, you should be able to:

- distinguish between spending, output, and income.

- describe what spending categories make up aggregate demand.

- distinguish between investment spending as a part of aggregate demand and as financial investment.

- explain why, except for some technical complications, national product and national income are necessarily equal.

- explain how disposable income differs from national income.

- derive a consumption function given data on consumption and disposable income.

- compute the marginal propensity to consume at various levels of income.

- explain why the marginal propensity to consume is equal to the slope of the consumption function.

- distinguish between factors that result in a *movement along* the consumption function and factors that result in a *shift* of the function.

- explain why consumption spending is affected by a change in the level of prices even if real income is unchanged.

- describe why permanent and temporary changes in taxes of the same magnitude would be expected to have different impacts on consumption spending.

- explain why investment spending is so volatile.

- describe how income and prices, both domestic and foreign, affect the demand for imports and exports.

- explain how a change in the exchange rate will affect net exports.

Chapter Review

This chapter introduces two key concepts that economists use when discussing the determination of an economy's output: aggregate demand and the consumption function. These concepts will be fundamental to the material in later chapters.

The total amount that all consumers, business firms, government agencies, and foreigners are willing to spend on goods and services produced by the domestic economy is called aggregate

(1) _____. Economists typically divide this sum into four components: consumption expenditures, investment spending, government purchases, and net exports. Food, clothing, movies, and haircuts are examples of (consumption/investment/government) expenditures. New factories, office buildings, machinery, and houses would be examples of _____ spending. Red tape, filing cabinets, and the services of bureaucrats are examples of _____ purchases. American wheat and tractors sold abroad are examples of (exports/imports), and American purchases of French wines, Canadian paper, and Mexican oil are examples of _____. The difference between exports and imports is called _____. Economists use national income accounts to keep track of these components of demand. The appendix to this chapter provides an introduction to these accounts.

There is a close analogy between the demand for a single product and aggregate demand. As seen in the study of consumer demand in microeconomics, economists argue that demand should be seen as a schedule showing how the quantity demanded depends upon a number of factors, including price. In later chapters we will see that aggregate demand is also a schedule showing how the demand by everyone for newly produced goods and services is affected by a variety of factors, including the overall level of prices or, for short, the price level.

Two other concepts that are closely related to aggregate demand are national product and national

(2) income. National product is simply the output of the economy. National income is the (before/after)-tax income of all the individuals in the economy. Disposable income is the income of individuals after _____ have been paid and any _____ payments from the government have been counted. The circular flow diagram shows that national product and national income are two ways of measuring the same thing: Producing goods and selling them results in income for the owners and employees of firms.

Economists use the concept of a consumption function to organize the determinants of consumption expenditures. Specifically, the consumption function is the relation between aggregate

(3) real consumption expenditures and aggregate real (disposable/national) income, holding all other determinants of consumer spending constant. Higher disposable income leads to (more/less) consumption spending. A change in disposable income leads to a (shift in/movement along) the consumption function. A change in one of the other factors that affect consumer spending, such as

wealth, the price level, real interest rates, or expectations of future income, leads to a(n) _____

_____ the consumption function.

An increase in the price level affects consumption spending and is an important reason why

aggregate demand, _____ + _____ + _____ + _____ − _____, is a schedule. If prices are   (4)

higher, we expect (<u>more/less</u>) consumption spending. Consumption spending changes because

the value of many consumer assets is fixed in money terms, and an increase in the price level will

(<u>increase/decrease</u>) the purchasing power of these assets. It is important to remember that higher

prices will lead to lower real consumption expenditures even if real disposable income is constant.

Consider a situation where prices double. If income doubles, there is no change in the purchasing

power of consumers' income, but there is a loss to consumers from the decline in the purchasing

power of their money fixed assets. It is this latter decline that leads to a shift in the consumption

function in response to a change in the price level.

A change in income taxes changes disposable income, and the consumption function tells us how

a change in disposable income will affect consumption spending. For example, a reduction in income

taxes would (<u>increase/decrease</u>) disposable income. After computing the change in disposable   (5)

income, one could estimate the initial impact on consumption spending by multiplying the change

in disposable income by the marginal propensity to consume. A permanent increase in taxes would

be expected to have a (<u>larger/smaller</u>) effect on consumption expenditures than a temporary tax

increase of the same magnitude because the permanent increase changes consumers' long-run

income prospects by (<u>more/less</u>) than the temporary increase. The same argument works in reverse

and implies that temporary tax changes have a (<u>larger/smaller</u>) impact on consumption expenditures

than do permanent tax changes. One must also remember that while it may be easy to calculate

the movement along the consumption function from a change in taxes, other factors influencing

consumption are likely to be changing at the same time, making it difficult to predict the final change

in consumption spending.

We have seen the important role that income plays as a determinant of consumption expenditures.

There is no such central factor influencing investment expenditures. Instead, investment expenditures

are influenced by a variety of factors, including interest rates, taxes, technical change, the strength of

the economy, and business confidence. If any of these factors change, investment spending is likely to

change.

Net exports are the difference between exports and imports. Exports reflect foreign demand for

American production and imports come from American demand for foreign goods and services. It

should not be surprising that both are influenced by income and prices. The tricky part is keeping

straight whose income influences which demand, and how changes in American and foreign prices

influence net exports.

Important Terms and Concepts Quiz

Choose the best definition for each of the following terms.

1. _____ Aggregate demand
2. _____ Consumer expenditure (*C*)
3. _____ Investment spending (*I*)
4. _____ Government purchases (*G*)
5. _____ Net exports (*X – IM*)
6. _____ National income
7. _____ Disposable income (*DI*)
8. _____ Transfer payments
9. _____ Consumption function
10. _____ Marginal propensity to consume
11. _____ Movement along the consumption function
12. _____ Shift of the consumption function
13. _____ Money fixed asset

a. Relation between aggregate real consumption expenditures and aggregate real disposable income
b. Income of individuals after taxes and transfer payments
c. Purchases of newly produced goods and services by all levels of government
d. Total amount spent by consumers on newly produced goods and services
e. Change in consumption due to a change in disposable income
f. Gross national product divided by price level
g. Total amount consumers, firms, government agencies, and foreigners are willing to spend on final goods and services
h. Total spending by firms on new plants and equipment plus spending by consumers on new homes
i. Change in consumption divided by change in disposable income
j. Asset whose value is fixed in terms of dollars
k. Exports minus imports
l. Total before-tax earnings of all individuals in economy
m. Change in consumption due to a change in any factor affecting consumption other than disposable income
n. Government grants to individuals

● Basic Exercises

Note that the first three problems are based on income and consumption data for individual families rather than aggregate income and consumption. Along with the fourth problem, they will give you practice using and understanding the MPC.

1. **Table 8-1** reports some data on disposable income and consumption.
   a. For each change in disposable income, compute the marginal propensity to consume by dividing the change in _____ by the change in _____.
   b. The average propensity to consume is defined as the ratio of consumption expenditures to disposable income or APC = $C \div DI$. For example, when disposable income is $20,000, the average propensity to consume is .90 = $18,000 ÷ $20,000. Use the data on disposable income and consumption to fill in the column for the APC.

Table 8-1

Disposable Income and Consumption Spending

Disposable Income	Change in Disposable Income	Marginal Propensity to Consume	Change in Consumption Expenditures	Consumption Expenditures	Average Propensity to Consume
$20,000				$18,000	_____
$40,000	$20,000	_____	$15,000	$33,000	_____
$60,000	$20,000	_____	$15,000	$48,000	_____
$80,000	$20,000	_____	$15,000	$63,000	_____
$100,000	$20,000	_____	$15,000	$78,000	_____

Figure 8-1

Consumption Function

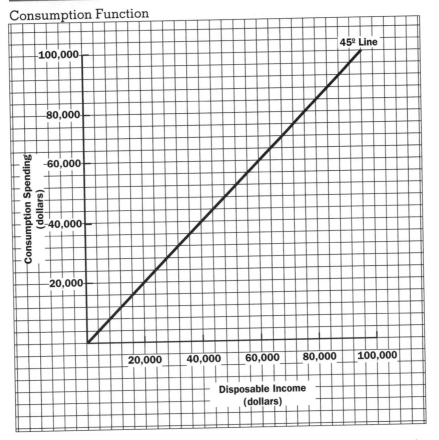

c. Are the average and marginal propensities equal? Do the differences surprise you? Can you explain them? Perhaps steps d through f will help.

d. Use the graph of **Figure 8-1** to draw the consumption function consistent with the data in Table 8-1. (Locate each income-consumption data pair and then draw a line connecting the points.)

e. The MPC is represented by what part of your graph?

f. The APC can be represented by the slope of a ray from the origin to a point on the consumption function. Remember the slope of any straight line, including a ray, is the vertical change over the horizontal change. When measured from the origin, the vertical change of a ray to a point on the consumption function is *C* and the horizontal change is *DI*. Thus the slope of the ray, $(C \div DI)$, is the APC. Draw rays to represent the APC for incomes of $20,000 and $100,000. How does the slope of your rays change as income increases? Is this change consistent with changes in the APC you calculated in step c?

2. Imagine an economy made up of 100 families each earning $20,000, and 100 families each earning $100,000. Each family consumes according to the consumption function described in Table 8-1.

   a. Fill in the following:

   Consumption of a family earning $20,000   _____

   Consumption of a family earning $100,000   _____

   Aggregate consumption of the 200 families   _____

   b. What is the APC of the richer families?   _____

   What is the APC of the poorer families?   _____

   c. Randy argues that since the lower-income families are spending a greater proportion of their income than the higher-income families, a redistribution of income from high- to low-income families will increase total consumption expenditures. Test Randy's assertion by assuming that the government takes $5,000 from each high-income family and gives it to each low-income family, and that all families adjust their consumption in line with the consumption function described in Table 8-1. Then fill in the following:

   Consumption of a family with $25,000 income _____

   Consumption of a family with $95,000 income _____

   Aggregate consumption of the 200 families _____

   d. Explain why in this example aggregate consumption is unaffected by the redistribution of income.

3. (Optional) Use the data in Table 8-1 to compute an algebraic expression for the consumption function.

   Consumption = _____ + 0. _____ 3 (disposable income)

4. The lower line in Figure 8-2 shows the location of the consumption function of Baulmovia in 2004. In 2004, Baulmovian disposable income was $6.0 trillion and consumption spending was $5.5 trillion. In 2005, there was a significant surge in consumer confidence that shifted the consumption function to the higher line in Figure 8-2. In 2005, Baulmovian disposable income was $6.5 trillion and consumption spending was $6.05 trillion.

   Consider an estimate of MPC that is calculated by looking at the change in consumption spending and the change in disposable income from 2004 to 2005.

   a. Change in *C* _____ change in *DI* _____ MPC _____

   b. How does this estimate of MPC compare to the slope of either consumption function? Explain any differences.

Figure 8-2

Consumption Functions for 1997 and 1998

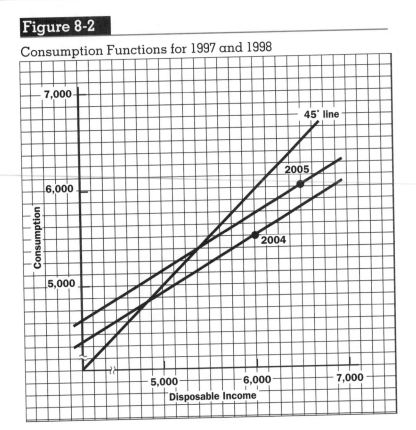

Self-Tests for Understanding

Test A

Circle the most appropriate answer.

1. Which of the following is not a part of aggregate demand?
   a. consumption expenditures
   b. national income
   c. net exports
   d. investment expenditures

2. When thinking about aggregate demand, economists use the term investment to refer to all except which one of the following?
   a. the newly built house that Roberta just bought
   b. the stock in General Electric that Ralph bought with his summer earnings
   c. the new factory that is being built on the edge of town
   d. the new machinery that Sherry bought to start her own company

3. Which of the following would be an example of a government transfer payment?
   a. wages paid to government bureaucrats
   b. a tax refund for excess withholding
   c. the purchase of paper clips by a government agency
   d. Social Security payments

4. In a circular flow diagram all but which one of the following would be depicted as an injection into the stream of spending?
   a. the Defense Department purchases a new airplane
   b. Michelle and Mathew purchase an existing house
   c. Alice's spending to rebuild her restaurant after a fire
   d. the new computerized machine tools that Elaine's company buys for its new assembly line

5. National income refers to
   a. consumers' income after taxes.
   b. the sum of everyone's before-tax income.
   c. employee wage and salary payments.
   d. the income of federal government employees.

6. Starting with the before-tax income of individuals, one calculates disposable income by
   a. adding taxes.
   b. subtracting transfer payments.
   c. adding taxes to transfer payments.
   d. subtracting taxes and adding transfer payments.

7. A graphical representation of how consumption spending varies with changes in disposable income is called the
   a. aggregate demand curve.
   b. income-expenditure schedule.
   c. consumption function.
   d. Phillips curve.

8. A change in which one of the following would be associated with a movement along the consumption function?
   a. current disposable income
   b. wealth
   c. the price level
   d. expected future income

9. A change in all but which one of the following would be associated with a shift in the consumption function?
   a. wealth
   b. interest rates
   c. current disposable income
   d. the price level

10. MPC refers to the
    a. *Y*-axis intercept of the consumption function.
    b. slope of the consumption function.
    c. ratio of consumption spending to income.
    d. slope of a ray from the origin to a point on the consumption function.

11. If MPC is 0.7, then a $100 billion change in disposable income will be associated with what change in consumption spending?
    a. $20 billion
    b. $30 billion
    c. $70 billion
    d. $100 billion

12. If a $100 billion increase in disposable income results in a $75 billion increase in consumption spending, then MPC is
    a. 0.25.
    b. 0.50.
    c. 0.75.
    d. 1.0.

13. If consumption spending declines by $45 billion when disposable income declines by $50 billion, what is MPC?
    a. 0.9
    b. 0.1
    c. −0.1
    d. −0.9

14. If an increase in prices is matched by an increase in incomes such that there is no change in real disposable income, then
    a. there should be no effect on consumption spending.
    b. the increase in prices will lead to a movement along the consumption function.
    c. one should expect MPC to decline.
    d. the impact of the change in prices on the purchasing power of money fixed assets should lead to a shift in the consumption function.

15. If MPC is 0.8, a $100 billion change in the wealth of consumers will lead to a(n)
    a. $100 billion change in consumption spending.
    b. $80 billion change in consumption spending.
    c. movement along the consumption function.
    d. shift in the entire consumption function.

16. An increase in real interest rates
    a. always leads to a decrease in consumption spending as it provides an increased incentive for greater saving.
    b. can be modeled as a movement along the consumption function.
    c. always leads to an increase in consumption spending as the higher interest rate allows savers to reach fixed objectives with smaller savings.
    d. does not appear to have influenced consumption spending very much one way or the other.

17. Which type of tax change would be expected to have the largest impact on consumption spending?
    a. a one-time tax rebate
    b. a one-time tax surcharge
    c. a permanent reduction in tax rates
    d. a reduction in tax withholding "to get money into the hands of consumers" that is enacted with no change in taxes due at the end of the year

18. Investment spending as measured in the national income accounts
    a. is a fairly constant proportion of GDP.
    b. includes all transactions on the New York Stock Exchange.
    c. is quite volatile as it is influenced by business confidence.
    d. is high correlated with disposable income.

19. An increase in foreign income should lead to a(n)
    a. increase in exports.
    b. decrease in exports.
    c. decrease in imports.
    d. increase in imports.

20. An increase in American prices should lead to a(n)
    a. decrease in imports.
    b. decrease in net exports.
    c. increase in exports.
    d. increase in net exports.

Test B

Circle T or F for true or false.

T F 1. Aggregate demand is the aggregate of individual household consumption decisions.

T F 2. The consumption function reflects the close relationship between consumption spending and national output.

T F 3. Disposable income equals national income minus taxes.

T F 4. A change in consumption divided by the change in disposable income that produced the change in consumption is called the marginal propensity to consume.

T F 5. An increase in the level of prices is likely to reduce consumption expenditures.

T F 6. The effect of a change in the level of prices on consumption would be viewed graphically as a shift in the consumption function.

T F 7. By increasing household wealth, a big increase in the stock market is likely to lead to a movement along the consumption function.

T F 8. The magnitude of the impact of a change in taxes on consumption expenditures is likely to depend on whether consumers view the change in taxes as permanent or temporary.

T F 9. A temporary decrease in taxes is likely to have a smaller impact on consumption than will a permanent decrease.

T   F 10. The demand for exports is likely to be influenced by foreign income while the demand for imports is influenced by domestic income.

| Appendix | *National Income Accounting*

Learning Objectives
After completing this appendix, you should be able to:

- describe the three alternative ways of measuring GDP and explain why, except for bookkeeping or statistical errors, they give the same answer.

- explain how the national income accounts treats production that is not sold on markets.

- explain why national income accounting treats government purchases of goods and services differently from government transfer payments.

- explain the difference in theory and practice between the following macro measurements: GDP, NNP, and national income.

Important Terms and Concepts

National income accounting

Gross domestic product (GDP)

Gross private domestic investment

National income

Net national product (NNP)

Depreciation

Appendix Review

Although included in an appendix, this material on national income accounting deserves special treatment. When working through this material, do not lose sight of the forest for the trees. The forest is composed of broad income concepts, such as gross domestic product (GDP) and national income, what each of these concepts measures and how they relate to one another. This appendix is an introduction to the forest rather than to each individual tree.

The national income accounts measure economic activity: the production of goods and services and the incomes that are generated as a result. Accurate measurement of production and income is an important prerequisite to attempts to understand and control the economy. National income accounts are centered around measurement of gross domestic product (GDP). Consumption (C), investment (I), government purchases of goods and services (G), and net exports ($X - IM$) are the individual components of GDP. National income is an alternative measure of total economic activity.

GDP is defined as the sum of the money values of all _____ goods and services that   (1) are (<u>produced/sold</u>) during a specified period of time, usually one year. Economists use money values or market prices to add up the very different types of output that make up GDP. Some production—government output and inventories—require special treatment as they are not sold on markets.

The emphasis on final goods and services is important because it avoids double counting of intermediate goods. (The need to avoid double counting is also the key to why the three alternative ways of measuring GDP are conceptually equivalent.) It is important to remember that GDP is a statement of production, not sales. It is only production that creates new goods available for consumption or investment. Thus GDP, as a measure of production, is the appropriate measure of how much new consumption or investment our economy can enjoy.

There are three ways to measure GDP. Perhaps the simplest way to measure GDP is to add up the purchases of newly produced final goods and services by private individuals and firms[em]for consumption and investment—by the government and by foreigners. For the United States in 2004, this sum of $C + I + G + (X - IM)$ was estimated to be about $10.7 trillion.

(2)   Net exports are (<u>imports/exports</u>) minus _____. We add exports to $C + I + G$ because, even though bought by foreigners, exports are American products and GDP is a measure of total production in the United States. We subtract imports because C and I and G include spending on imports, and we want a measure that reflects only those goods and services (<u>purchased/produced</u>) in the United States.

All of a firm's sales receipts eventually end up as income for someone, directly in the case of workers, creditors, and firm owners, and indirectly in the case of payments to suppliers, who in turn use this money to pay their workers, creditors, and so forth. Thus, instead of measuring GDP as purchases of final goods and services, we could equivalently add up all incomes earned in the production of goods and services. This sum of factor incomes plus indirect business taxes is also called

(3) national _____ and is the second way to measure GDP.

National Income is conceptually similar to GDP but differs from U.S. national income accounts because of several items: A) Conceptually national income and net national product (NNP) should be equal but as each is estimated separately there is often a small statistical discrepancy. B) The difference

(4) between net national product and gross national product is _____, which refers to the portion of current total production that is used to replace those parts of the capital stock that have deteriorated as a result of current production. If GNP were all one edible good, we could eat NNP while maintaining our productive capacity. Eating GNP would reduce our productive capacity as we would not be replacing worn-out plants and machines. C) National income and hence gross national product measures the income of American nationals whether they are in the United States or not and excludes the income of foreign nationals working in the United States. Adjusting for income that Americans receive from business activities abroad and for income that foreigners receive for business activities in the United States gives us gross domestic product, i.e., it measures the production of final goods and services within the borders of the United States.

To measure GDP as the money value of final goods and services, one would start by collecting sales data for final goods. The second way of measuring GDP, total factor incomes, would start with the collection of income data from firms and individuals. The third way of measuring GDP looks at the difference between a firm's sales receipts and its purchases from other firms. This difference, also called a firm's _____ _____, is the amount of money a firm has to pay the factors of production that it has employed, including the profits firm owners pay themselves. Thus, the sum of total value added in the economy is the third way to measure GDP. (5)

Important Terms and Concepts Quiz

Choose the best definition for each of the following terms.

1. _____ National income accounting

2. _____ Depreciation

3. _____ Value added

a. Bookkeeping and measurement system for national economic data
b. Value of an economy's capital used up during a year
c. Revenue from sale of product minus amount paid for goods and services purchased from other firms
d. Loss on value of business assets from inflation

• Basic Exercises

These problems are designed to give you practice in understanding alternative ways of measuring GDP.

1. Consider the following two-firm economy. Firm A is a mining company that does not make purchases from firm B. Firm A sells all its output to firm B, which uses the output of Firm A to make goods that it sells to consumers.

	Firm A	Firm B
Total sales	$500	$1,700
Wages	400	800
Profits	100	400
Purchases from other firms	0	500

a. What are the total sales for the economy? $ _____

b. What is the total value of sales for final uses? $ _____

c. What is the total of all factor incomes? $ _____

d. What is value added for firm A? $ _____

e. What is value added for firm B? $ _____

f. What is the total value added of both firms? $ _____

g. What is GDP? $ _____

h. What is national income? $ _____

2. Table 8-2 contains information on a three-firm economy. Firm A sells only to other firms. Firm B has both an industrial and a household division. Firm C sells only to final consumers. Note also that production by firm C was greater than sales, thus the entry showing the addition to inventories. Simple addition shows that the sum of factor incomes, in this case wages and profits, is equal to $4,700. Answer the following questions to see if the two other ways of measuring GDP give the same answer. The tricky part of this question is the treatment of production that has not been sold, but added to inventories. You may want to review the discussion of inventories in the appendix before answering the following questions.

Table 8-2

	Firm A	Firm B	Firm C
Total Sales	$1,000	$2,500	$3,000
Sales to firm B	$400		
Sales to firm C	$600	$1,000	
Sales to consumers		$1,500	$3,000
Change in inventories			$200
Wages	$750	$1,800	$1,200
Profits	$250	$300	$400

a. Calculate value added for each firm and the sum of value added for all firms.

Value Added, firm A _____

Value Added, firm B _____

Value Added, firm C _____

Sum _____

b. GDP is defined as the production of newly produced final goods and services. It is typically calculated by summing sales of newly produced final goods and services. Sales to consumers are an important part of final sales but they only total $4,500. What is missing to get to GDP of $4,700?

● Self-Tests for Understanding

Test A

Circle the most appropriate answer.

1. GDP is
   a. the sum of all sales in the economy.
   b. the sum of all purchases in the economy.
   c. the sum of money value of all newly produced final goods and services produced during a year.
   d. equal to $C + I + G + X + IM$.

2. Conceptually, GDP can be measured by all but which one of the following?
   a. Add up all factor payments by firms in the economy.
   b. Add up all purchases of final goods and services, $C + I + G + (X - IM)$.
   c. Add up total sales of all firms in the economy.
   d. Add up value added for all firms in the economy.

3. When measuring GDP, money values are for the most part determined by
   a. the cost of production.
   b. market prices.
   c. estimates prepared by national income accountants who work for the U.S. Commerce Department.
   d. banks and Eastern money interests.

4. Which of the following is not valued at market prices when computing GDP?
   a. imports
   b. investment
   c. government output
   d. exports

5. Which of the following would add to this year's GDP?
   a. Nick purchases a new copy of the Baumol/Blinder textbook for this course.
   b. Ashley purchases a used copy of the Baumol/Blinder textbook for this course.
   c. Susan purchases 100 shares of GM stock.
   d. Steve sells his three-year-old car.

6. Which of the following transactions represents the sale of a final good as opposed to sale of an intermediate good?
   a. Holly sells peaches from her farm to the Good Food Packing and Canning Company.
   b. Good Food sells a load of canned peaches to Smith Brothers Distributors.
   c. Smith Brothers sells the load of canned peaches to Irving's Supermarket.
   d. You buy a can of peaches at Irving's.

7. Which of the following events results in an addition to gross private domestic investment?
   a. Managers of the Good Earth, a newly formed food co-op, buy a used refrigerator case for their store.
   b. Sony's office in Tokyo buys a new IBM computer.
   c. The U.S. Air Force purchases a new plane for the president.
   d. Southwest Airlines purchases 20 new planes so it can expand its service.

8. Gross private domestic investment includes all but which one of the following?
   a. the new home purchased by Kimberly and Jason
   b. Ryan's purchase of a used fax machine for his new business
   c. the increase in the inventory of newly produced but unsold cars
   d. the construction of a new plant to manufacture microchips for Intel

9. When measuring GDP, government purchases include all but which one of the following?
   a. salaries paid to members of Congress
   b. newly produced red tape purchased by government agencies
   c. Social Security payments to older Americans
   d. concrete for new highway construction

10. If net exports are negative it means that
    a. the national income accountant made a mistake.
    b. depreciation is greater than net exports.
    c. Americans are consuming too many foreign goods.
    d. imports exceed exports.

11. Which accounts for the largest proportion of national income?
    a. profits
    b. employee compensation
    c. rents
    d. interest

12. In the national income accounts, transfer payments are
    a. subtracted from national income in the calculation of disposable income.
    b. included in *G*, government purchases of goods and services.
    c. added to wages when computing national income.
    d. not a direct component of GDP, and are reflected in GDP only when they influence consumption spending.

13. Which of the following adds to consumption spending as measured by the national income accountants?
    a. Howard buys a used CD at Play It Again Sam.
    b. Rachel builds a new store to house her business.
    c. Tyrone buys three new suits when he gets a job as a marketing representative.
    d. Hilary sells the computer she bought when she first came to campus four years ago.

14. Which of the following is not part of the difference between GDP and national income?
    a. depreciation
    b. income earned by foreigners working in the United States
    c. profits
    d. income earned by Americans from foreign business activities

15. Depreciation explains the difference between
    a. GNP and NNP.
    b. NNP and National Income.
    c. GDP and National Income.
    d. savings and investment.

16. Value added by a single firm is measured as total sales revenue
    a. minus factor payments.
    b. plus indirect business taxes.
    c. plus depreciation.
    d. minus the purchase of intermediate goods.

17. Additions to inventory
    a. add to next year's GDP when the goods are actually sold.
    b. are simply ignored when calculating GDP.
    c. add to current GDP.
    d. are priced at zero since they have not been sold.

18. When measuring GDP, government outputs are
    a. appropriately valued at zero.
    b. valued by estimates of their market prices.
    c. valued at the cost of inputs needed to produce them.
    d. added to transfer payments to measure G in $C + I + G + X - IM$.

Test B

Circle T or F for true or false.

T F   1. GDP is designed to be a measure of economic well-being, not a measure of economic production.

T F   2. If you measured GDP by adding up total sales in the economy, you would be double or triple counting many intermediate goods.

T F   3. Production that is not sold but is instead added to inventories is not counted in GDP.

T F   4. If GM started its own steel company rather than continuing to buy steel from independent steel companies, GDP would be lower because intrafirm transfers are not part of GDP but all interfirm sales are.

T F   5. Since the output of government agencies is not sold on markets, it is not included in GDP.

T F   6. Value added is the difference between what a firm sells its output for and the cost of its own purchases from other firms.

T F   7. The difference between GDP and national income is net exports.

T F   8. Adding up value added for all firms will underestimate GDP as it ignores the production of intermediate goods.

T F   9. Corporate profits are the largest component of national income.

T F 10. The sum of value added for all firms in the economy is equal to the sum of all factor incomes—wages, interest, rents, and profits.

Supplementary Exercises

1. Consider the following nonlinear, consumption function.

$$C = 120DI^{1/2}$$

Restricting yourself to positive values for disposable income, graph this function. What happens to MPC as income increases? Can you find an explicit expression for MPC as a function of income? (Knowledge of simple calculus will be helpful.) Use this new consumption function to re-answer Basic Exercise question 2 about income redistribution. Does your answer change? If so, why?

• Economics in Action

Do Americans Save Enough?

Do Americans save too little? It would certainly seem so. From 1960 to 1989, household savings as measured in the national income accounts averaged 9 percent of disposable income. Savings have declined continuously since then, averaging only 1 percent of disposable income in 2004.

While Americans have always saved less than individuals in other industrialized countries, the decline in savings has come at a time when there is increasing concern about the ability of Americans to provide for their own retirement and concerns about future growth rates for the economy as a whole. It also occurred at a time when there were increasing tax incentives to increase savings. Indeed by 2004 economists Elizabeth Bell, Adam Carasso, and C. Eugene Steuerle estimated that government spending on tax incentives to increase savings were greater than savings themselves. It appeared that rather than increasing savings, there were substantial portfolio adjustments in search of tax advantages.

As we have seen, savings, investment, and economic growth are closely related. Higher levels of investment are likely to mean higher levels of economic growth. If a country is to invest more, it seems obvious that it must consume less, that is, it must save more. Savings levels as low as 1 percent seem only to spell disaster for the future.

Some were less concerned and argued that the decline in household savings during the 1990s was hardly surprising and only part of the story. Families with significant holdings of stock saw substantial increases in their wealth even without increased saving. Economic theory has always recognized that an increase in wealth is likely to lead to an increase in consumption spending at the expense of a reduction in savings.

Economists Dean Maki and Michael Palumbo looked at stock holdings and savings behavior. They found the decline in household savings was concentrated among the wealthiest families who had the largest holdings of stock and other assets with significant price appreciation over the 1990s.

The decline in personal savings did not lead to a decline in private investment as a proportion of GDP. How can this be? First, a fair amount of U.S. national savings is done by businesses rather than households, and business savings showed no decline over the 1990s. Second, national savings is also influenced by the state of the government's budget. Government budgets, especially that of the federal government, showed a significant move to surplus over the 1990s, adding to rather than subtracting from national savings, although since 2000 increasing federal government deficits have meant that on net government savings now subtracts from national savings. Finally, a country can sustain or increase the level of private investment even in the facing of declining domestic savings if it is willing to borrow from other countries. This is exactly what the United States did over the 1990s as the trade deficit, the excess of imports over exports, increased as a proportion of GDP.

Those who are concerned about savings are also concerned about whether the gains in the stock market represent permanent increases in wealth or transitory gains from unrealistic stock price increases. They also point out that while a country can sustain levels of investment by foreign borrowing, increasing international indebtedness may only be planting the seeds for future trouble.

1. Who is right, those concerned that America is saving too little or those who say that traditional ways of looking at this issue are inappropriate?

2. Should we be concerned about increased international borrowing?

3. Should Americans save more? If so, what policy measures would you endorse to encourage savings?

4. Why do you think that savings-linked tax advantages have not increased aggregate personal savings?

Sources: David Leonhardt, "A Blasphemy Spreads: Debts are O.K.," *New York Times,* January 19, 2002. Edmund L. Andrews, "Savings: Lots of Talk But Few Dollars," *New York Times,* March 13, 2005.

Study Questions

1. What are the four major components of GDP? (Why are imports subtracted when everything else is added?)

2. What is the difference between national income and disposable income?

3. How is MPC different from the proportion of disposable income that is spent on consumption?

4. MPC can be represented by what part of the consumption function?

5. Why does a change in the price level or in expected future incomes lead to a shift in the consumption function rather than a movement along the function?

6. If planning a reduction in income taxes to increase consumption spending by $200 billion, what difference would it make if MPC were 0.75 or 0.90? Would you expect any differences if the reduction in taxes were to be permanent or temporary? Why?

7. What are the different ways one can measure GDP?

8. Economists often use national income or GDP interchangeably as a measure of the level of aggregate economic activity. What is the difference between national income and GDP?

9. Why is investment spending so volatile? Does the volatility of investment mean that policy changes by the government have no impact on investment?

10. "Exports will change with changes in foreign but not domestic income. They will also change if foreign or domestic prices change." How can it be that exports respond to domestic prices but not domestic income?

11. How do imports respond to changes in domestic income, foreign income, domestic prices, and foreign prices?

Economics Online

Check here for the most recent estimates of GDP: http://www.bea.gov/

The Economic Report of the President is issued every year in February. The Report includes extensive tables with historical data on macroeconomic activity including Gross Domestic Product and its components. Use the following URL to access copies of the Economic Report of the President and its statistical tables back to 1995.

http://www/gpoaccess.gov/eop/download.html

Demand-Side Equilibrium: Unemployment or Inflation?

9

Important Terms and Concepts

Equilibrium

Expenditure schedule

Induced investment

$Y = C + I + G + (X - IM)$

Income-expenditure (or 45° line) diagram

Aggregate demand curve

Full-employment level of GDP (potential GDP)

Recessionary gap

Inflationary gap

Coordination of saving and investment

Coordination failure

Multiplier

Induced increase in consumption

Autonomous increase in consumption

Learning Objectives
After completing this chapter, you should be able to:

- draw an expenditure schedule, given information about consumption spending, investment spending, government purchases, and net exports.

- determine the equilibrium level of income on the demand side and explain why the level of income tends toward its equilibrium value.

- describe how a change in the price level affects the expenditure schedule and the equilibrium level of income on the demand side.

- describe how the impact of a change in prices on the expenditure schedule can be used to derive the aggregate demand curve.

- explain why equilibrium GDP can be above or below the full-employment level of GDP.

- explain why any autonomous increases in expenditures will have a multiplier effect on GDP.

- explain why the multiplier expression, $1/(1 - MPC)$, is oversimplified.

- explain the difference between an autonomous and an induced increase in consumption expenditures.

- explain how and why economic booms and recessions tend to be transmitted across national boundaries.

- describe how any change in autonomous spending leads to a shift in the aggregate demand curve.

• Chapter Review

This chapter is an introduction to explicit models of income determination. The model discussed in this chapter is relatively simple and is not meant to be taken literally. Do not be put off by the simplicity of the model or its lack of realism. Careful study now will pay future dividends in terms of easier understanding of later chapters, in which the implications of more complicated models are described.

The central focus of this chapter is on the concept of the equilibrium level of income and output. (You may want to review the material in Chapter 8 on the equality of national income and national output.) The models discussed in this chapter show us how spending decisions are reconciled with production decisions of firms to determine the equilibrium level of GDP on the demand side.

When considering the determination of the equilibrium level of GDP, it is important to distinguish between output and income on the one hand and total spending on the other hand. If total spending exceeds current production, firms will find that their inventories are decreasing. They are then likely

(1) to take steps to (decrease/increase) production and output. Analogously, if total spending is less than current output, firms are likely to find their inventories _____, and they are likely to take steps to _____ production.

The concept of equilibrium refers to a situation in which producers and consumers are satisfied with things the way they are and see no reason to change their behavior. Thus the equilibrium level of GDP must be a level of GDP at which firms have no reason to increase or decrease output; that is,

(2) at the equilibrium level of GDP, total spending will be (less than/equal to/greater than) output. The determination of the equilibrium level of output thus reduces to

A. describing how total spending changes as output (and income) changes, and

B. finding the one level of output (and income) at which total spending equals output. In the simplified model discussed in this chapter, there are four components to total spending: consumption, investment, government purchases, and net exports.

The income-expenditure diagram is a useful tool for analyzing the determination of the

(3) equilibrium level of output. Output (and income) is measured along the (horizontal/vertical) axis, and spending is measured on the _____ axis. To find the equilibrium level of output (and income) we need to know how total spending changes as output (and income) change, and we need to know where total spending equals output. The relationship between total spending, $C + I + G + (X - IM)$, and income is given by the expenditure schedule. The 45° line shows all possible points of equilibrium as it is the line where the vertical distance, i.e., spending, is equal to the horizontal distance, i.e., output and income.

The one place where actual spending as shown by the expenditure schedule is equal to output

(4) is given by the _____ of the expenditure schedule and the 45° line. This is the equilibrium level of output because it is the only level of output where total spending is equal to

output. At any other level of output, total spending will not be equal to output. You should be sure that you understand why the economy tends to move to the equilibrium level of output rather than getting stuck at a level of income and output where total spending is either larger or smaller than output. Consider what happens to business inventories when spending is greater or less than output. Do not get confused between this tendency to move to the equilibrium level of output on the income-expenditure diagram and the real possibility that the economy can end up at a point away from full employment.

Any particular expenditure schedule relates total spending to income for a given level of prices. If prices change, total spending will change, even for the same level of real income. In particular, a higher price level is apt to mean (<u>less/more</u>) consumption spending because of the decline in the   (5) purchasing power of the money assets of consumers. A change in the price level will also affect net exports. Specifically, higher prices (<u>increase/reduce</u>) exports and _____ imports as domestically produced goods are (<u>less/more</u>) price competitive vis-à-vis foreign goods. These changes in consumption spending and net exports will lead to a (<u>downward/upward</u>) shift in the expenditure schedule and a new equilibrium of income that is (<u>higher/lower</u>) than before. In the opposite case, a lower price level would (<u>decrease/increase</u>) consumption spending and _____ net exports. The result will be a (<u>higher/lower</u>) equilibrium level of income.

The relationship between the price level and the equilibrium level of income given by the income-expenditure diagram is called the aggregate demand curve. The aggregate demand curve is derived from the income-expenditure diagram and, from the viewpoint of demand, shows how the equilibrium level of income changes when the _____ _____ changes. The qualifier "from the   (6) viewpoint of demand" is important. Complete determination of the equilibrium level of income/output and the equilibrium price level comes from the interaction of the aggregate demand and aggregate supply curves.

At this point we are considering only the demand side of the economy. Nothing that has been said so far implies that, with regard to demand, the equilibrium level of output must equal the full-employment level of output. It may be larger or it may be smaller. It all depends upon the strength of aggregate demand. In particular, if savings plans at full employment are greater than investment plans, spending will be (<u>less/more</u>) than full employment output and equilibrium on the demand   (7) side will result in a(n) _____ gap. The importance of savings and investment plans in determining equilibrium means that recessions and inflation can be seen as failures of coordination. If the equilibrium level of output exceeds the full-employment level of output, the difference is called a(n) _____ gap.

What happens to the equilibrium level of income if demand changes? From the perspective of the income-expenditure diagram, the change in the equilibrium level of GDP will be a multiple of the original change in spending. In particular, our analysis will be concerned with parallel shifts in the expenditure schedule that are represented graphically as a change in the vertical axis intercept of the expenditure schedule. A parallel shift in the expenditure schedule shows the same change in spending

(8) at all levels of income and is thus a change in (<u>autonomous/induced</u>) spending. Spending that changes when income changes, such as the response of consumption spending to a change in income, is called a(n) _____ change.

Multiplier analysis shows that the equilibrium level of GDP changes by a multiple of the change in autonomous spending, which is where we get the term "multiplier." The basic reason for this multiplier result is relatively simple: Increased spending by one sector of the economy means increased sales receipts for other sectors of the economy. Higher sales receipts will show up in bigger paychecks or profits or both—in short, higher incomes. These higher incomes will then induce more consumer spending, which in turn will result in still higher incomes and more consumption spending by others, and so on and so on.

What determines the value of the multiplier? There are several alternative, but equally valid, ways of answering this question. In the text, the value of the multiplier is determined by summing the increments to spending and income that follow from the original autonomous change in spending. When consumption is the only induced spending, the oversimplified multiplier expression turns out

(9) to be $1/(1 - $ _____ $)$.

Here is an alternative derivation of the same result. We know that in equilibrium national output, or income, will equal total spending:

$$Y = C + I + G + (X - IM).$$

Now assume that there is an autonomous increase in investment spending that induces subsequent increases in consumption spending. At the new equilibrium, we know that the change in the equilibrium level of national output must equal the change in total spending. If net exports and government purchases do not change, the change in total spending will have two parts. One is the autonomous change in investment spending and the other is the induced change in consumption spending. We know that

Change in equilibrium level of income	=	Autonomous change in investment spending	+	Induced change in consumption spending

It is possible to represent this symbolically. Let ΔY represent the change in the equilibrium level of income and ΔI represent the autonomous change in investment spending. What about the induced change in consumption spending? The discussion of the consumption function in

(10) Chapter 8 told us that consumption spending will change as disposable _____ changes. Further, with the use of the concept of the marginal propensity to consume, we can represent the change in consumption spending as the product of the change in disposable income multiplied by

the _____. When taxes do not vary with income, $\Delta DI = \Delta Y$ and we can represent the change in consumption as $\Delta Y \times MPC$. If we substitute all these symbols for the words above, we see that

$$\Delta Y = \Delta I + (\Delta Y \times MPC).$$

We can now solve this equation for the change in income by moving all terms in ΔY to the left-hand side of the equation:

$$\Delta Y - (\Delta Y \times MPC) = \Delta I.$$

If we factor out the ΔY we can rewrite the expression as

$$\Delta Y(1 - MPC) = \Delta I.$$

We can now solve for ΔY by dividing both sides of the equation by $(1 - MPC)$.

$$\Delta Y = \Delta I [1 / (1 - MPC)].$$

Note that ΔI is the initial change in autonomous spending and $1/(1 - MPC)$ is the multiplier. The change in the equilibrium level of income is found by multiplying these two terms. That is

$$\begin{array}{c} \text{Change in} \\ \text{equilibrium level of} \\ \text{income} \end{array} = \begin{array}{c} \text{Autonomous change in} \\ \text{investment spending} \end{array} \times \text{Multiplier}$$

Although our derivation was different, the multiplier expression we just identified, $1/(1 - MPC)$, is the same as the one in the text and is subject to the same limitations.[1] That is, this expression is oversimplified. There are four important reasons why real-world multipliers will be (<u>smaller/larger</u>)   (11) than our formula. These reasons are related to the effects of _____, international _____, _____ taxes, and the _____ system.

The simplified multiplier expression we derived above is applicable when analyzing a shift in the expenditure schedule in the 45° line diagram. As such, this expression assumes that prices (<u>do/do not</u>) change. To complete our analysis on the demand side, we need to see how our multiplier (12) analysis affects the aggregate demand curve. The multiplier analysis we have done by using the income-expenditure diagram shows us that if prices are constant, the equilibrium level of income will change following any change in autonomous spending. This result is true at all price levels and implies that a vertical shift in the expenditure schedule following a change in autonomous spending leads to a (<u>movement along/shift in</u>) the aggregate demand curve. In fact, it leads to a (<u>horizontal/vertical</u>) shift in the aggregate demand curve. The magnitude of the shift can be computed with the help of the multiplier, as shown in Figure 9-12 in the text.

---

[1]A more general expression for the multiplier is $1/(1 - \text{slope of the expenditure schedule})$. The multiplier is based on summing the rounds of spending induced by an autonomous increase in spending. In the model of this chapter only consumption spending changes as income changes. Appendix B examines what happens when imports vary with income. We will see then that the slope of the expenditure schedule is flatter and the multiplier is smaller.

Important Terms and Concepts Quiz

Choose the best definition for each of the following terms.

1. _____ Equilibrium level of GDP
2. _____ Expenditure schedule
3. _____ Induced investment
4. _____ Income-expenditure diagram
5. _____ Aggregate demand curve
6. _____ Recessionary gap
7. _____ Inflationary gap
8. _____ Potential GDP
9. _____ Coordination failure
10. _____ Multiplier
11. _____ Induced increase in consumption
12. _____ Autonomous increase in consumption

a. Graph of quantity of national product demanded at each possible price level
b. Line showing relationship between GDP and total spending
c. Full-employment level of GDP
d. Increase in consumer spending not due to an increase in income
e. When equilibrium GDP exceeds full-employment GDP
f. Level of output where aggregate demand equals total production
g. Investment spending that changes with changes in GDP
h. Ratio of change in equilibrium GDP to change in autonomous spending that causes GDP to change
i. When full-employment GDP exceeds equilibrium GDP
j. Two-variable graph that allows plotting of total real expenditures against real income
k. Savings plans at full employment differ from investment plans at full employment
l. Increase in consumer spending due to an increase in disposable income
m. Table or graph showing how saving depends on consumption

● Basic Exercises

These exercises are designed to give you practice with the income-expenditure diagram and deriving the aggregate demand curve.

1. **Equilibrium Level of Income**

   This exercise shows you how the expenditure schedule is derived and how it helps to determine the equilibrium level of income. For this exercise it is assumed that prices are constant with the price level having a value of 100.

   a. Use the data on consumption spending in **Table 9-1** to show how consumption spending varies with income in **Figure 9-1**.
   b. Add investment spending to the line drawn in Figure 9-1 to show how consumption plus investment spending varies with income.
   c. Now draw the expenditure schedule by adding G and (X − IM) to the line drawn in step b.
   d. Next, draw a line representing all the points where total spending and income could be equal. (This is the 45° line. Do you know why?)
   e. The 45° line represents all the points that could be the equilibrium level of income. Now circle the one point that is the equilibrium level of income. What is the equilibrium level of income on your graph?

Table 9-1

Data for Expenditure Schedule

Y	Tx	DI	C	I	G	X	IM	Total Spending C + I + G + X − IM
9,500	1,800	7,700	6,500	1,500	1,750	1,200	1,350	_____
9,750	1,800	7,950	6,700	1,500	1,750	1,200	1,350	_____
10,000	1,800	8,200	6,900	1,500	1,750	1,200	1,350	_____
10,250	1,800	8,450	7,100	1,500	1,750	1,200	1,350	_____
10,500	1,800	8,700	7,300	1,500	1,750	1,200	1,350	_____
10,750	1,800	8,950	7,500	1,500	1,750	1,200	1,350	_____
11,000	1,800	9,200	7,700	1,500	1,750	1,200	1,350	_____

Figure 9-1

Expenditure Schedule

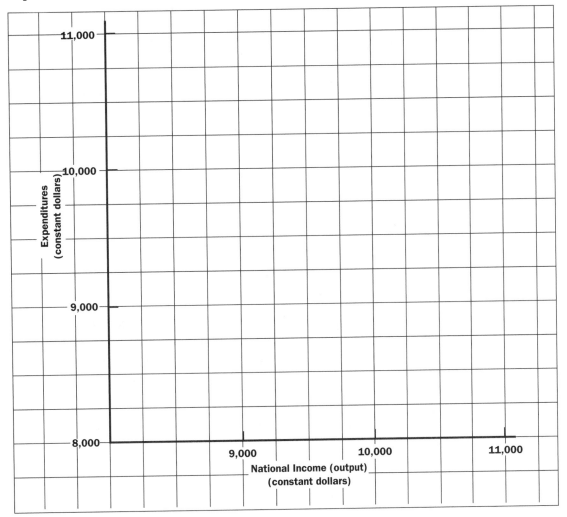

f. Check your answer by filling in the Total Spending column in Table 9-1 to see where total spending equals income. You should get the same answer from Table 9-1 as you do from the graph.

121

g. Why isn't the equilibrium level of output $9,750 billion? If for some reason national output and income started out at $9,750 billion, what forces would tend to move the economy toward the equilibrium you determined in questions e and f?

h. Using the data in Table 9-1 and assuming that the full-employment level of output income is $10,250 billion, is there an inflationary or recessionary gap? How large is the gap? If the full-employment level of income were $9,800 billion, how large would the inflationary or recessionary gap be?

2. **The Multiplier**

a. Assume now that an increase in business confidence leads to an increased level of investment spending of $1,600 billion at all levels of national income. Complete **Table 9-2** and draw the new expenditure schedule in Figure 9-1 to see what happens to the equilibrium level of income and consumption spending at the new equilibrium level of income.

| Table 9-2 |

Data for Expenditure Schedule Following Increase in Investment Spending

Y	Tx	DI	C	I	G	X	IM	Total Spending C + I + G + X − IM
9,500	1,800	7,700	6,500	1,600	1,750	1,200	1,350	_____
9,750	1,800	7,950	6,700	1,600	1,750	1,200	1,350	_____
10,000	1,800	8,200	6,900	1,600	1,750	1,200	1,350	_____
10,250	1,800	8,450	7,100	1,600	1,750	1,200	1,350	_____
10,500	1,800	8,700	7,300	1,600	1,750	1,200	1,350	_____
10,750	1,800	8,950	7,500	1,600	1,750	1,200	1,350	_____
11,000	1,800	9,200	7,700	1,600	1,750	1,200	1,350	_____

b. What is the value of the multiplier for this increase in autonomous investment spending? _____ (Remember that the multiplier is defined as the ratio of the change in the _____ _____ of _____ divided by the change in _____ _____ that produced the change in income.)

c. Now let us verify that the value of the multiplier that you found in question b is the same as the simplified formula $1/(1 - MPC)$. To do this we will first need to calculate the MPC for the economy in Tables 26-1 and 26-2. Write the value of the MPC here: _____. (If you do not remember how to calculate the MPC, review the discussion of the consumption function in the textbook and in this Study Guide.)

d. Now calculate the value of the multiplier from the oversimplified formula $1/(1 - MPC)$. Write your answer here: _____.

e. (Optional) The multiplier can also be calculated as $1/(1 - $ slope of expenditure schedule$)$. What is the slope of the expenditure schedule in Tables 9-1 and 9-2? Does this way of calculating the multiplier give you the same answer as in part d?

3. **Derivation of the Aggregate Demand Curve**

This exercise explores the implications of changes in the price level. It is designed to show how a change in the price level implies a shift in the expenditure schedule and can be used to derive the aggregate demand curve.

Figure 9-2

Aggregate Demand Curve

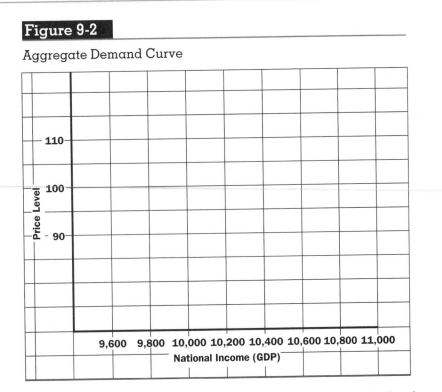

a. The data in Table 9-1 assumed that prices were constant with the price level at a value of 100. Mark the point in **Figure 9-2** that shows the price level of 100 and the equilibrium level of income you found when answering questions e and f of Exercise 1.

b. Economic research has determined that if prices rose to 110, consumption spending and net exports would decline by a total of $100 billion at every level of real income. **Table 9-3** shows the relevant information. Each entry in the column for a price level of 110 should be 100 less than the values you calculated for total spending in question 1.f. What is the new equilibrium level of income on the income-expenditure diagram with this higher price level? Mark the point in Figure 9-2 that shows the price level of 110 and this new equilibrium level of income.

c. This same research determined that if prices fell to 90, consumption spending and net exports would increase over amounts shown in Table 9-1 by a total of $100 billion at every level of real income. What is the new equilibrium level of income on the income-expenditure diagram for this lower price level? Mark the point in Figure 9-2 that shows the price level of 90 and this new equilibrium level of income.

Table 9-3

Total Spending at Different Price Levels

Real Income (Output)	Total Spending (Price Level = 90)	Total Spending (Price level = 110)
9,500	9,700	9,500
9,750	9,900	9,700
10,000	10,100	9,900
10,250	10,300	10,100
10,500	10,500	10,300
10,750	10,700	10,500
11,000	10,900	10,700

d. The points you have marked in Figure 9-2 help to trace what curve?

e. Connect these points to verify that your curve has a (<u>negative/positive</u>) slope.

4. The Multiplier and the Aggregate Demand Curve

Question 2 asked you to consider the impact of an increase in investment spending. We saw then that an increase in investment spending shifts the expenditure schedule and leads to a new equilibrium on the income-expenditure diagram. What about the aggregate demand curve? **Table 9-4** shows the impact of the price level on total spending following the increase in investment spending. Use this information from Tables 9-2 and 9-4 about the equilibrium level of income on the income expenditure diagram when the price level equals 90, 100, and 110 to draw the new aggregate demand curve in Figure 9-2. How does this curve differ from the initial aggregate demand curve you drew in question 3?

Table 9-4

Total Spending at Different Price Levels
Following Increase in Investment Spending

Real Income (Output)	Total Spending (Price Level = 90)	Total Spending (Price level = 110)
9,500	9,800	9,600
9,750	10,000	9,800
10,000	10,200	10,000
10,250	10,400	10,200
10,500	10,600	10,400
10,750	10,800	10,600
11,000	11,000	10,800

● Self-Tests for Understanding

Test A

Circle the most appropriate answer.

1. Of production, income, and spending, _____ and _____ are always equal while _____ equals the other two only in equilibrium.
   a. spending and income; production
   b. production and spending; income
   c. income and production; spending

2. The expenditure schedule is a relationship between
   a. the equilibrium level of national income and prices.
   b. consumption spending and national income.
   c. total spending and national income.
   d. consumption spending and prices.

3. The expenditure schedule is derived by showing how which of the following vary with income? (There may be more than one correct answer.)
   a. *C*—consumption
   b. *DI*—disposable income
   c. *G*—government purchases
   d. *I*—investment spending
   e. *IM*—imports
   f. *T*—taxes
   g. *X*—exports

4. If investment spending were now higher at all levels of income, the expenditure schedule would
   a. shift down.
   b. show no change.
   c. shift up.

5. Induced investment means the expenditure schedule
   a. is flatter than before.
   b. shifts up.
   c. shifts down.
   d. is steeper than before.

6. In the income-expenditure diagram, the equilibrium level of output is given by the intersection of the expenditure schedule and the
   a. consumption function.
   b. aggregate demand curve.
   c. 45° line.
   d. level of full-employment output.

7. When total spending is less than output,
   a. inventories are likely to be increasing.
   b. inventories are likely to be decreasing.
   c. there will be a shift in the expenditure schedule.
   d. firms are likely to raise prices.

8. When total spending is equal to output,
   a. the resulting level of output is called the full-employment level of output.
   b. the level of income is given by the intersection of the expenditure schedule and the 45° line.
   c. there is never an inflationary gap.
   d. the expenditure schedule and the aggregate demand curve coincide.

9. At the equilibrium level of income which one of the following is not necessarily true?
   a. The expenditure schedule will intersect the 45° line.
   b. There will be no unexpected changes in business inventories.
   c. There will be no unemployment.
   d. The equilibrium level of output and the price level will together determine one point on the aggregate demand curve.

10. If, at the full-employment level of income, consumers' savings plans are equal to firms' investment plans, then
    a. the equilibrium level of income will be equal to the full-employment level of income.
    b. there will be an inflationary gap.
    c. firms will find their inventories increasing.
    d. the economy will be producing less than potential output.

11. There is a recessionary gap when the equilibrium level of income is
    a. less than potential GDP.
    b. equal to the full-employment level of GDP.
    c. greater than potential GDP.

12. A lower price level will _____ the equilibrium level of income on the income-expenditure diagram.
    a. decrease
    b. not affect
    c. increase

13. The aggregate demand curve is a relationship between the price level and
    a. consumption spending.
    b. the equilibrium level of income on the income-expenditure diagram.
    c. full-employment GDP.
    d. the interest rate.

14. A lower price level will lead to which of the following? (There may be more than one correct answer.)
    a. an increase in exports
    b. a shift in the consumption function
    c. a shift in the expenditure schedule
    d. a shift in the aggregate demand curve

15. The multiplier is defined as the ratio of the change in
    a. autonomous spending divided by the change in consumption expenditures.
    b. the equilibrium level of income divided by the increase in consumption spending.
    c. the equilibrium level of income divided by the change in autonomous spending that produced the change in income.
    d. consumption spending divided by the change in autonomous spending.

16. The multiplier shows that
    a. any increase in induced spending will be a multiple of the increase in income.
    b. an autonomous increase in spending will increase income by a multiple of the increase in autonomous spending.
    c. to influence income, any change in autonomous spending must be a multiple of the induced changes in spending.
    d. an induced change in spending will lead to a multiple increase in income.

17. The oversimplified multiplier formula is
    a. 1/MPC.
    b. 1/(MPC − 1)
    c. MPC(1 − MPC)
    d. 1/(1 − MPC)

18. The secret behind the multiplier is
    a. the government's printing press.
    b. understanding that an autonomous increase in investment spending leads to an autonomous increase in consumption spending.
    c. understanding that any increase in autonomous spending induces additional increases in spending as income increases.
    d. the gnomes of Zurich.

19. Actual multipliers will be less than theoretical multipliers because of which of the following? (There may be more than one correct answer.)
    a. inflation
    b. accounting practices
    c. international trade
    d. the government deficit
    e. income taxes
    f. price controls
    g. the financial system

20. An autonomous change in spending can be modeled as a(n)
    a. horizontal shift in the expenditure schedule.
    b. tilt in the slope of the expenditure schedule.
    c. vertical shift in the expenditure schedule.
    d. increase in MPC.

21. If MPC were 0.6 and prices did not change, the multiplier would be
    a. 1/0.6 = 1.67.
    b. 0.6.
    c. 1/(1 − 0.6) = 2.5.
    d. 1/(1 + 0.6) = 0.63.

22. The textbook multiplier would be largest if MPC were
    a. 0.73.
    b. 0.89.
    c. 0.45.
    d. 0.67.

23. The multiplier is useful in calculating the
    a. slope of the consumption function.
    b. horizontal shift in the aggregate demand curve following an increase in autonomous spending.
    c. vertical shift of the expenditure schedule following a change in autonomous spending.
    d. shift of the consumption function following an increase in autonomous spending.

24. The multiplier response following a decrease in investment spending would have what impact on the aggregate demand curve?
    a. horizontal shift to the left
    b. no impact
    c. horizontal shift to the right

Test B

Circle T or F for true or false.

T F   1. The expenditure schedule refers to a relationship between total spending and the level of output (and income).

T F   2. The equilibrium level of GDP never equals the full-employment level of GDP.

T F   3. If total spending exceeds national output, the resulting decrease in inventories should lead firms to reduce the level of output and production.

T F   4. The intersection of the expenditure schedule and the 45° line determines one point on the aggregate demand curve.

T F   5. The term recessionary gap refers to a situation in which the equilibrium level of GDP is less than the full-employment level of GDP.

T F   6. Because consumers usually invest their savings at financial institutions, there can be no difference between desired savings and desired investment for the economy.

T F   7. The aggregate demand curve refers to a relationship between the price level and the equilibrium level of income as determined on the income-expenditure diagram.

T F   8. An increase in the level of prices will lead to a movement along the expenditure schedule.

T F   9. The multiplier is defined as the ratio of a change in autonomous spending divided by the resulting change in the equilibrium level of income.

T F 10. Multiplier responses mean that the equilibrium level of national income is likely to change by less than any change in autonomous spending.

T F 11. Multiplier increases illustrated on the income-expenditure diagram are based on the assumption that prices do not change.

T F 12. Actual multiplier responses to changes in autonomous spending are likely to be less than that suggested by the formula $1/(1 - MPC)$.

T F 13. If income increases because of an autonomous increase in investment spending, the resulting increase in consumption spending is called an induced increase.

T F 14. The impact of a shift in the aggregate demand curve on prices and real output will depend upon the slope of the aggregate supply curve.

| Appendix A | *The Simple Algebra of Income Determination*

Basic Exercises

This exercise is meant to illustrate the material in the Appendix to Chapter 9.

If we are willing to use algebra we can use equations rather than graphs or tables to determine the equilibrium level of output. If we have done all our work accurately, we should get the same answer regardless of whether we use graphs, tables, or algebra.

The following equations are consistent with the numbers in Table 9-1:

(1) C = $340 + 0.8\ DI$
(2) DI = $Y - T$
(3) T = $1,800$
(4) I = $1,500$
(5) G = $1,750$
(6) X = $1,200$
(7) IM = $1,350$
(8) Y = $C + I + G + (X - IM)$

1. Equation 1 is the consumption function. It shows how consumption spending changes with changes in disposable income. To derive the expenditure schedule we need to figure out how spending changes with changes in national income. Start by substituting equations 2 and 3 for disposable income and taxes into equation 1 to see how C varies with Y.

    (9) $C =$ _____ + _____ Y.

2. Now use equation 9, along with equations 4, 5, 6, and 7, to show how total spending varies with Y.

    (10) $C + I + G + (X - IM) =$ _____ + _____ Y.

3. Equation 10 is the expenditure schedule. Equation 8 is the 45° line. To find the one level of income where spending equals output (and income), substitute the right-hand side of equation 10 for the right-hand side of equation 8 and solve for the equilibrium level of Y.

    $Y =$ _____

    Substituting the right-hand side of equation 10 for the right-hand side of equation 8 is the algebraic way of finding the intersection of these two lines.

4. Now assume that investment increases by 100 to 1,600, that is equation 4 changes to $I = 1600$. Repeat steps 2 and 3 to solve for the new equilibrium level of income. What is the change in the equilibrium level of income? What is the value of the multiplier?

| Appendix B | *The Multiplier with Variable Imports*

The following questions are meant to illustrate the major point of Appendix B: When the demand for imports increases with domestic GDP, the multiplier will be smaller.

1. **Table 9-5** is similar to Table 9-1 except that imports increase with income. Compute total spending to verify that the equilibrium level of income in Table 9-5 is the same as in Table 9-1.

Table 9-5

Expenditure Schedule Data with Variable Imports

Y	Tx	DI	C	I	G	X	IM	Total Spending C + I + G + X − IM
9,500	1,800	7,700	6,500	1,500	1,750	1,200	1,325	_____
9,750	1,800	7,950	6,700	1,500	1,750	1,200	1,338	_____
10,000	1,800	8,200	6,900	1,500	1,750	1,200	1,350	_____
10,250	1,800	8,450	7,100	1,500	1,750	1,200	1,363	_____
10,500	1,800	8,700	7,300	1,500	1,750	1,200	1,375	_____
10,750	1,800	8,950	7,500	1,500	1,750	1,200	1,388	_____
11,000	1,800	9,200	7,700	1,500	1,750	1,200	1,400	_____

2. **Table 9-6** is based on the assumption that investment spending has increased by $125. The new equilibrium level of income is _____.

Table 9-6

Expenditure Schedule Data with Variable Imports Following Increase in Investment Spending

Y	Tx	DI	C	I	G	X	IM	Total Spending C + I + G + X − IM
9,500	1,800	7,700	6,500	1,625	1,750	1,200	1,325	_____
9,750	1,800	7,950	6,700	1,625	1,750	1,200	1,338	_____
10,000	1,800	8,200	6,900	1,625	1,750	1,200	1,350	_____
10,250	1,800	8,450	7,100	1,625	1,750	1,200	1,363	_____
10,500	1,800	8,700	7,300	1,625	1,750	1,200	1,375	_____
10,750	1,800	8,950	7,500	1,625	1,750	1,200	1,388	_____
11,000	1,800	9,200	7,700	1,625	1,750	1,200	1,400	_____

3. We calculate the multiplier as before: the change in the equilibrium level of income divided by the change that changed income. Now the multiplier is _____.

4. Explain any difference between this multiplier and the one you calculated in question 2 of the Basic Exercises.

Supplementary Exercises

1. Use all of the equations in Appendix A but assume that consumption depends upon income with a one-period lag. That is

$$C = 300 + 0.8DI\,(-1)$$

a. Confirm that the equilibrium level of income is 10,000. That is, if income last period was 10,000, then total spending, $C = I + G + (X - IM)$, will equal 10,000 this period.

b. Now assume that investment spending increases by 100 to 1,600. Assuming that consumption responds with the one-period lag, simulate your model to investigate how the change in investment spending affects this economy over time. Does the level of income appear to converge to a new equilibrium value? What is that value? What is the multiplier for the change in investment spending? How does the multiplier from your simulation compare to the oversimplified formula of $1/(1 - \text{MPC})$?

c. Investigate the impact of increases and decreases in net exports. Investigate the impact of a change in government purchases. Investigate the impact of autonomous changes in consumption spending, that is, a change in the constant term of the consumption function.

d. What happens if the MPC changes? You will need first to determine the initial equilibrium level of income for given levels of investment spending, net exports, and autonomous consumption spending. Then simulate your model to see how the change in the MPC affects the multiplier.

Economics in Action

Autonomous and Induced Changes in Consumption Spending

The multiplier shows how an autonomous increase in spending, through its impact on income, induces additional spending. The final result is that the equilibrium level of income increases by more than, or by a multiple of, the original autonomous change. We have also seen the close link between disposable income and consumption spending. Indeed, the induced changes in consumption spending are a critical part of the multiplier process.

Can changes in consumption spending ever initiate multiplier changes or are they only a part of a process that must be initiated by some other element of spending? To answer this question one must distinguish between factors that shift the consumption function and factors that lead to a movement along the consumption function. As a particular example, let's consider material from the 2004 Report of the Council of Economic Advisers.

Early each year, the President's Council of Economic Advisers issues its annual report. The council's report is published along with the Economic Report of the President. The volume's statistical appendix reports numerous data series that measure the macroeconomic performance of the economy. The council's report itself includes commentary on recent developments, a forecast for the upcoming year, and a detailed study of two or three topics of interest. The report is a mixture of politics and economic analysis as it is, in part, a brief for the policies of the president.

The February 2004 Report included the following comments about consumption spending during 2003.

> Consumer spending increased briskly in 2003...
>
> The pickup in spending growth in the second half of the year corresponded to an increase in the rate of growth of household income...Other factors also likely contributed to the strengthening of consumer spending over the course of 2003. The robust performance of equity markets and solid gains in home prices bolstered

wealth... Consumer sentiment was depressed early in the year by the prospect of war with Iraq. Sentiment jumped in April and May following the successful resolution of major combat operations and then was little changed until November, when it picked up noticeably. By the end of the year, household sentiment was somewhat higher than it had been at the end of 2002 and much higher than it was just prior to the war with Iraq... [P]ersonal saving was likely depressed by the boost to consumption from low interest rates both directly through the availability of low-interest-rate loans on durable goods and indirectly through the funds made available by cash-out mortgage refinancings.

The report cites several factors as helping to explain consumer spending: household income, consumer wealth and increased consumer confidence over the year, increases in house prices, lower interest rates and associated mortgage refinancing.

1. Which of these factors reflects a movement along an unchanged consumption function and which reflects a shift in the consumption function? Which would initiate a multiplier process and which would be part of the multiplier response to an autonomous change in spending?

2. What does the most recent Report say about autonomous and induced elements of consumption spending and other categories of spending?

SOURCE: *Economic Report of the President*, February 2004 (Washington, D.C.: United States Government Printing Office), p. 84–89.

• Study Questions

1. The expenditure schedule shows how total spending changes with domestic income. What categories of spending does the expenditure schedule need to include?

2. What would happen to the expenditure schedule if the marginal propensity to consume were larger or smaller? Why?

3. What would happen to the expenditure schedule if there were a change in any of the following: investment spending, government purchases of goods and services, exports, or imports?

4. What would happen to the expenditure schedule if investment spending or imports increased as national income increases?

5. According to the text, equilibrium occurs at the intersection of the expenditure schedule and the 45° line. Why there? What prevents points to the left or right of the intersection from also being points of equilibrium?

6. Why do we say the expenditure schedule is drawn for a given level of prices?

7. What happens to the expenditure schedule if prices increase or if they decrease?

8. Plotting different price levels and the corresponding equilibrium level of income from the income-expenditure diagram results in what curve?

9. Looking just at the expenditure schedule, how can you represent a change in autonomous spending? A change in induced spending?

10. How can it be that a change in autonomous spending results in an even larger change in the equilibrium level of income?

11. What happens to the value of the multiplier if the MPC is larger? Smaller? Why?

12. What are the four shortcomings of the multiplier formula $1/(1 - MPC)$?

13. Do these shortcomings mean that the formula overstates or understates the likely value of the multiplier?

14. What is the mechanism by which a recession in Europe may lead to a decline in output in the United States?

15. What is the relation between the multiplier analysis on the income-expenditure diagram following an autonomous change in spending and the resulting shift of the aggregate demand curve?

Bringing in the Supply-Side: Unemployment *and* Inflation?

10

Important Terms and Concepts

Aggregate supply curve

Productivity

Recessionary gap

Inflationary gap

Self-correcting mechanism

Stagflation

Learning Objectives
After completing this chapter, you should be able to:

- describe how the aggregate supply curve is derived from an analysis of business costs and why it slopes upward.

- distinguish between factors that will lead to a movement along or a shift in the aggregate supply curve.

- use the aggregate demand/aggregate supply graph to determine the equilibrium price level and the equilibrium level of real GDP.

- use the aggregate demand/aggregate supply graph to analyze how factors that shift either the aggregate demand curve or the aggregate supply curve will affect the equilibrium level of prices and output.

- use the aggregate demand curve/ aggregate supply graph to explain what kinds of shifts in the aggregate demand

curve and the aggregate supply curve can give rise to a period of stagnation.

- explain how an inflationary gap will self-destruct.

- explain how a recessionary gap will self-destruct.

- use the aggregate demand/aggregate supply diagram to show

  o demand-side inflation tends to be associated with a booming economy.

  o supply-side inflation tends to be associated with a slowing economy.

  o how favorable supply-side shocks enable an economy to have high employment and low inflation at the same time.

  o how increases in prices reduce the value of the multiplier.

Chapter Review

In Chapter 4 we first learned that for individual commodities, equilibrium price and quantity are determined by the intersection of the relevant demand and supply curves. The same logic holds when analyzing the economy as a whole. The level of prices and aggregate output is determined by the intersection of the aggregate demand and aggregate supply curves. We have also learned how the aggregate demand curve can be derived from analyzing how changes in the price level affect the spending decisions that underlie the expenditure schedule. In this chapter we will derive the aggregate supply curve and show how the price level and aggregate output are determined.

The aggregate supply curve is a schedule, showing for each possible price level, the total quantity of goods and services that all businesses are willing to supply during a specified period of time, holding all other factors influencing aggregate supply constant. You should note that the same logic applies here as to discussions of the supply decisions of individual firms. Businesses will adjust supply in pursuit of profits.

If prices rise while production costs per unit of output remain unchanged, we expect firms to (1) (increase/decrease) output. If prices stayed higher and production costs did not increase at all, would there be any limit to the increase in profits firms could derive from increases in output? Even if the prices of inputs do not increase, microeconomic analysis suggests that production costs will rise as firms try to expand output, putting a limit on the profitable increase in output. (Remember that in the short run, the supply curve for an individual firm is the upward-sloping portion of the firm's marginal cost curve.) The increase in output induced by an increase in the price level is a (movement along/shift in) the aggregate supply curve. Any change in production costs in the face of an otherwise unchanged price level—for example, an increase in energy prices imposed by a foreign supplier or an increase in money wages—will also affect profits and will lead to an adjustment in the quantity of goods and services that businesses are willing to supply. This time, however, the change in supply is a(n) _____ _____ the aggregate supply curve. The aggregate supply curve would also shift following a change in productivity or in the available supplies of labor or capital. For example, as investment increases the stock of capital, the aggregate supply curve will shift to the (left/right).

Now, having derived both the aggregate demand curve and the aggregate supply curve, we are in a position to use both to determine the final equilibrium level of prices and aggregate output, or GDP. See **Figure 10-1** for example, where the equilibrium price level of 100 and the equilibrium level (2) of GDP of $10,000 billion are given by the (intersection/slope) of the aggregate demand and supply curves. A higher price level, say, 110, implies (a) a lower quantity of aggregate demand as consumers respond to the loss of purchasing power of their money assets and net exports (increase/decrease) following the increase in domestic prices, and (b) a larger quantity of aggregate supply as firms respond to higher prices. Clearly, more supply and less demand cannot be a point of equilibrium,

Figure 10-1

Aggregate Demand and Aggregate Supply

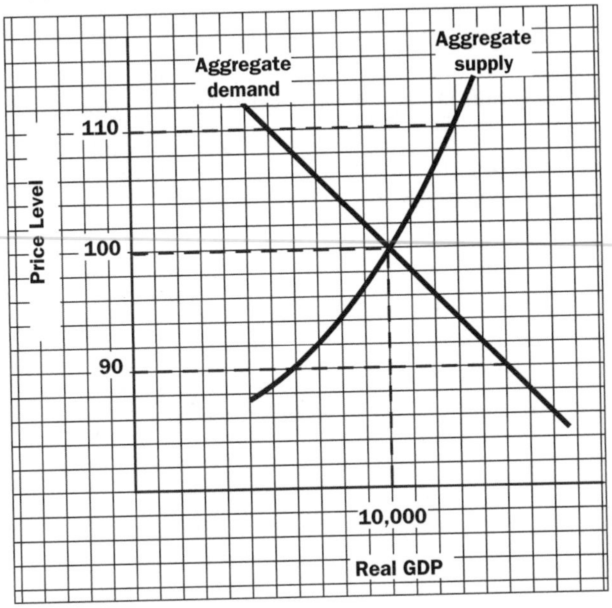

Figure 10-2

Aggregate Demand and Aggregate Supply

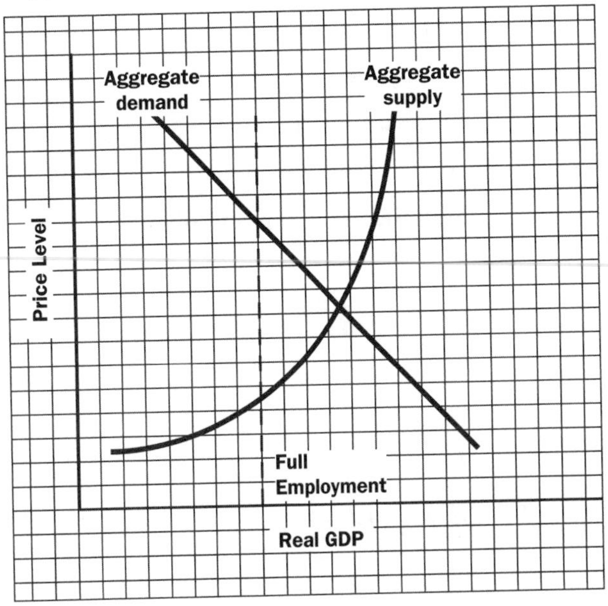

since firms would experience continual (increases/decreases) in inventories. The result is likely to be reduced output and price reductions that move the economy back toward equilibrium. Similarly, a lower price level, such as 90, would induce analogous, although opposite, reactions.

Nothing in the analysis so far guarantees that the intersection of the aggregate demand and aggregate supply curves will be at the level of output corresponding to full employment. If the final equilibrium level of output is different from the full-employment level of output, the result is either a recessionary gap or an inflationary gap. Consider **Figure 10-2,** which shows a(n) _____ gap. As unemployment falls below frictional levels and material inputs (3) become scarce, higher input prices will shift the aggregate supply curve (inward/outward) leading to a (movement along/shift in) the aggregate demand curve, (higher/lower) prices, (higher/lower) output, and the eventual elimination of the inflationary gap. Note that the simultaneous increase in prices and wages does not prove that increasing wages cause inflation. Both are best seen as a symptom of the original inflationary gap.

If the aggregate demand and aggregate supply curves intersect to the left of the full-employment level of output, there will be a(n) _____ gap. The rigidity of wages and other (4) input prices in the face of unemployment means that while a recessionary gap will eventually self-destruct, the process may be slow and painful.

Stagflation refers to the simultaneous occurrence of increasing prices and increasing unemployment. The previous analysis suggests that stagflation is a natural result of the self-destruction of a(n) (inflationary/recessionary) gap. Stagflation can also occur as a result of adverse shifts in the (5) aggregate _____ curve. Favorable shifts in the aggregate supply curve will result in (falling/rising) prices and _____ GDP.

Important Terms and Concepts Quiz

Choose the best definition for each of the following terms.

1. _____ Aggregate supply curve
2. _____ Productivity
3. _____ Recessionary gap
4. _____ Inflationary gap
5. _____ Self-correcting mechanism
6. _____ Stagflation

a. Economy's way of restoring equilibrium through inflation or deflation
b. Equilibrium real GDP exceeds the full-employment level of GDP
c. Amount of output produced by a unit of input
d. Equilibrium level of real GDP falls short of potential GDP
e. Inflation that occurs while the economy is growing slowly or in recession
f. Graph of total quantity of goods and services produced at each possible price level
g. Amount of input required to produce a unit of output

● Basic Exercises

This exercise first reviews the derivation of the aggregate demand curve and then uses both the aggregate demand and aggregate supply curves to determine the equilibrium level of income.

1. **Figure 10-3** shows an income-expenditure diagram in the top half and a price level–aggregate output diagram in the bottom half. The middle expenditure schedule in the top half duplicates the original situation described in Basic Exercise 1 of the previous chapter and assumes that the price level with this expenditure schedule is 100. The dashed line extending into the bottom figure shows how this output level, together with its associated price level, can be plotted in the lower diagram. It is one point on the aggregate demand curve.

   a. A decrease in the price level to 90 would increase consumption spending because a reduction in prices (decreases/increases) the purchasing power of consumer money assets and _____ net exports. These changes shift the expenditure schedule up. The new expenditure schedule, for a price level of 90, is shown in the top half of Figure 10-3. What is the equilibrium level of income in the income-expenditure diagram for a price level of 90?

   b. Plot the combination of prices and output from part a in the lower diagram. This is a second point on the aggregate demand curve.

   c. A price level of 110 would depress consumer spending and net exports, shifting both the consumption function and the expenditure schedule. Use the expenditure schedule for a price level of 110 to plot a third point on the aggregate demand curve.

   d. Draw the aggregate demand curve by connecting the three points now plotted in the lower diagram.

   e. Using the aggregate demand curve you have just derived and the aggregate supply curve that is already drawn, what is the equilibrium level of prices and real GDP?

   f. If the level of full-employment output were $10 trillion, would there be an inflationary gap or recessionary gap? How, if at all, might such a gap self-destruct and where would the price level and real GDP end up?

   g. If the level of full-employment output were $10.125 trillion, would there be an inflationary gap or recessionary gap? How, if at all, might such a gap self-destruct and where would the price level and real GDP end up?

Figure 10-3

Deriving the Aggregate Demand Curve

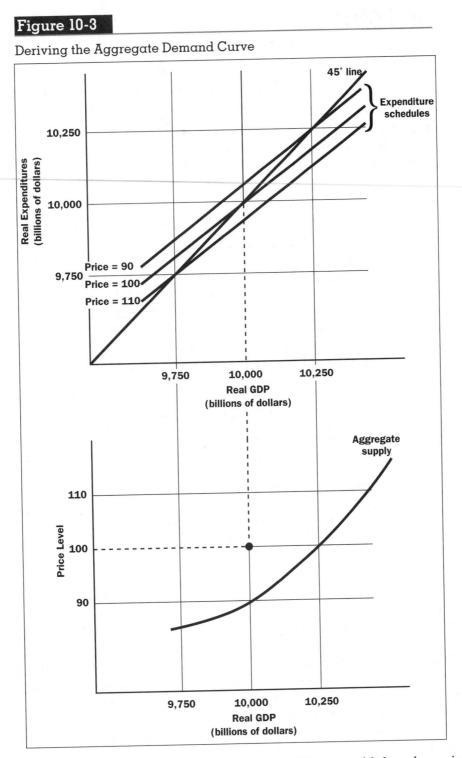

h. If the level of full-employment output were $10.250 trillion, would there be an inflationary or recessionary gap? How, if at all, might such a gap self-destruct and where would the price level and real GDP end up?

Figure 10-4

Adjustments Following a Shift in the Aggregate Demand Curve

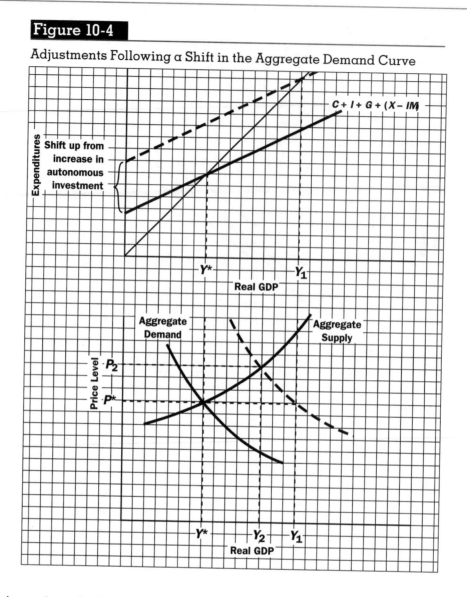

2. This exercise reviews the impact of higher prices on the multiplier. Consider **Figure 10-4.** The heavy lines show an initial expenditure schedule and the associated aggregate demand curve. The initial equilibrium is at a level of income Y^*, and price level P^*. The dashed expenditure schedule comes from an increase in investment spending. Note that the shift in the expenditure schedule leads to a shift in the aggregate demand curve. In fact, the initial new equilibrium on the income-expenditure diagram, Y_1, is equal to the (horizontal/vertical) shift of the aggregate demand curve in the lower half of the diagram.
   a. Is the combination Y_1, P^* the final equilibrium?
   b. If Y_1, P^* is not the final equilibrium, describe what will happen during the transition to the final equilibrium.

3. In **Table 10-1**, fill in the blanks as indicated to analyze the response to each change. In the first two columns use S or M for "shift in" or "movement along." In the last two columns use + or –.

Table 10-1

Adjustments to External Shocks

	Aggregate Demand Curve	Aggregate Supply Curve	Equilibrium Real GDP	Equilibrium Price Level
A reduction in business investment spending				
An increase in the price of many basic commodities used as inputs in the production of final goods and services				
An increase in the demand for exports caused by an economic boom abroad				
An increase in labor productivity due to a technological breakthrough				
A reduction in consumer spending due to a fall in the stock market				
A large increase in energy prices				

• Self-Tests for Understanding

Test A

Circle the most appropriate answer.

1. The aggregate supply curve
   a. slopes down to the right.
   b. has a positive slope.
   c. slopes up to the left.
   d. has a negative slope.

2. The slope of the aggregate supply curve reflects the fact that
   a. inflation reduces the value of the oversimplified multiplier.
   b. the costs of important inputs, such as labor, are relatively fixed in the short run.
   c. the marginal propensity to consume is less than 1.0.
   d. recessionary gaps take a long time to self-destruct.

3. The aggregate supply curve will shift following changes in all but which of the following?
   a. the price level
   b. wage rates
   c. technology and productivity
   d. available supplies of factories and machines

4. Which of the following will shift the aggregate supply curve outward?
   a. lower prices
   b. higher wages
   c. higher energy prices
   d. improvements in technology that increase labor productivity

5. The price level and the equilibrium level of real GDP
   a. are determined by the intersection of the aggregate demand and aggregate supply curves.
   b. will always occur at full employment.
   c. can be found in the income-expenditure diagram.
   d. do not change unless the aggregate demand curve shifts.

6. A change in the price level
   a. will lead to a shift in the aggregate supply curve.
   b. will lead to a shift in the aggregate demand curve.
   c. reflects a shift in the aggregate demand curve and/or aggregate supply curve.
   d. will always lead to stagnation.

7. A higher price level will lead to which of the following? (There may be more than one correct answer.)
   a. a reduction in the purchasing power of consumers' money fixed assets
   b. a downward shift in the consumption function
   c. an increase in imports
   d. a decrease in exports
   e. a downward shift in the expenditure schedule

8. An inflationary gap occurs
   a. when the equilibrium level of GDP exceeds potential GDP.
   b. whenever there is an upward shift in the expenditure schedule.
   c. whenever aggregate supply exceeds aggregate demand.
   d. during periods of high unemployment.

9. From an initial position of full employment, which one of the following will not lead to a recessionary gap?
   a. a shift in the aggregate supply curve in response to an increase in energy prices
   b. a reduction in investment spending due to a decline in business confidences
   c. a reduction in consumer spending due to an adverse shift in consumer expectations
   d. an increase in exports that follows a business expansion in Europe

10. Which of the following is not associated with the elimination of an inflationary gap?
    a. rising prices
    b. falling output
    c. increased employment
    d. rising wages

11. Which of the following is most likely to lead to an inflationary gap?
    a. an increase in government purchases of goods and services to fight a recession
    b. an increase in exports that occurs when unemployment rates are high
    c. a significant reduction in energy prices
    d. any increase in spending that shifts the aggregate demand curve to the right when GDP is at or beyond potential GDP

12. In the face of a recessionary gap, the economy's self-correcting mechanism reflects the effects of
    a. weak labor markets.
    b. trade deficits.
    c. government deficits.
    d. an MPC that is less than 1.0.

13. Which of the following is most likely to lead to stagflation?
    a. a reduction in investment spending due to a decline in business confidence
    b. an increase in exports that occurs when unemployment rates are high
    c. a significant increase in energy prices
    d. a technological breakthrough that lowers production costs

14. Which of the following lead(s) to an increase in net exports? (There may be more than one correct answer.)
    a. decrease in exports
    b. decrease in imports
    c. increase in imports
    d. increase in exports

15. From an initial position of equilibrium, exports increase by $100 billion as Europe experiences a business boom. This change will lead to which of the following? (There may be more than one correct answer.)
    a. an increase in net exports
    b. an upward shift of the expenditure schedule
    c. a shift to the right in the aggregate supply curve
    d. a shift to the right in the aggregate demand curve

16. At the new equilibrium following the increase in exports, U.S. GDP will be _____ and the U.S. price level will be _____.
    a. higher; lower
    b. lower; lower
    c. higher; higher
    d. lower; higher

17. The economy will experience increases in output with little inflation whenever
    a. the aggregate supply curve shifts to the left.
    b. the aggregate demand curve shifts to the right.
    c. both the aggregate demand and supply curves shift to the right in a similar fashion.
    d. the expenditure schedule becomes steeper.

18. Year-to-year changes in GDP and prices are probably best seen as the result of
    a. shifts in the aggregate demand curve that move the economy along an unchanged aggregate supply curve.
    b. shifts in the aggregate supply curve that move the economy along an unchanged aggregate demand curve.
    c. shifts in both the aggregate demand and aggregate supply curves.

19. Prices rise following an increase in autonomous spending whenever the
    a. marginal propensity to consume is less than 1.0.
    b. multiplier is greater than 1.0.
    c. aggregate demand curve has a negative slope.
    d. aggregate supply curve has a positive slope.

20. The aggregate demand curve–aggregate supply curve diagram shows that the multiplier will be smaller than suggested by the original shift of the expenditure schedule whenever the
    a. aggregate demand curve slopes down and to the right.
    b. aggregate demand curve slopes up and to the right.
    c. aggregate supply curve slopes up and to the right.
    d. MPC is less than 1.0.

Test B

Circle T or F for true or false.

T F   1. The aggregate supply curve shows for each possible price the total quantity of goods and services that the nation's businesses are willing to supply.

T F   2. The aggregate supply curve slopes upward because businesses will expand output as long as higher prices make expansion profitable.

T F   3. An increase in the capital stock from business investment will shift the aggregate supply curve to the right.

T F   4. The impact of unemployment on wages and prices is part of the process by which recessionary gaps self-destruct.

T F   5. If the aggregate supply curve shifts to the left, the result will be stagnation.

T F   6. The economy's self-correcting mechanisms ensure that the aggregate demand and aggregate supply curves will always intersect at potential output.

T F   7. If the aggregate demand and supply curves intersect to the left of the full employment level of output there will be a recessionary gap.

T F   8. A period of excessive aggregate demand is likely to be followed by a period of stagnation as the inflationary gap self-destructs.

T F   9. During the elimination of an inflationary gap, the real cause of inflation is excessive wage demands on the part of labor.

T F 10. Analysis of the aggregate supply curve shows that the multiplier derived from the income-expenditure diagram typically understates the final change in output.

Supplementary Exercise

The following equations are consistent with Basic Exercise 1.

$T = 1,800$
$DI = Y - T$
$C = 790 + 0.8DI - 4.5P$
$I = 1,500$
$G = 1,800$
$X - IM = -150 - 0.5P$
$C + I + G + (X - IM) = Y \ (45° \text{ line})$

Aggregate supply curve: $Y = 7,750 + 25P$

T = taxes
DI = disposable income
C = consumption expenditures
I = investment expenditures
G = government purchases
X = exports
IM = imports
Y = GDP
P = price level

1. Use the consumption function along with the level of investment spending, government purchases, and net exports to determine an expression for the expenditure schedule. (Don't forget to substitute for disposable income and note that this expression will involve the variable P. Remember a single Expenditure Schedule assumes that the price level does not change. When P changes, the Expenditure Schedule will shift.)

2. Use the expenditure schedule and the equation for the 45° line to determine an expression for the aggregate demand curve.

3. Now use both the aggregate demand curve and the aggregate supply curve to determine the equilibrium level of prices and GDP.

4. Resolve the system on the assumption that investment expenditures decrease to 1,450.

Economics in Action

How Variable Is the Aggregate Supply Curve?

What explains fluctuations in GDP—shifts in the aggregate demand curve or shifts in the aggregate supply curve? Keynesian analysis focuses on shifts in aggregate demand as the major source of fluctuations in output. In this view, the aggregate supply curve shifts out year by year more or less regularly and deviations from potential or full-employment output are largely the result of shifts in the aggregate demand curve that are greater or less than the shift in the aggregate supply curve. In recent years an alternative view has argued that the growth of potential output and the associated shifts in the aggregate supply curve may be less regular and more variable than had been suspected.

What difference does it make whether potential output grows smoothly or fluctuates from year to year? Estimates of potential output and the difference of actual output from potential are an important determinant of changes in fiscal and monetary policy. For example, when the economy is operating below potential, expansionary policies that increase aggregate demand can increase output and employment. If the aggregate supply curve is relatively flat, the increase in output may have little impact on prices. The magnitude of changes in fiscal and monetary policy to increase aggregate demand will be influenced by estimates of the shortfall from potential output.

But if GDP is low in part because of an adverse shift in the aggregate supply curve, then expansionary policy that ignores the decrease in potential output could turn out to be too expansionary, push the economy above potential, and create unwanted inflationary pressures. On the other hand, if GDP increased above traditional estimates of potential output because of a favorable shift in the aggregate supply curve, stabilization policy that tried to reduce aggregate demand because of a concern about possible inflationary pressures would unnecessarily increase unemployment.

Why is it so difficult to figure out how the aggregate supply curve is shifting? As economists John Boschen and Leonard Mills point out, potential GDP is not directly observable. Neither is the aggregate demand curve or the aggregate supply curve. The levels of output and prices that we observe give us information about where these curves intersect, but by themselves do not identify one curve or the other. In order to identify the aggregate supply curve one needs to use economic theory and make appropriate assumptions about factors that affect aggregate supply, just as we have done with regard to factors that affect aggregate demand. These theories of the aggregate supply curve are then tested by comparing implications of the models with data from the real world. Models of the aggregate supply curve are still relatively new and estimates of the importance of supply-side factors in explaining fluctuations in output cover a wide range. A number of these estimates suggest that a one-third of the variation in output might be attributed to variability in the growth of potential GDP while others range as high as 50 to 70 percent.

1. What are the implications for stabilization policy if fluctuations in the aggregate supply curve account for 10 percent or 50 percent of the fluctuations in output?

SOURCES: John Boschen and Leonard Mills, "Monetary Policy with a New View of Potential GNP," *Business Review*, Federal Reserve Bank of Philadelphia (July/August 1990), pp. 3-10; and Satyajit Chatterjee, "Productivity Growth and the American Business Cycle," *Business Review*, Federal Reserve Bank of Philadelphia (September/October 1995), pp. 13–22.

● Study Questions

1. Why is the aggregate supply curve drawn sloping upward to the right?

2. What factors influence the position of the aggregate supply curve?

3. What market forces move the economy to the equilibrium level of output and prices given by the intersection of the aggregate demand curve and aggregate supply curve?

4. Evaluate the following statement: "All periods of inflation are caused by excessive demands for high wages on the part of labor."

5. What is the process by which an inflationary gap self-destructs?

6. Is an adverse supply shock likely to give rise to an inflationary gap or a recessionary gap? Why?

7. What are some of the reasons the economy's self-correcting mechanisms might work slowly in the face of a recessionary gap?

8. What is meant by stagnation and when is it likely to occur?

9. How do considerations of aggregate supply affect the value of the multiplier?

10. How might shifts in the aggregate supply curve help to explain the experience of the later 1990s when inflation and unemployment declined at the same time?

Managing Aggregate Demand: Fiscal Policy

11

Important Terms and Concepts

Fiscal policy	Effect of income taxes on the multiplier	Automatic stabilizers	Supply-side tax cuts

Learning Objectives
After completing this chapter, you should be able to:

- describe the process by which a change in government purchases of goods and services will lead to a shift in the expenditure schedule and the aggregate demand curve.

- describe the process by which a change in taxes will lead to a shift in the expenditure schedule and the aggregate demand curve.

- explain why income taxes reduce the value of the multiplier.

- explain why the multiplier for a change in income taxes will be less than the multiplier for a change in government purchases of goods and services.

- explain how automatic stabilizers help to reduce fluctuations in GDP when there are changes in autonomous spending.

- explain why economists treat government transfer payments like negative taxes, not

like government purchases of goods and services.

- describe the process by which a change in government transfer payments will lead to a shift in the aggregate demand curve.

- explain why active stabilization policy need not imply that government must get bigger and bigger.

- use the aggregate demand and supply diagram to show how supply-side tax cuts hope to reduce the impact on prices associated with stabilization policy to eliminate a recessionary gap.

- describe the kernel of truth in supply-side economics.

- discuss the reservations that most economists have in regard to supply-side economics.

• Chapter Review

The models of income determination in earlier chapters included a rather passive government. This chapter uses a more realistic model of taxes and provides a framework for considering how and when the government should vary spending and taxes. The government's plans for spending and taxes are

(1) called (<u>fiscal/monetary</u>) policy. The only trick is to understand how government spending and taxes affect the curves we have already derived, that is, how government spending and taxes affect the expenditure schedule, the aggregate demand curve, and the aggregate supply curve. After this, the analysis proceeds exactly as before: For a given price level, the equilibrium level of income on the income-expenditure diagram is determined by the intersection of the (<u>consumption/expenditure</u>) schedule and the 45° line. A change in prices will affect consumption spending and net exports. The different price levels and the associated equilibrium levels of income on the income-expenditure diagram can be combined to form the aggregate _____ curve. This curve together with the aggregate _____ curve will determine the final equilibrium for income and prices. A change in the government's fiscal policy will shift one or more of the curves and lead to new equilibrium values for income and prices.

There are three important ways government fiscal policy influences total spending in the economy:

A. The government purchases goods and services.

B. The government collects *taxes*, reducing the spending power of households and firms. Particular taxes may affect incentives for working, saving, investing, or spending.

C. The government gives *transfer payments* to some individuals, e.g., Social Security payments, thereby increasing their disposable income.

Government purchases of goods and services are a direct addition to total spending in the

(2) economy; that is, they shift the expenditure schedule (<u>up/down</u>) by the full amount of the purchases. Thus, if government spending increased by $1, the expenditure schedule would shift up by $_____. (An increase in autonomous consumption spending, investment spending or net exports of $1 would also shift the expenditure schedule up by $_____.) Thus, changes in government spending shift the expenditure schedule in exactly the same way as other changes in autonomous spending and should have similar multiplier effects.

(3) Government taxes (<u>are/are not</u>) a direct component of spending on currently produced goods and services. Personal income taxes affect consumption spending through their impact on disposable income. Following a decrease in personal income taxes, consumers' disposable income will be (<u>higher/lower</u>). The initial effect on consumption spending will depend in part

on whether consumers view the tax change as permanent or temporary. The largest impact will come from a (permanent/temporary) tax cut. The change in consumption spending following the reduction in taxes will be determined by the marginal propensity to consume, which is (less than/equal to/greater than) 1.0. Thus, changes in personal income taxes affect spending, but indirectly through their effect on consumption expenditures. A change in corporate income taxes will change corporate profits after taxes, and is likely to affect _____ expenditures.

The third important function of the government that affects total spending is the magnitude of government transfer payments. These payments, like taxes, are not a direct element of total spending on goods and services. Also, like personal taxes, they affect total spending because they affect people's disposable _____ and thus their _____ spending. Remember that taxes   (4) are earned but not received while transfers are received but not earned. Thus in the models we will be working with, disposable income is equal to GDP (minus/plus) taxes (minus/plus) transfers, and transfers can be thought of as negative taxes. An important feature of income taxes (and some transfer payments) is that they vary with GDP. Taxes go (down/up) and transfer payments go _____ as GDP goes up.

We have seen that the multiplier process arises because any autonomous increase in spending means higher income for those who supply the newly demanded goods. These higher incomes will lead to more consumption spending, and so on, and so on. This process continues to take place, but it is important to remember that each round of spending produces an increase in income *before* taxes. With income taxes some of the increase in before-tax income goes to pay taxes, and after-tax income (or disposable income) will increase by (more/less) than it would in an economy with fixed taxes.   (5) Thus, each induced round of consumption spending will be (smaller/larger) than before.

To summarize, in an economy with income taxes and transfer payments that vary with income, each round in the multiplier process will be smaller than before, and thus the multiplier effect on income, from any increase in autonomous spending, will be (smaller/larger) than before. The   (6) impact of income taxes on the multiplier is another important reason why our earlier formula for the multiplier, $1/(1 - MPC)$, was oversimplified.

We can see these same results graphically on the income-expenditure diagram. Up to now we have assumed that taxes did not vary with income. A $1 change in GDP meant a $1 increase in disposable income and led to an increase in consumption spending given by the MPC. Since in these models consumption spending was the only type of spending that changed when GDP changed, the slope of the expenditure schedule was equal to the _____. Now when we consider the impact   (7) of income taxes, we see that a $1 increase in GDP leads to a(n) (smaller/equal/larger) increase in disposable income and a(n) _____ increase in consumption spending than before. The result is a (flatter/steeper) expenditure schedule.

As we saw earlier, the multiplier can be derived from the slope of the expenditure schedule. The slope of the expenditure schedule can be written as

$$\text{Slope of the Expenditure Schedule} = \frac{\Delta C}{\Delta GDP} + \frac{\Delta I}{\Delta GDP} + \frac{\Delta G}{\Delta GDP} + \frac{\Delta X}{\Delta GDP} + \frac{\Delta IM}{\Delta GDP}$$

Earlier we had assumed that all terms except $\frac{\Delta C}{\Delta GDP}$, were zero. Let us look more closely at $\frac{\Delta C}{\Delta GDP}$, which we can rewrite as

$$\frac{\Delta C}{\Delta GDP} = \left(\frac{\Delta C}{\Delta D}\right) \times \left(\frac{\Delta D}{\Delta GDP}\right)$$

The first term on the right-hand side of the equal sign is the marginal propensity to consume. If taxes do not vary with income, the second term will equal 1.0. An income tax means the second term

(8) is (<u>greater than/equal to/less than</u>) 1.0 and the slope of the expenditure schedule is less than the marginal propensity to consume.[1]

We have now added government purchases of goods and services, taxes, and transfers to our model of income determination. Taken together, these variables are an important determinant of the equilibrium level of income. Changes in these variables, just like the changes in autonomous spending we considered in earlier chapters, will have multiplier effects on the equilibrium level of GDP. The deliberate manipulation of fiscal policy variables may help the government achieve its desired objectives for GDP and prices. Manipulation of government fiscal policy variables for GDP objectives is an example of stabilization policy. For example, if the government wants to increase GDP, it can decide

(9) to (<u>increase/decrease</u>) government purchases of goods and services, _____ personal taxes, _____ corporate taxes, or _____ transfer payments to individuals.

One of the reasons it is so difficult to agree on fiscal policy is that there are so many choices, all of which could have the same impact on national income, but very different impacts on other issues, such as the size of the public versus private sector, the burden of taxes between individuals and corporations, the composition of output between consumption and investment spending, and the amount of income redistribution through transfers to low-income families.

One might believe that if we could decide upon the amounts of government purchases, taxes, and transfers, effective fiscal policy would be simply a technical matter of choosing the right numbers so that the expenditure schedule would intersect the 45° line, and the aggregate demand curve would intersect the aggregate supply curve at full employment. In actuality, uncertainties about (a) private components of aggregate demand, (b) the precise size of the multiplier, (c) exactly what level of GDP is associated with full employment, (d) the time it takes for changes in fiscal policy to affect spending,

---

[1]This analysis also helps us see how induced spending affects the slope of the expenditure schedule. For example, if investment spending increases when GDP increases, then $\Delta I/\Delta GDP$ will be greater than zero and the expenditure schedule will be steeper. If imports increase with increases in GDP, then $\Delta IM/\Delta GDP$ will be greater than zero and the slope of the expenditure schedule will be flatter.

and (e) the vagaries of the political process all mean that fiscal policy will continue to be subject to much political give and take. One hopes that appropriate economic analysis will contribute to a more informed level of debate.

Changes in government spending or tax rates shift the aggregate demand curve, directly in the case of government purchases and indirectly through impacts on private spending in the case of taxes and transfer payments. Any shift in the aggregate demand curve, including shifts from changes in fiscal policy, affects both prices and output as we move along the aggregate _____ curve. (10) Thus, expansionary fiscal policy, designed to increase GDP, is also likely to (increase/decrease) prices. Supply-side fiscal policies attempt to minimize the impact on prices through changes that shift the aggregate supply curve at the same time that they shift the aggregate demand curve.

Since 1980, there has been much attention given to supply-side tax cuts. Most economists have a number of reservations about the exaggerated claims of ardent supporters of supply-side tax cuts: Specific effects will depend on exactly which taxes are reduced; increases in aggregate supply are likely to take some time, while effects on aggregate demand will be much quicker. By themselves supply-side tax cuts are likely to lead to increased income inequality and to bigger, not smaller, government budget deficits. Do not let these serious objections to exaggerated claims blind you to the kernel of truth in supply-side economics: Marginal tax rates are important for decisions by individuals and firms. In particular situations, reductions in marginal tax rates can improve economic incentives.

Important Terms and Concepts Quiz

Choose the best definition for each of the following terms.

1. _____ Fiscal policy
2. _____ Automatic stabilizers
3. _____ Government transfer payments
4. _____ Supply-side tax cuts

a. All income is taxed at a single rate

b. Money the government gives to individuals in the form of outright grants

c. The government's plan for spending and taxes

d. Tax policy designed to shift the aggregate supply curve to the right

e. Features of the economy that reduce its sensitivity to shifts in demand

Basic Exercises

This exercise is designed to show how changes in government purchases and taxes will have multiplier effects on the equilibrium level of income and how these multipliers can be used to help determine appropriate fiscal policy. To simplify the numerical calculations, the exercise focuses on the shift in the expenditure schedule, holding prices constant. That is, we will consider how changes in fiscal policy shift the aggregate demand curve.

Table 11-1 has data on GDP, taxes, disposable income, consumption, investment, government spending, exports, and imports. This table is similar to Table 11-1 except that here taxes vary with income while in Table 11-1 they did not.

Table 11-1

Constant Prices

Income (Output) Y	Taxes T	Disposable Income DI	Consumption Spending C	Investment Spending I	Government Purchases G	Exports X	Imports IM	Total Spending C + I + G + (X − IM)
9,500	1,675	7,825	6,600	1,500	1,750	1,200	1,350	_____
9,750	1,738	8,013	6,750	1,500	1,750	1,200	1,350	_____
10,000	1,800	8,200	6,900	1,500	1,750	1,200	1,350	_____
10,250	1,863	8,388	7,050	1,500	1,750	1,200	1,350	_____
10,500	1,925	8,575	7,200	1,500	1,750	1,200	1,350	_____
10,750	1,988	8,763	7,350	1,500	1,750	1,200	1,350	_____
11,000	2,050	8,950	7,500	1,500	1,750	1,200	1,350	_____

1. Complete the column for total spending to determine the equilibrium level of GDP $ _____

2. Assume now that government purchases decrease by $200 to $1550 as shown in **Table 11-2.** Following the decrease in government purchases, the new equilibrium level of income is $ _____.

Table 11-2

Constant Prices

Income (Output) Y	Taxes T	Disposable Income DI	Consumption Spending C	Investment Spending I	Government Purchases G	Exports X	Imports IM	Total Spending C + I + G + (X − IM)
9,500	1,675	7,825	6,600	1,500	1,550	1,200	1,350	_____
9,750	1,738	8,013	6,750	1,500	1,550	1,200	1,350	_____
10,000	1,800	8,200	6,900	1,500	1,550	1,200	1,350	_____
10,250	1,863	8,388	7,050	1,500	1,550	1,200	1,350	_____
10,500	1,925	8,575	7,200	1,500	1,550	1,200	1,350	_____
10,750	1,988	8,763	7,350	1,500	1,550	1,200	1,350	_____
11,000	2,050	8,950	7,500	1,500	1,550	1,200	1,350	_____

3. The multiplier for this decrease in government purchases is _____. (This multiplier can be computed by dividing the change in the equilibrium level of income by the change in

government purchases.) How does the value for the multiplier compare with the value for the multiplier in Basic Exercise of Chapter 9? The only difference here is that taxes are assumed to vary with income. In particular the marginal propensity to consume is the same in Tables 28-1, 28-2, and Tables 26-1 and 26-2.

4. Now let us use the multipliers computed in question 3 to figure out what changes in government purchases would be necessary to raise the equilibrium level of income from its initial value given in question 1 to its full-employment level of $10,750.

   The necessary increase in government purchases is $_____.

   (You can answer this question by figuring out what appropriate change in government purchases when multiplied by the relevant multiplier will equal the desired change in income.) Alternatively one could have lowered taxes to stimulate demand. How would you choose between using changes in government purchases of goods and services and changes in taxes when you want to use fiscal policy to influence aggregate demand?

5. What is the new equilibrium level of income if, from the initial equilibrium given in question 1, investment expenditures rather than government purchases fall by $200? (Now investment spending will be $1,700 while government purchases stay at $1,800. Create a new version of Table 11-1 if necessary.) What can one say about multipliers for autonomous changes in public versus private purchases of goods and services?

● Self-Tests for Understanding

Test A

Circle the most appropriate answer.

1. Fiscal policy involves decisions about all but which one of the following?
   a. income tax rates
   b. the magnitude of transfer payments
   c. interest rates
   d. government purchases of goods and services

2. The impact of transfer payments on disposable income suggests that an increase in transfer payments will have the same effect as a(n)
   a. increase in taxes.
   b. increase in government purchases of goods and services.
   c. decrease in government purchases of goods and services.
   d. decrease in taxes.

3. A simultaneous reduction in income taxes and transfer payments of $15 billion will leave aggregate disposable income
   a. lower than before the change.
   b. unchanged.
   c. higher than before the change.

4. An increase in government purchases will
   a. shift the expenditure schedule down.
   b. leave the expenditure schedule unchanged.
   c. shift the expenditure schedule up.

5. A decrease in taxes will
   a. shift the expenditure schedule down.
   b. leave the expenditure schedule unchanged.
   c. shift the expenditure schedule up.

6. An increase in transfer payments will
   a. shift the expenditure schedule down.
   b. leave the expenditure schedule unchanged.
   c. shift the expenditure schedule up.

7. Income taxes mean that the difference between GDP and disposable income will _____ as GDP increases.
   a. decrease
   b. stay the same
   c. increase

8. When taxes, transfers, investment spending, net exports, and government purchases do not vary with GDP, the slope of the expenditure schedule will be
   a. less than the MPC.
   b. equal to the MPC.
   c. greater than the MPC.

9. If a system of fixed taxes and transfers is replaced with taxes and transfers that vary with income, the slope of the expenditure schedule will be
   a. less than before.
   b. unchanged.
   c. greater than before.

10. The initial impact of a change in income taxes is on _____ and _____.
    a. imports; exports
    b. disposable income; investment
    c. investment; consumption
    d. disposable income; consumption

11. Equal reductions in government purchases and taxes are likely to
    a. shift the expenditure schedule down.
    b. leave the expenditure schedule unchanged.
    c. shift the expenditure schedule up.

12. If the basic expenditure multiplier is 2.0 and if the government wishes to decrease the level of GDP by $80 billion, what decrease in government purchases of goods and services would do the job?
    a. $20 billion
    b. $40 billion
    c. $80 billion
    d. $160 billion

13. Instead of decreasing government purchases, the same objectives, in terms of reducing GDP, could also be achieved by
    a. reducing government transfer payments.
    b. reducing taxes.
    c. increasing both taxes and government transfer payments by equal amounts.
    d. reducing both taxes and government transfer payments by equal amounts.

14. Which of the following would help eliminate a recessionary gap?
    a. decrease in taxes
    b. decrease in transfer payments
    c. decrease in government purchases
    d. increase in tax rates

15. A 10 percent reduction in income tax rates would
    a. lower the value of the basic expenditure multiplier.
    b. not affect the value of the basic expenditure multiplier.
    c. raise the value of the basic expenditure multiplier.

16. An increase in tax rates will lead to all but which one of the following?
    a. a decrease in the value of the multiplier
    b. a movement along the aggregate demand curve
    c. a reduction in the equilibrium level of GDP
    d. a shift of the expenditure schedule

17. Which of the following is not an example of an automatic stabilizer?
    a. unemployment compensation
    b. the corporate income tax
    c. a special program to build more highways enacted to help combat a recession
    d. personal income taxes

18. Political conservatives could still argue for active stabilization policy as long as the government agreed to _____ during periods of boom and _____ during recessions.
    a. increase taxes; increase government spending
    b. increase government spending; lower taxes
    c. lower government spending; lower taxes
    d. lower taxes; increase government spending

19. Supply-side tax cuts are designed to increase output without raising prices by shifting the
   a. expenditure schedule.
   b. aggregate demand curve.
   c. aggregate supply curve.
   d. 45° line.

20. Critics of supply-side tax cuts would agree with all but which one of the following?
   a. Supply-side tax cuts are likely to increase inequality in the distribution of income.
   b. Supply-side tax cuts will substantially reduce the rate of inflation.
   c. Supply-side tax cuts are likely to mean bigger deficits for the federal government.
   d. Supply-side tax cuts will have a larger initial impact on aggregate demand than on aggregate supply.

Test B

Circle T or F for true or false.

T   F   1. An increase in income tax rates will increase the multiplier.

T   F   2. When taxes increase with increases in income, a $1 change in GDP will mean a smaller change in disposable income.

T   F   3. Income taxation reduces the value of the multiplier for changes in government purchases but does not affect the multiplier for changes in investment.

T   F   4. Since taxes are not a direct component of aggregate demand, changes in taxes do not have multiplier effects on income.

T   F   5. Changes in government purchases of goods and services and in government transfer payments to individuals are both changes in government spending and thus have the same multiplier effects on the equilibrium level of income.

T   F   6. Reducing tax rates would help to eliminate an inflationary gap.

T   F   7. Active stabilization policy implies that the government must get bigger and bigger.

T   F   8. Automatic stabilizers reduce the sensitivity of the economy to shifts in aggregate demand.

T   F   9. Only the aggregate supply curve will shift following a supply-side tax cut that increases investment spending by firms.

T   F   10. There is general agreement among economists that supply-side tax cuts will increase output with little impact on prices.

| Appendix A | *Graphical Treatment of Taxes and Fiscal Policy*

Basic Exercises

Table 11-3

Constant Prices

Income (Output) Y	Taxes T	Disposable Income DI	Consumption Spending C	Investment Spending I	Government Purchases G	Exports X	Imports IM	Total Spending C + I + G + (X − IM)
9,500	1,425	8,075	6,800	1,500	1,550	1,200	1,350	_____
9,750	1,488	8,263	6,950	1,500	1,550	1,200	1,350	_____
10,000	1,550	8,450	7,100	1,500	1,550	1,200	1,350	_____
10,250	1,613	8,638	7,250	1,500	1,550	1,200	1,350	_____
10,500	1,675	8,825	7,400	1,500	1,550	1,200	1,350	_____
10,750	1,738	9,013	7,550	1,500	1,550	1,200	1,350	_____
11,000	1,800	9,200	7,700	1,500	1,550	1,200	1,350	_____

The following problem is meant to illustrate the material in Appendix A. Table 11-3 is the same as Table 11-2 except that taxes are lower at each possible level of income.

1. A comparison of consumption spending in Tables 11-2 and **11-3** when Y = 9,500 shows the initial impact on consumption spending when taxes are reduced. Taxes decreased by $250, disposable income increased by $250, and consumption spending increased by _____. The increase in consumption spending should equal the MPC times the increase in disposable income. Does it?

2. What is the new equilibrium level of income following the reduction in taxes? _____

3. Was the reduction in taxes analyzed in questions 1 and 2 self-financing? That is, was the increase in GDP stimulated by the reduction in taxes large enough so that on balance there was no decrease in government tax revenues? (Be sure to compare tax receipts at the equilibrium level of income in Table 11-2 with tax receipts at the equilibrium in Table 11-3.)

Figure 11-1

Expenditure Schedule

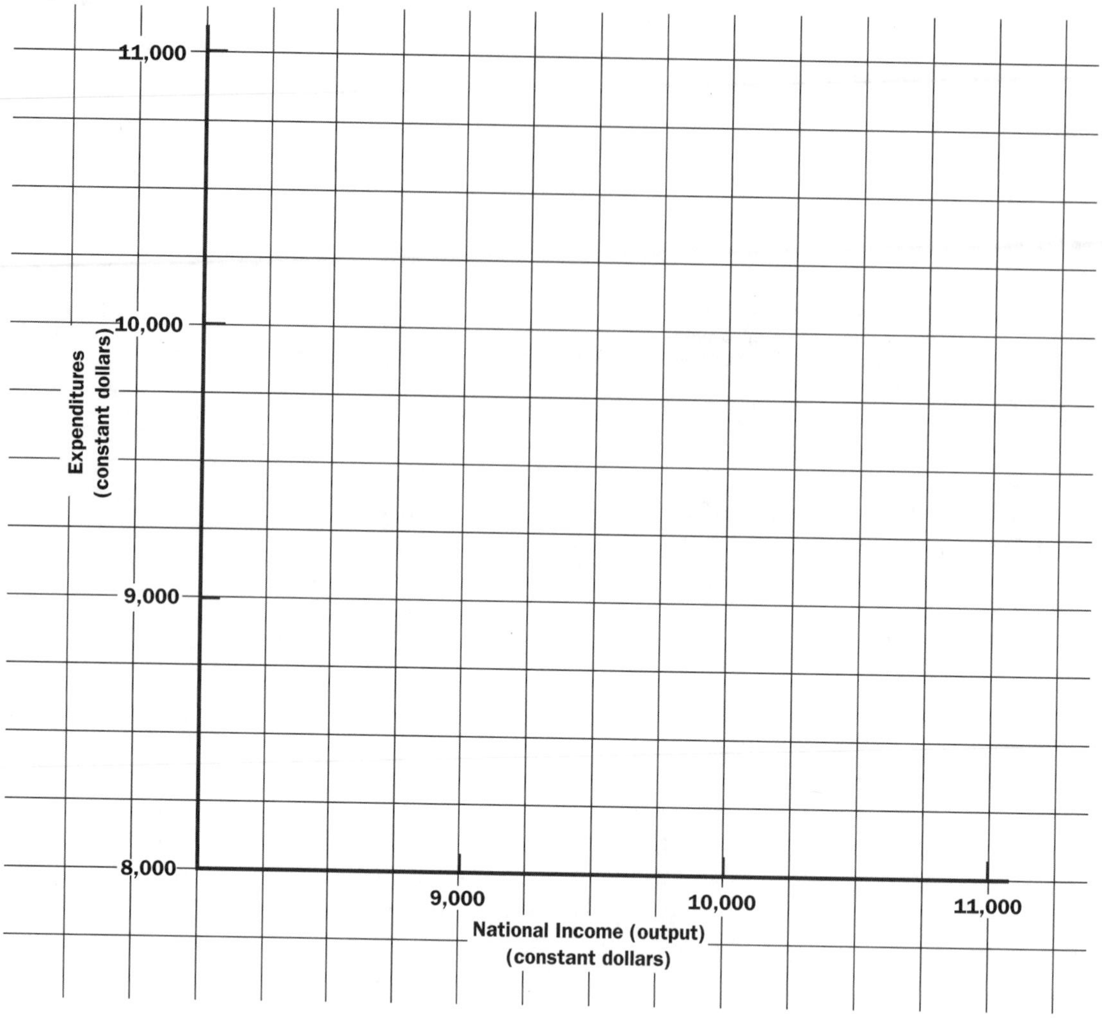

4. Use **Figure 11-1** to show the impact of variable taxes on the slope of the expenditure schedule and thus on the value of the multiplier. Start by plotting the expenditure schedule from Table 11-1. Label this expenditure schedule "Fixed Taxes." Now plot the expenditure schedule from Table 11-1. Label this expenditure schedule "Variable Taxes." Which expenditure schedule is steeper? Now assume that investment spending increases by 200. Carefully draw new expenditure schedules that are 200 higher than before. Be sure you do not change the slope of each expenditure schedule. What happens to the equilibrium level of income following the shift of the Fixed Taxes expenditure schedule? What happens to the equilibrium level of income following the shift of the Variable Taxes expenditure schedule? Explain the differences.

| Appendix B | *Algebraic Treatment of Fiscal Policy and Aggregate Demand*

● Basic Exercises

This exercise is meant to illustrate the material in the Appendix to Chapter 11. Just as in other chapters, we can use equations rather than graphs or tables to determine the equilibrium level of output and relevant multipliers. If we have done our work accurately, we should get the same answer regardless of whether we use graphs, tables, or algebra.

The following equations underlie the numerical example in the Basic Exercise.

$C = 340 + 0.8DI$

$T = -700 + 0.25Y$

$DI = Y - T$

$Y = C + I + G + (X - IM)$

1. What is the equilibrium level of income if investment spending is $1,500 billion, net exports are –$150 billion, and government purchases are $1,750 billion? Be sure that $C + I + G + (X - IM) = Y$.

2. Assume that both across-the-board taxes and government purchases decline by $50 billion so that government purchases are $1,700 billion and the tax equation is

$$T = -750 + 0.25Y.$$

   Is the equilibrium level of income unchanged following the balanced reduction in the size of the government? Why? What about the government deficit $(G - T)$?

3. Calculate the multiplier for each of the following:
   - change in investment spending
   - change in government purchases
   - change in exports
   - change in fixed taxes (that is, change in intercept of tax equation)

4. Explore the implications for fixed and variable taxes by replacing the equation for T with $T = 1,800$. Now there are only fixed taxes. First calculate the equilibrium level of income when $G = 1,750$. Then consider the simultaneous reductions in G and T described in question 2. Now consider the various multipliers in question 3. How, if at all, do answers differ when there are only fixed taxes?

● Supplementary Exercises

1. In his analysis of the impact of the 1964 tax cut, which reduced taxes on a permanent basis, Arthur Okun estimated that the MPC was 0.95.[2] At the same time, Okun estimated that the basic expenditure multiplier, applicable for any increase in autonomous spending, was only

---

[2]Arthur M. Okun, "Measuring the Impact of the 1964 Tax Cut," in W. W. Heller, ed., *Perspectives on Economic Growth* (New York: Vintage Books, 1968), pp. 25-49.

2.73, not 20, which comes from the oversimplified formula of $1/(1 - MPC)$. How can such a large MPC be consistent with such a small multiplier?

2. The 1964 reduction in personal taxes was about $10 billion. Okun estimated that this tax reduction raised GDP by $25.9 billion. The ratio of the change in GDP to the change in taxes was only 2.59, not 2.73, the value of the basic expenditure multiplier. How can you account for this discrepancy?

(*Hint:* In his analysis, Okun assumed prices did not change, so price effects on consumption expenditures are not part of the answer. You should think about whether the basic expenditure multiplier—the multiplier for a shift in the expenditure schedule—is the appropriate multiplier to apply directly to the change in taxes.)

3. What is it like to advise the president of the United States about economic policy? Martin S. Feldstein was chairman of the Council of Economic Advisers during the Reagan administration. You might enjoy reading his observations on the workings of the council and serving as chairman of the council in "The Council of Economic Advisers and Economic Advising in the United States" (*The Economic Journal*, September 1992, pp. 1223–1234).

● Economics in Action

Growth and Taxes

What is the relation between taxes and economic growth? Do high taxes impede growth and would countries be unambiguously better off if they lowered taxes?

For some, the answers to these questions are obviously yes. Reporting in *The New York Times*, Anna Bernasek suggests that the evidence for this viewpoint is cloudy at best. While taxes may affect individual behavior, Bernasek argues that "there is surprisingly little evidence that tax rates are an important factor in determining the nation's economic prosperity." She quotes economists William Easterly and Sergio Rebelo who in 1993 concluded, "the evidence that tax rates matter for growth is disturbingly fragile."

More recently economist Joel Slemrod and Jon Bakija looked at the relationship between marginal tax rates and productivity. They found that over the period 1950 to 2002, periods with the highest growth in productivity were also periods with the highest tax rates. In addition, high tax countries tend to be the most affluent.

While no economist would suggest that these findings are a license to increase taxes without limit, Bernasek suggests that the findings of Easterly, Rebelo, Slemrod, and Bakija "call into question why, if taxes are so bad for growth, their effect doesn't show up more prominently." All of this is not to suggest that some behaviors are not influenced by tax rates. For example, changes in investment tax policy appear to influence the timing of business investment in order to maximize tax advantages. However tax advantages for personal saving appears to have had little impact on aggregate household savings.

Economist Peter Lindert would not be surprised by Bernasek's report. In a recent book, *Growing Public,* he explores the links between high taxes, high levels of social spending, and economic growth. Lindert argues that some forms of social spending, e.g., spending on education, can improve economic growth and nations with high levels of taxes and spending are often careful to choose efficient tax schemes that minimize adverse impacts. In many European countries this has meant high sin taxes—taxes on smoking and drinking—and relatively lighter taxes on capital that could easily move from one country to another should tax rates get too high.

Bernasek worries that a belief in lowering tax rates to spur economic growth could result in spiraling deficits and pressures to reduce important public investments in areas like infrastructure, education, and basic research.

1. What do you think is the relationship between tax rates and growth rates? What evidence supports and contradicts your position? If a country wanted to support a high level of social spending, what forms of taxation would be the most efficient and do the least damage to growth prospects?

Sources: Anna Bernasek, "Economic View: Do Taxes Thwart Growth? Prove It?," *The New York Times*, April 3, 2005. Peter Lindert, *Growing Public*, (Cambridge University Press: 2004).

• Study Questions

1. How does the multiplier for a change in government spending compare to the multipliers in earlier chapters for changes in investment spending, net exports, and the autonomous component of consumption spending?

2. Why do income taxes reduce the value of the multiplier?

3. What is meant by the term *automatic stabilizers*? In what sense are they automatic? In what sense do they stabilize the economy?

4. If you were charged with recommending changes in government purchases, taxes, and transfers to shift the aggregate demand curve to the right, what sorts of changes in each of these elements of fiscal policy would do the job?

5. How would you choose between the alternatives you proposed when answering question 4?

6. Why is designing fiscal policy to achieve full employment subject to such intense political debate rather than being a technical exercise best left to economists?

7. "Active stabilization policy—the deliberate use of fiscal policy to avoid recessions and inflation—must inevitably lead to bigger and bigger government." Do you agree or disagree? Why?

8. What are some examples of supply-side tax cuts? Explain how and why each of your examples is expected to affect the aggregate supply curve.

9. If supply-side tax cuts could increase the equilibrium level of output without increasing prices, they would be a superior instrument for short-run stabilization policy. Are supply-side tax cuts likely to work in this way? Why or why not? If not, what are supply-side tax cuts good for?

10. What would be necessary if tax cuts were to be self-financing? How likely are these conditions to be met in practice?

Economics Online

Reports of the Congressional Budget Office analyzing the president's budget proposals, summarizing the economic and budget outlook, and reporting on special studies are published on a regular basis. They are available online at

http://www.cbo.gov

12

Money and the Banking System

Important Terms and Concepts

Run on a bank	Fiat money	Deposit insurance	Liability
Barter	M1	Moral hazard	Balance sheet
Money	M2	Federal Deposit Insurance Corporation (FDIC)	Net worth
Medium of exchange	Near moneys		Deposit creation
Unit of account	Liquidity	Required reserves	Excess reserves
Store of value	Fractional reserve banking	Asset	Money Multiplier
Commodity money			

Learning Objectives
After completing this chapter, you should be able to:

- explain the advantages of using money over barter.

- distinguish between various functions of money. Which are unique to money? Which are shared with other assets?

- list the desirable features of objects serving as money.

- distinguish between commodity money and fiat money.

- explain the differences between M1 and M2 as measures of money.

- describe the historical origins of fractional reserve banking and explain why the industry is so heavily regulated today.

- explain how the banking system as a whole can create deposits, given an initial injection of bank reserves.

- use the required reserve fraction to derive the oversimplified deposit creation multiplier.

- explain why the deposit creation multiplier, based on the required reserve fraction, is oversimplified.

Chapter Review

Whether the love of money is the root of all evil or not, there is no argument that money has an important influence on the way our economy operates. The right amount of money can help to keep employment up and prices stable. Too much money may lead to excessive inflation; too little money may lead to excessive unemployment. This chapter is an introduction to money. What is it? Where did it come from? What role do banks play in the creation of money? The next chapter discusses how the government regulates the amount of money in the economy, and the chapter after that discusses the influence of money on economic activity.

It is possible that a society could be organized without money. If everyone were self-sufficient there would, by definition, be no trading between individuals and no need for money. If people concentrated their productive activities on what they did best and traded with each other to get goods they did not produce themselves, they might be able to get along without money. Direct trading of

(1) goods for goods, or goods for services, is called _____. For it to be successful there must be a double coincidence of wants. As societies become more complicated and people become ever more specialized, it is clear that barter becomes (<u>less difficult/more difficult</u>).

When a society uses a standard object for exchanging goods and services, a seller will provide goods or services to a buyer and receive the standard object as payment. The efficiency of such a system should be obvious. You no longer have to find someone who not only has what you want but also wants what you have. Anyone who has what you want will now do. Economists would call the

(2) standard object _____. If the object serving as money has intrinsic value in nonmonetary uses, such as gold or jewelry, it is called _____ money. When objects serve as money it is useful that they be divisible, of uniform quality, durable, storable at little or no cost, and compact. Many commodity monies fail on one or more of these criteria. Today money has little intrinsic value and is called _____ money. Such money has value because everyone believes that everyone else will exchange goods and services for it. The bedrock for this foundation of faith is that the government will stand behind the money and limit its production.

When it comes to measuring the quantity of money, exactly where one draws the line is a bit unclear. We have defined money as a standard object used for exchanging goods and services. On this count, the sum of all coins and currency outside of banks plus the wide variety of checking accounts at banks and credit unions surely belongs in any measure of money. The measure that focuses on these

(3) items is known as _____. If one also includes savings accounts (because funds in savings accounts can easily be transferred into checking accounts), money market deposit accounts, and money market mutual funds, one is measuring _____.

Consider the data on elements of M1 and M2 for June 2004.

Currency (including travelers' checks)	$686.1 billion
Checkable deposits	652.7 billion
Savings deposits, including money market deposit accounts	4,190.2 billion
Money market mutual funds	754.3 billion[1]

How big is

M1? $ _____ billion

M2? $ _____ billion

(4)

Given the importance of bank deposits in all measures of money, it is important to understand how the banking system can create money. Banks subject to deposit reserve requirements must hold reserves that are at least as great as some stated percentage of their deposits. Reserves can be either cash in a bank's vaults or money that the bank has on deposit at its local Federal Reserve Bank. We will learn more about the Federal Reserve System in the next chapter. The stated percentage is the required reserve ratio. Thus, only some of the money used to open or to add to a bank deposit must be kept by the bank to meet reserve requirements. The rest can be used to make loans in the search for more profits. This system is known as fractional reserve banking.

The multiple creation of deposits is the counterpart to bank (lending/borrowing). Assume (5) that banks are subject to a 10 percent reserve requirement. Following a new deposit of $1,000, the maximum amount of the new deposit that this bank could lend out and still meet the reserve requirement is $_____. As the proceeds of the loan are deposited in other banks, new deposits will be created. For the banking system as a whole, the maximum amount of loans that can be made, and thus the maximum amount of deposits that can be created following an increase in bank reserves, is limited by the _____ _____. The precise sequence of the multiple deposit creation process is illustrated in the Basic Exercise for this chapter.

Mathematical formulas have been devised to determine the maximum increase in deposits that can be created by the banking system following an increase in bank reserves:

Maximum increase in deposits = Initial increase in bank reserves × (1/_____ _____) (6)

The deposit creation formula is oversimplified for two reasons:

A. The formula assumes that the entire proceeds of each loan will eventually be re-deposited in the banking system. If some of the proceeds of a loan do not get re-deposited, then the deposit creation multiplier will be (larger/smaller). (7)

[1]H.6 Statistical Release, Board of Governors of the Federal Reserve System, H.6 Money Stock Measures, http://www.federalreserve.gov/releases/h6/hist/. Accessed April 6, 2005.

B.   The formula also assumes that every bank makes as large a loan as possible; that is, each bank is assumed to make no changes in its holdings of _____ reserves. If banks increase their holdings of such reserves, then the money creation formula would be (<u>larger/smaller</u>).

The discussion of the deposit creation multiplier showed how deposits can be created following an increase in bank reserves. The emphasis was on how a change in reserves leads to a change in deposits. One should not be surprised to learn that *total* deposits in all banks are similarly limited by *total* reserves. The cash deposit discussed in the text results in an increase in total reserves of the banking system. However, most increases in reserves at one bank are offset by a decrease in reserves at some other bank, with no change in reserves of the banking system as a whole. Consider Derek, who takes money out of his account at Bank A. Derek uses the money to buy a home computer, and the dealer deposits this money in her bank, Bank B. While Bank B experiences an increase in reserves, Bank A shows a decrease. The process of multiple deposit creation initiated at Bank B is offset by a process of (8) multiple deposit _____ starting with Bank A. On net there is (<u>some/no</u>) increase in reserves and deposits for the banking system as a whole. The important factor for expanding deposits is new reserves available to the banking system. We will learn in the next chapter how the Federal Reserve is able to influence the volume of reserves available to the banking system.

Important Terms and Concepts Quiz

Choose the best definition for each of the following terms.

1. _____ Run on a bank
2. _____ Barter
3. _____ Unit of account
4. _____ Money
5. _____ Medium of exchange
6. _____ Store of value
7. _____ Commodity money
8. _____ Fiat money
9. _____ M1
10. _____ M2
11. _____ Near moneys
12. _____ Liquidity
13. _____ Fractional reserve banking
14. _____ Deposit insurance
15. _____ Moral hazard
16. _____ FDIC
17. _____ Required reserves
18. _____ Asset
19. _____ Liability
20. _____ Balance sheet
21. _____ Net worth
22. _____ Deposit creation
23. _____ Excess reserves
24. _____ Money multiplier

a. Reserves in excess of the legal minimum
b. Item an individual or firm owns
c. Many depositors concurrently withdrawing cash from their accounts
d. Item used to hold wealth from one point in time to another
e. Ease with which an asset can be converted into cash
f. System where bankers keep reserves equal to only a portion of total deposits
g. Standard unit for quoting prices
h. Value of all assets minus the value of all liabilities
i. Ratio of newly created deposits to new reserves
j. System of exchange where people trade one good for another without using money
k. Sum of coins, paper money, checkable deposits, money market mutual funds, and most savings account balances
l. Accounting statement listing assets on the left-hand side and liabilities and net worth on the right-hand side
m. Standard object used in exchanging goods and services
n. Object, without value as commodity that serves as money by government decree
o. Liquid assets that are close substitutes for money
p. System that guarantees depositors against loss if bank goes bankrupt
q. Process by which banking system turns one dollar of reserves into several dollars of deposits
r. Item an individual or firm owes
s. Sum of coins, paper money, and checkable deposits
t. Object used as a medium of exchange that also has substantial value in nonmonetary uses
u. Minimum amount of reserves a bank must hold
v. Government agency that insures depositors' checking and savings accounts
w. People with insurance are less vigorous in protecting against the insured risk
x. System of money based on electronic bookkeeping entries

• Basic Exercises

This exercise is designed to help you understand the multiple creation of bank deposits by working through a specific simplified example.

Table 12-1

Balance Sheet Changes

	(1) Bank A	(2) Bank A	(3) Bank B	(4) Bank B	(5) Bank C
Assets					
Reserves	$10,000	_____	_____	_____	_____
Loans	0	_____	_____	_____	_____
Liabilities					
Deposits	$10,000	_____	_____	_____	_____
Addendum					
Required reserves	_____	_____	_____	_____	_____
Excess reserves	_____	_____	_____	_____	_____

NOTE: Required reserve ratio is 10 percent.

1. Column 1 of **Table 12-1** is partly filled in for you to show the changes in the balance sheet of Bank A immediately following Janet's cash deposit of $10,000. At this point, bank deposits have increased by $ _____. Assuming the required reserve fraction is 10 percent, fill in the last two rows of column 1, showing the initial changes in required and excess reserves.

2. Assume that Bank A responds to Janet's deposit by making as large a loan as it can to Earl, given the required reserve ratio. Now fill in column 2 to represent the changes in Bank A's balance sheet after the loan has been made and Earl has taken the proceeds of the loan in cash.

3. Earl uses the money from the loan to buy a car and the car dealer deposits this cash in Bank B. Fill in column 3 to represent the changes in Bank B's balance sheet following this cash deposit. At this point, total bank deposits have increased by $_____ .

4. Assume now that Bank B also makes as large a loan as possible. Fill in column 4 to represent changes in Bank B's balance sheet after it makes the loan and this latest borrower takes the proceeds in cash.

5. Assume that the proceeds of this loan eventually get deposited in Bank C. Fill in column 5 to represent the changes in the balance sheet of Bank C following the increase in deposits. At this point total bank deposits have increased by $ _____.

6. Fill in the following sequence of increased deposits following the initial increase at Bank A, assuming that each bank makes the largest possible loan.

    Increased deposits at Bank A $10,000

    Increased deposits at Bank B _____

    Increased deposits at Bank C _____

    Increased deposits at Bank D _____

    Increased deposits at Bank E _____

    If you have not made any mistakes, you will notice that each increase in deposit is less than the previous increase and can be expressed as $(1.0 - 0.1) \times$ (the previous increase in deposits) or $(1.0 -$ reserve requirement ratio) $\times$ (the previous increase in deposits).

    Mathematically this is an infinite geometric progression with decreasing increments. If we carried the sum out far enough it would approach a limit given by $10,000 ÷ _____, or $_____. (You might try testing this result by using a computer to calculate the sum for a very large number of terms.) This specific numerical example illustrates the more general principle that the multiplier for the maximum increase in deposits following an increase in bank reserves is $1 ÷$ _____ _____ _____.

• Self-Tests for Understanding

Test A

Circle the most appropriate answer.

1. Money serves all but which one of the following functions?
    a. medium of exchange
    b. hedge against inflation
    c. unit of account
    d. store of value

2. Which of the following is not an example of commodity money?
    a. gold coins
    b. cigarettes
    c. a $10 bill
    d. diamonds

3. Where was paper money first used?
   a. China
   b. Egypt
   c. India
   d. Italy

4. Which of the following does not belong in M1?
   a. the coins in your pocket
   b. Jodi's checking account
   c. the cash in the vault at the bank downtown
   d. the travelers' check that Heather has left over from last summer

5. The difference between M2 and M1 includes which of the following?
   (There may be more than one correct answer.)
   a. checking accounts
   b. money market mutual fund balances
   c. marketable U.S. government debt
   d. savings deposits

6. Liquidity is defined as the
   a. viscosity of financial assets.
   b. ease with which assets can be converted to money.
   c. net worth of a financial institution.
   d. ratio of liabilities to assets.

7. Which of Randy's assets is the most liquid?
   a. the U.S. savings bond his grandparents gave him
   b. his collection of 1950s baseball cards
   c. the $20 bill in his wallet
   d. the 100 shares of Microsoft stock he bought last summer

8. A bank's (or your) net worth is found by
   a. summing up all assets.
   b. adding total assets to total liabilities.
   c. dividing total assets by total liabilities.
   d. subtracting total liabilities from total assets.

9. Which of the following is not an asset for a bank?
   a. excess reserves
   b. holdings of U.S. government securities
   c. checking account balances held by depositors
   d. mortgage loans made by the bank

10. The key item that makes a bank's balance sheet balance is its
    a. holdings of excess reserves.
    b. assets.
    c. required reserves.
    d. net worth.

11. If a bank holds more reserves than required, the difference is
    a. the bank's net worth.
    b. liquidity.
    c. solvency.
    d. excess reserves.

12. Banks could increase profits by
    a. holding more commodity money and less fiat money.
    b. holding fewer excess reserves in order to make more loans.
    c. reducing their liabilities.
    d. substituting M2 for M1.

13. If Damien deposits cash that he used to keep under his mattress into his checking account, the initial deposit will result in
    a. an increase in M1.
    b. a decrease in M2.
    c. an increase in the net worth of the banking system.
    d. no change in M1 or M2.

14. The most important government regulation of banks in terms of limiting the multiple creation of deposits is
    a. bank examinations and audits.
    b. limits on the kinds of assets that banks can buy.
    c. the required reserve ratio.
    d. requirements to disclose the volume of loans to bank officials.

15. If the minimum reserve requirement ratio for all bank deposits is 5 percent, then the maximum multiple creation of deposits by the banking system as a whole following a cash deposit of $2,000 would be
    a. $100 = (0.05) \times ($2,000)$.
    b. $2,100 = (1 + 0.05) \times ($2,000)$.
    c. $2,105 = ($2,000)/(1 - 0.05)$.
    d. $40,000 = ($2,000)/(0.05)$.

16. If the reserve requirement ratio is 10 percent instead of 5 percent, then the maximum multiple creation of deposits would be
    a. smaller than in question 15.
    b. larger than in question 15.
    c. the same as in question 15.

17. If banks hold some of every increase in deposits in the form of excess reserves, then the amount of deposits actually created following a cash deposit would be
    a. less than that indicated in question 15.
    b. the same as that indicated in question 15.
    c. more than that indicated in question 15.

18. If the required reserve ratio is 20 percent and Rachel deposits $100 in cash in the First National Bank, the maximum increase in deposits by the banking system as a whole is
    a. 0.
    b. $20.
    c. $100.
    d. $500.

19. If the required reserve ratio is 20 percent and Sharon deposits $100 in the First National Bank by depositing a check from her mother written on the Second National Bank, the maximum increase in deposits by the banking system as a whole is
    a. 0.
    b. $20.
    c. $100.
    d. $500.

20. If a bank's total reserve holdings are $35 million and it has $12 million of excess reserves, then its required reserves are
    a. $12 million.
    b. $23 million.
    c. $35 million.
    d. $47 million.

Test B

Circle T or F for true or false.

T F 1. A major advantage of the use of money rather than barter is that money avoids the problems of finding a "double coincidence of wants."

T F 2. Fiat money in the United States may be redeemed for gold from the U.S. Treasury.

T F 3. Many assets serve as a store of value but only money is also a medium of exchange.

T F 4. In periods with high rates of inflation, money is a good store of value.

T F 5. Banks could increase their profitability by holding higher levels of excess reserves.

T F 6. The existence of deposit insurance is an important reason for the dramatic decline in the number of bank failures in the United States since the 1930s.

T F 7. The term moral hazard refers to situations where insurance causes people to be less vigilant in guarding against possible losses.

T F 8. Multiple deposit creation applies to increases in the money supply but reductions in the money supply can come about only through government taxation.

T F 9. Required reserves are part of a bank's liabilities, whereas excess reserves are part of a bank's assets.

T F 10. If a bank's liabilities exceed its assets, the bank is said to have negative net worth.

Supplementary Exercises

1. If the required reserve ratio is 20 percent and banks want to hold 10 percent of any increase in deposits in the form of excess reserves and people want to hold $1 more in currency for every $10 increase in deposits, what is the eventual increase in deposits following a $1,000 cash deposit in the First National Bank? What is the eventual increase in the money supply?

2. If M is the required reserve fraction, E is the ratio of excess reserves to deposits, and C is the ratio of currency to deposits, what is the formula that relates the change in deposits to a change in reserves?

Economics in Action

The Reform of Deposit Insurance

As described in the text, the establishment of federal deposit insurance had a dramatic effect on the number of bank failures. Some critics argue that experience during the 1980s suggests that we may have had too much of a good thing. Economist Edward J. Kane has been especially critical of the actions of federal government officials, both elected and appointed, concerning deposit insurance. He was one of the first to describe the collapse of the Federal Savings and Loan Insurance Corporation (FSLIC), the deposit insurance agency for S&Ls, as resulting from a combination moral hazard and principal-agent problem.[2]

Moral hazard arose because deposit insurance provided an incentive for some S&Ls to engage in risky behavior. The period of high interest rates in the late 1970s and early 1980s had left these institutions with little or negative net worth. Owners of these institutions saw high-risk but potentially high-return loans as their only salvation. Insurance protected their depositors. Negative net worth meant that their own investment in the S&L had already been wiped out. They literally had nothing to lose by engaging in risky behavior.

Kane also charges that Congress and bank regulators (the agents) failed to act in the best interest of U.S. taxpayers (the principals). Kane charges that at critical points, and with the support and encouragement of key members of Congress, the FSLIC allowed bankrupt institutions to continue in business. Succumbing to lobbying pressures to focus on the original book value of assets rather than current market value allowed officials to pretend that bankrupt institutions were still solvent. The result was that problems were deferred as the cost of appropriate action increased. Opposition to increased federal spending and the impact on the deficit that would accompany the official closing of failed institutions further contributed to delay.

What is an appropriate stance for deposit insurance? There have been a large number of proposals. They include the mandatory use of market prices to value assets; mandatory and higher net worth requirements for financial institutions; automatic rules for closing insolvent institutions that remove the element of discretion on the part of regulators; deposit insurance premiums that vary with the riskiness of a bank's portfolio; and public notice of the results of bank examinations.

---

[2]*Moral hazard* refers to the tendency of insurance to make people less concerned with the risks associated with their behavior—after all, it's covered by insurance. Principal-agent relationships occur whenever one party, the principal, has to hire others, the agents, to act on the principal's behalf. An example would be stockholders who hire executives to manage corporations. It is often difficult for the principals (stockholders) to monitor the behavior of their agents (executives) to ensure that the agents act to promote the principals' interests and not their (the agents') own.

A number of observers have also argued that the present deposit insurance limit is so high that depositors have little incentive to concern themselves with the riskiness of a bank's portfolio. If a smaller amount, perhaps the first $25,000 or $50,000 of deposits, were insured and it was clear that deposits above this level had no insurance protection, depositors with large balances, especially businesses, would have a real incentive to pay attention to the riskiness of their bank's assets. According to this view, a bank that was imprudent would (and should) suffer a run on its deposits with little reason to expect that the run would spill over and harm sound banks.

1. What changes, if any, do you think there should be to the system of deposit insurance? Why? How far should the government go to protect depositors? How does one design a system of deposit insurance that addresses the problem of moral hazard?

You might want to consult the following:

Edward J. Kane, *The S&L Insurance Mess: How Did It Happen,* (Washington, D.C.: The Urban Institute Press, 1991).

Lawrence J. White, *The S&L Debacle,* (New York: Oxford University Press, 1991).

Gary H. Stern and Ron Feldman, "Too Big to Fail: The Hazards of Bank Bailouts," *The Region,* (Federal Reserve Bank of Minneapolis, December 2003). Available online at http://woodrow.mpls.frb.fed.us/pubs/region/03-12/tbtf.cfm. This article is one of a number of papers on deposit insurance reform at http://woodrow.mpls.frb.fed.us/research/studies/tbtf/.

● Study Questions

1. What functions does money share with other assets, and what functions are unique to money?

2. How does fiat money differ from commodity money? In particular, how do they compare with regard to the list of desirable characteristics discussed in the text?

3. Where would you draw the line if asked to come up with a measure of money for the American economy?

4. Rank the following in terms of their liquidity and justify your ranking: a 12-month savings certificate, the balance in your checking account, a corporate bond issued by Intel, some leftover travelers' checks from your most recent trip, a share of stock in DuPont, a $20 bill, and a piece of lakeside vacation property.

5. What is full-bodied money? Is money in the United States today full-bodied? If not, where does its value come from?

6. If the government is going to insure deposits, it seems natural that it be allowed to examine a bank's books and put limits on some types of loans to control its risk. Alternatively, the need for deposit insurance could be eliminated if reserve requirements were set at 100 percent. What do you think would happen to bank service charges if reserve requirements were 100 percent? What other changes might you expect? In particular think about the incentive to create alternatives to bank deposits.

7. How can you tell when something is an asset or a liability?

8. As every banker wants her assets to exceed her liabilities, in what sense does a bank's balance sheet balance?

9. As the government controls the printing press, how can banks create money?

10. In what ways is the deposit creation multiplier, $1/m$, oversimplified? Does adjusting for these complications make the deposit creation multiplier larger or smaller?

Economics Online

The latest information on the size of M1 and M2 can be found at

http://www/federalreserve.gov/releases/H6

The Federal Reserve Bank of San Francisco hosts an online museum of American currency, the American Currency exhibit, at

http://www.frbsf.org/currency/

Banknotes.com's World Currency Gallery displays pictures of money from around the world.

http://www.banknotes.com/images.htm

Managing Aggregate Demand: Monetary Policy

13

Important Terms and Concepts

Monetary policy

Central bank

Federal Reserve System

Federal Open Market Committee
(FOMC)

Central bank independence

Open market operations

Equilibrium in the market for
bank reserves

Federal funds rate

Bond prices and interest rates

Federal Reserve lending to banks

Discount rate

Reserve requirements

Why the aggregate demand
curve slopes down

Learning Objectives
After completing this chapter, you should be able to:

- distinguish between the concepts "money" and "income."

- explain why older arguments about whether a country's central bank should be independent have been replaced by arguments about how central banks should be accountable to the public.

- draw and explain the logic behind both the supply-of-bank-reserves and the demand-for-bank-reserves schedules.

- analyze the impact of open market operations using the demand-for- and supply-of-bank reserves.

- explain how bond prices and interest rates are related.

- describe the impact of open market operations on bond prices and interest rates.

- explain why the Fed's control of the size of bank deposits is not exact.

- use the expenditure schedule along with the aggregate demand and supply curves to describe how changes in monetary policy affect the economy's macroeconomic equilibrium.

- explain how the impact of higher prices on the demand for bank reserves helps to explain why the aggregate demand curve has a negative slope.

• Chapter Review

In the preceding chapter we learned how deposits are created by the actions of banks. In this chapter we will see how actions taken by the Federal Reserve System can influence interest rates and the economy's overall macroeconomic equilibrium. The emphasis in this chapter is on building models. In subsequent chapters we will use these models to understand policy issues.

(1)   The Federal Reserve System was established in 1914 and is the nation's _____ bank. There are _____ district banks throughout the country, with headquarters in Washington, D.C. The people in charge in Washington are the seven members of the _____ of _____ of the Federal Reserve System. Major decisions about open market operations are made by the FOMC, or the _____ _____ _____ Committee. Decisions about government spending and taxes are the nation's (fiscal/monetary) policy. Policy actions by the Federal Reserve constitute the nation's _____ policy. Older arguments about how much independence a country's central bank should enjoy have been replaced by arguments about how to hold independent central banks accountable to the public.

We saw in the preceding chapter that the multiple creation of bank deposits is limited by the required reserve ratio and by the volume of bank reserves. Reserve requirements help to determine the deposit creation multiplier. The Fed's other two major policy instruments—open market operations and lending to banks—directly affect total bank reserves. We have seen that controlling reserve requirements and the volume of bank reserves do not allow for the precise   control of the

(2) bank deposits (or the stock of money) because of possible changes in (excess/required) reserve holdings by banks and in currency holdings by the public. In contrast, the Fed has greater ability to hit specific interest rate targets through the use of open market operations.

A reduction in reserve requirements does not change total bank reserves, but it will initially

(3) result in a(n) (increase/decrease) in noninterest-earning excess reserves. Multiple deposit creation will take place as banks try to put these nonearning excess reserves to work. Banks can add to their reserve holdings by borrowing directly from the Fed. The Fed influences the volume of borrowing by changing the interest rate it charges banks. In the United States, the interest rate for these borrowings is called the _____ _____.

(4)   Open market operations—the purchase and sale of government _____ —represent the most important and most commonly used instrument of monetary policy. Open market operations affect bank behavior by adding to or subtracting from the amount of bank reserves. The essence of an open market purchase is that the Fed creates bank reserves when it (buys/sells) a government security. The result is a(n) (increase/decrease) in noninterest-earning excess reserves, and the usual multiple deposit creation process is set in motion. An open market sale has exactly opposite effects. Payment

to the Fed for government securities means a(n) (<u>reduction/increase</u>) in bank reserves and initiates a process of multiple deposit (<u>creation/destruction</u>).

The impact of open market operations on interest rates can be analyzed by considering the demand and supply for bank reserves. Open market operations are the major determinant of the supply of reserves while the need for banks to hold reserves at least as great as that demanded by the Fed's minimum reserve requirement is the major determinant of the demand for bank reserves. In addition, there is an active inter-bank market for reserves, the market for federal funds, where banks with excess reserves can lend reserves to banks that need to borrow to meet their reserve requirement. The price associated with these transactions is the interest rate borrowing banks pay for the use of excess reserves from other banks. This interest rate is called the _____ _____   (5) rate. An open market purchase will shift the supply curve of bank reserves to the (<u>left/right</u>) and (<u>increase/lower</u>) the federal funds rate. An open market sale will have exactly opposite effects. Changes in the federal funds rate from either type of open market operation will then influence other interest rates.

What exactly is entailed in an open market purchase? It is easiest to consider a case where the Fed buys Treasury bills from a bank. When it does this, the Fed pays for the Treasury bill by crediting the bank with additional reserves. Initially our selling bank will have more reserves without an increase in deposits or required reserves, will likely to step up its own loan operations, and will be more likely to lend reserves to other banks in the market for federal funds.

When the Fed buys Treasury bills, this action will typically increase the price of Treasury bills. Simple mathematics shows that an increase in the price of Treasury bills will be associated with a(n) (<u>decrease/increase</u>) in interest rates. When the price of a security paying a fixed number of   (6) dollars per year in interest increases, the rate of return on that security, as measured by the ratio of the interest payments to the price of the security, must decline.

The mathematics of the relationship between bond prices and interest rates is explored in more detail in the Supplementary Exercises to this chapter.

With an understanding of how open market operations can affect the federal funds rates, we are in a position to see how changes in monetary policy affect aggregate demand. Policy shifts in the (<u>supply/demand</u>)-of-reserves schedule will change interest rates as we move along the   (7) _____-for-reserves schedule. The change in interest rates will affect interest-sensitive categories of demand, especially investment spending. Changes in investment spending lead to a (<u>shift in/movement along</u>) the expenditure schedule. The (<u>shift in/movement along</u>) the expenditure schedule will shift the aggregate (<u>demand/supply</u>) curve through the multiplier process. Overall macroeconomic equilibrium is reestablished at the new intersection of the aggregate demand curve and the aggregate supply curve. The division of effects, as between real output and prices, is determined by the slope of the aggregate _____ curve. This sequence of events is diagrammed at the end of this chapter in the text.[1]

The same reasoning helps us to understand two other important points:

Why the aggregate demand curve has a negative slope and why the multiplier formula $1/(1 - MPC)$ is oversimplified:

Higher prices not only reduce the purchasing power of money fixed assets and affect the international price competitiveness of American goods, but they also increase the demand for bank deposits. Unless the Fed is conducting monetary policy to fix the interest rate on federal funds, which it can do by shifting the supply schedule whenever the demand schedule shifts, the increase in the demand for bank deposits that derives from the higher price level will shift the demand-for-bank reserves schedule to the right, leading to an increase in interest rates and lower investment spending. Thus higher prices can affect aggregate demand through their impact on interest rates and investment as well as their impact on consumption and net exports.

The reduction in investment spending induced by the rise in interest rates is an additional important reason why the multiplier process of the income-expenditure diagram is oversimplified.

Expansionary monetary policy that lowers interest rates and increases investment spending will eventually affect the aggregate supply curve as investment projects are completed and add to the capital stock. We concentrate here on impacts on the aggregate demand curve as they are the most immediate.

---

[1]Expansionary monetary policy that lowers interest rates and increases investment spending will eventually affect the aggregate supply curve as investment projects are completed and added to the capital stock. We concentrate here on impacts on the aggregate demand curve as they are the most immediate.

Important Terms and Concepts Quiz

Choose the best definition for each of the following terms.

1. _____ Monetary policy
2. _____ Central bank
3. _____ Federal Reserve System
4. _____ Federal Open Market Committee
5. _____ Open market operations
6. _____ Equilibrium in the market for bank reserves
7. _____ Federal funds rate
8. _____ Discount rate
9. _____ Reserve requirement

a. Interest rate banks pay (get) when they borrow (lend) reserves from each other
b. A bank for banks responsible for the conduct of monetary policy
c. Branch of the U.S. Treasury responsible for minting coins
d. Quantity of bank reserves and federal funds rate where demand equals supply for bank reserves
e. Minimum amount of reserves a bank must hold
f. Chief policymaking committee of the Federal Reserve System responsible for open market operations
g. Actions Fed takes to affect bank reserves, interest rates, or both
h. Central bank of the United States
i. Interest rate Fed charges on loans to banks
j. Fed's purchase or sale of government securities

• Basic Exercises

Open Market Operations

1. This exercise is designed to review the mechanics and impact of open market operations.

   a. Use **Figure 13-1** to analyze the impact of an open market purchase. The purchase of a government security by the Fed results in a(n) (increase/decrease) in total bank reserves. This change in bank reserves can be represented as a shift of the supply-of-reserves schedule to the _____. (Draw a new supply-of-reserves schedule that represents the result of the open market purchase.) As a result of the open market purchase, interest rates will _____.

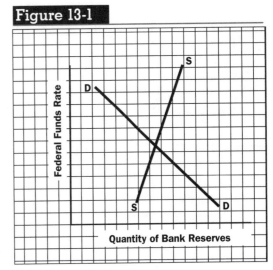

Figure 13-1

b. Use **Figure 13-2** to analyze the impact of an open market sale. The sale of a government security by the Fed results in a(n) (<u>increase/decrease</u>) in total bank reserves. This change in bank reserves can be represented as a shift of the supply-of-reserves schedule to the _____. (Draw a new supply-of-reserves schedule that represents the result of the open market sale. As a result of the open market purchase, interest rates will _____.

Figure 13-2

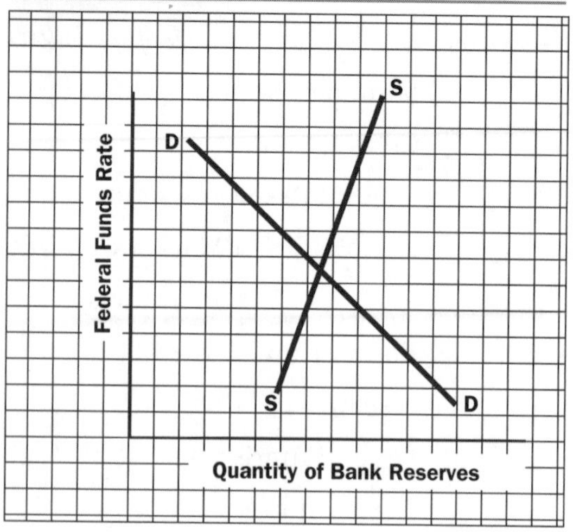

• Self-Tests for Understanding

Test A

Circle the most appropriate answer.

1. If Mary says she earns $78,000 a year, she is referring to her
   a. money.
   b. income.
   c. assets.
   d. wealth.

2. The Federal Reserve is responsible for the conduct of
   a. environmental policy.
   b. fiscal policy.
   c. international economic policy.
   d. monetary policy.

3. The Federal Reserve is a bank for
   a. the Treasury.
   b. households.
   c. businesses.
   d. banks.

4. Which of the following is *not* an instrument of monetary policy?
   a. Open market operations
   b. Lending to banks
   c. Antitrust actions to promote competition in banking
   d. Required reserve ratios

5. Who has direct responsibility for open market operations?
   a. The Board of Governors
   b. The Federal Open Market Committee
   c. The President of the United States
   d. The Banking Committee of the U.S. Senate

6. Open market operations involve the Fed buying and selling
   a. stocks in American companies.
   b. U.S. government securities.
   c. gold.
   d. corporate bonds.

7. Open market operations give the Fed the strongest control over
   a. interest rates on corporate bonds.
   b. the interest rate on 10-year government securities.
   c. the federal funds rate.
   d. mortgage interest rates.

8. An open market sale will shift the supply of bank reserves to
   a. the right.
   b. the left.

9. When making an open market purchase, the Fed gets the money to make the purchase from
   a. the Treasury.
   b. the Bureau of Printing and Engraving.
   c. cash in its vault.
   d. making a computer entry on its own books to credit the reserve account of the bank from which it purchases the security.

10. The impact of an open market purchase on the expenditure schedule reflects its initial impact on
    a. disposable income and consumption.
    b. taxes and government spending.
    c. interest rates and investment spending.
    d. sales and corporate profits.

11. An open market purchase will lead to all but which one of the following?
    a. Supply-of-bank reserves schedule shifts to the right.
    b. Expenditure schedule shifts up.
    c. Multiplier increases.
    d. Aggregate demand curve shifts to the right.

12. An open market sale will result in all but which one of the following?
    a. decrease in the quantity of bank reserves
    b. increase in interest rates
    c. lower investment spending
    d. higher price level

13. The immediate impact of a change in reserve requirements would be on the
    a. total volume of bank reserves.
    b. division of reserves (as between required reserves and excess reserves).
    c. account balances for the U.S. Treasury.
    d. discount rate.

14. The discount rate is the interest rate
    a. used by department stores when holding sales.
    b. the Fed charges banks that borrow reserves.
    c. banks use for their best customers.
    d. earned on checking accounts by depositors with large balances.

15. Which is the most frequently used instrument of monetary policy?
    a. changes in the discount rate
    b. open market operations
    c. changes in reserve requirements
    d. stricter bank examinations

16. Which of the following help to explain why the Fed does not have precise control of the money supply? (There may be more than one correct answer.)
    a. Banks may vary the amount of excess reserves they desire to hold.
    b. Open market operations can change the volume of bank reserves.
    c. Individuals and businesses change the amount of currency as opposed to bank deposits they want to hold.
    d. Changes in reserve requirements will affect the deposit creation multiplier.

17. The Fed is likely to have most success in hitting its target for the
    a. federal funds rate.
    b. quantity of bank deposits.
    c. level of GDP.
    d. rate of inflation.

18. An increase in interest rates from 8 percent to 9 percent would be associated with _____ in the price of existing bonds.
    a. a decline
    b. no change
    c. an increase

19. Changes in interest rates resulting from changes in monetary policy are likely to affect investment spending and initially lead to a shift in the _____. (There may be more than one correct answer.)
    a. expenditure schedule
    b. aggregate supply curve
    c. consumption function
    d. aggregate demand curve

20. Knowing that an increase in the level of prices will increase the demand for bank reserves helps to explain why
    a. the aggregate supply curve has a positive slope.
    b. the aggregate demand curve has a negative slope.
    c. equilibrium occurs at the intersection of the aggregate demand and aggregate supply curves.
    d. the multiplier response to a change in autonomous spending may be greater than 1.0.

Test B

Circle T or F for true or false.

T F 1. In recent years there has been a movement toward more independent central banks in a number of countries.

T F 2. Most power in the Federal Reserve System is held by the 12 district Federal Reserve banks.

T F 3. Monetary policy decisions by the Federal Reserve are subject to review by the president of the United States before being implemented.

T F 4. An open market purchase by the Fed lowers the rate on federal funds without changing the quantity of bank reserves.

T F 5. An open market sale that increases interest rates will increase bond prices.

T F 6. Changing the discount rate is the most frequently used instrument of monetary policy today.

T F 7. Since bank reserves do not earn interest, the demand for reserves is not affected by changes in interest rates.

T F 8. Higher interest rates would normally lead banks to reduce their holdings of excess reserves.

T F 9. The initial impact of changes in monetary policy on interest-sensitive categories of demand affects GDP and prices as the economy moves along a given aggregate supply curve.

T F 10. The impact of the price level on the demand for bank reserves, and hence interest rates, helps to explain why the aggregate demand curve has a negative slope.

• Supplementary Exercises

1. **An Algebraic Model of the Economy**

The following algebraic model builds on models from earlier chapters but this time includes explicit expressions for the demand for and supply of bank reserves. For simplicity the model assumes that the price level does not change. That is, it is equivalent to assuming that the aggregate supply curve is horizontal.

Consider an economy where consumption and investment spending are given by

$$C = 1{,}550 + 0.6DI$$

$$I = 2{,}000 - 50R$$

where R is the interest rate. In this economy, taxes are one-sixth of income and net exports are −150.

a. If government purchases are 1,500 and R is 8 (that is, 8 percent), what is the equilibrium level of income?

b. If the Fed lowers the interest rate to 4 percent, what happens to the equilibrium level of income?

c. The Fed can lower the interest rate by an appropriate increase in bank reserves; that is, an appropriate shift in the supply schedule for bank reserves. But what is appropriate? Assume the demand for bank reserves can be represented by

$$BRD = 0.02Y - 3R$$

where the term in Y reflects the impact of nominal GDP on the bank deposits and hence the required reserves of banks.

Let the supply of bank reserves be represented by

$$BRS = OMO + 2R$$

where OMO is the amount of bank reserves supplied by open market operations. If $OMO = 140$, what is the equilibrium level of income? Of R?

d. What increase in OMO is necessary to reduce the interest rate to 4 and produce the increase in Y you found in question 2?

2. **Bond Prices and Interest Rates**

   a. Consider a bond that pays $60 a year forever. If interest rates are 6 percent, such a bond should sell for $1,000 as ($60 ÷ $1,000) = .06. Assume now that interest rates fall to 4 percent. With interest payments of $60, what bond price offers investors a return of 4 percent? If interest rates rise to 10 percent, what must be the price of the bond paying $60 to offer investors a return of 10 percent?

   b. Bonds that pay only interest and never repay principal are called consols. Most bonds pay interest for a certain number of years and then repay the original borrowing or principal. Bond prices reflect the present value of those interest and principal payments as follows:

      where INT = interest payments

         r = interest rate

         PRIN = principal

         N = maturity, number of years of interest payments (also number of years to principal payment)

      Use a computer or financial calculator to verify that if INT = $60, PRIN = $1,000, $N = 10$, and $r = .06$, the present value of interest and principal payments = $1,000.

      Calculate the present value of interest and principal payments when $r = .04$ and when $r = .10$ while INT, PRIN, and N remain unchanged. These calculations show what would happen to the price of an existing bond if interest rates change. Do your results confirm the negative correlation between bond prices and interest rates discussed in the text?

   c. Redo the calculations in question b but for values of $N = 5$ and $N = 30$. Is the sensitivity of bond prices to a change in interest rates the same for all maturities?

3. **Federal Open Market Committee**

   The Federal Open Market Committee (FOMC) has 12 voting members: the seven members of the Board of Governors and five of the 12 district bank presidents. The president of the Federal Reserve Bank of New York is always a voting member of the FOMC. The remaining four votes rotate among the other 11 presidents. Presidents of nine banks share three votes. That is, each of these presidents is a voting member of the FOMC once every three years. Two bank presidents are voting members every other year. What banks do these two presidents represent?

Economics in Action

Structure and Accountability of the Federal Reserve

In October 1993, Congressman Henry Gonzales (D-Texas), Chairman of the House Banking Committee, convened a series of committee hearings to consider issues related to the structure and accountability of the Federal Reserve. Appointment procedures for presidents of the 12 district Federal Reserve Banks and the secrecy surrounding meetings of the Federal Open Market Committee (FOMC) were among the items of special concern to Congressman Gonzales.

With regard to the meetings of the FOMC, Congressman Gonzales proposed that decisions be disclosed within a week and that detailed transcripts and videotapes of each meeting be released within 60 days. He argued that his proposals would promote individual accountability and that "accurate information does not undermine markets. Partial information and leaked information undermine market efficiency."[2]

The FOMC now issues a press release announcing its decisions the same day that it meets. However, Alan Greenspan, chairman of the Board of Governors, and the other Federal Reserve representatives who appeared before the committee argued that videotaping would hinder free debate as individuals, concerned that their remarks might be misinterpreted and "cause unnecessary volatility in financial markets," would self-censor what they said. "Unconventional policy prescriptions and ruminations about the longer-term outlook for economic and financial market developments might never be surfaced . . . for fear of igniting a speculative reaction when the discussion was disclosed."[3]

The president of each district bank is appointed by the district bank's Board of Directors, subject to the approval of the Board of Governors in Washington, D.C. District bank presidents serve as voting members of the FOMC on a rotating basis. Critics of the Federal Reserve argue that, in view of their membership on the FOMC and the importance of monetary policy, district bank presidents should be selected or reviewed by elected officials rather than appointed bodies. Options might include appointment by the president and/or confirmation by the Senate. Again Chairman Greenspan spoke against these changes, arguing that the current system represents a deliberate choice by the Congress to isolate decisions about monetary policy from political pressures. He argued that the Federal Reserve is accountable to the Congress and the public through reporting requirements and the daily scrutiny of the business and financial press. However, he warned that "if accountability is achieved by putting the conduct of monetary policy under the close influence of politicians subject to short-term election-cycle pressures, the resulting policy would likely prove disappointing over time.. . . The public-private and regional makeup of the Federal Reserve was chosen by Congress, in preference to a unitary public central bank, only after long and careful debate. The system was designed to avoid an excessive concentration of authority in federal hands and to ensure responsiveness to local needs."[4]

1. When and in how much detail should decisions and minutes of the FOMC be released?

2. Is Greenspan right when he argues that the advance announcement of contingent plans limits their effectiveness?

3. Who should select district bank presidents? Should voting membership on the FOMC be restricted to members of the Board of Governors and exclude district bank presidents?

---

[2] "Greenspan Warns Against Easing Fed's Secrecy," *New York Times*, October 20, 1992.
[3] Testimony by Alan Greenspan, Chairman, Board of Governors of the Federal Reserve System, before the Committee on Banking, Finance, and Urban Affairs, U.S. House of Representatives, October 13, 1993.
[4] Ibid.

Study Questions

1. What is the difference between money and income?

2. How much independence do you think is desirable for the Fed? Why? How does one ensure accountability?

3. Use a demand and supply diagram to show how open market operations affect the quantity of bank reserves and interest rates.

4. Open market operations are the most used instrument of monetary policy. Reserve requirements are changed only infrequently and the changes in the discount rate tend to be passive rather than active. What do you think explains the heavy reliance on open market operations rather than other instruments of monetary policy?

5. Why do interest rates and bond prices move inversely to each other?

6. Why can't the Fed control the stock of money to the penny?

7. What are the links by which changes in monetary policy affect spending and thus output, employment, and prices? Use an expenditure diagram and an aggregate demand–aggregate supply diagram to illustrate your answer.

8. "Recognizing that an increase in prices increases the demand for bank reserves helps to explain why the aggregate demand curve has a negative slope." What is the logic behind this statement?

Economics Online

All 12 district Federal Reserve banks and the Board of Governors are online with their own Web pages. You can access a wide variety of reports and lots of data about the economy from these sites.

Atlanta	http://www.frbatlanta.org
Boston	http://www.bos.frb.org
Chicago	http://www.chicagofed.org
Cleveland	http://www.clevelandfed.org/
Dallas	http://www.dallasfed.org
Kansas City	http://www.kc.frb.org
Minneapolis	http://minneapolisfed.org
New York	http://www.ny.frb.org
Philadelphia	http://www.phil.frb.org
Richmond	http://www.rich.frb.org
St. Louis	http://www.stls.frb.org
San Francisco	http://www.frbsf.org
Board of Governors	http://www.federalreserve.gov

The Federal Open Market Committee has its own homepage with links to meeting dates, announcements, and minutes.

http://www.federalreserve.gov/fomc

Laurence Meyer, a former member of the Board of Governors, describes a typical meeting of the Federal Open Market Committee in this speech given as the Gillian Lecture at Willamette University in 1998.

http://www.federalreserve.gov/boarddocs/speeches/1998/199804022.htm

The Federal Reserve Bank of San Francisco maintains an online search engine for Federal Reserve publications from all banks, Fed in Print.

http://www.frbsf.org/publications/fedinprint/index.html

You can access lots of economic data at FRED, an online databank maintained by the Federal Reserve Bank of St. Louis:

http://research.stlouisfed.org/fred2/

The Debate over Monetary and Fiscal Policy

14

Important Terms and Concepts

Velocity

Equation of exchange

Quantity theory of money

Effect of interest rate on velocity

Monetarism

Effect of fiscal policy on interest rates

Lags in stabilization policy

Controlling M versus controlling r

Rules versus discretionary policy

Learning Objectives

After completing this chapter, you should be able to:

- compute velocity given data on nominal income and the stock of money.

- describe the determinants of velocity.

- explain the difference between the quantity theory and the equation of exchange.

- describe why the equation of exchange is not a theory of income determination and why monetarists' use of the same equation turns it into a theory of income determination.

- distinguish between lags affecting fiscal policy and those affecting monetary policy.

- explain why the Fed does not have precise control over both M and r.

- explain how and why the slope of the aggregate supply curve helps to determine the effectiveness of stabilization policy.

- explain how long lags might mean that efforts to stabilize the economy could end up destabilizing it.

- summarize the views of advocates and opponents of activist stabilization policy by the government.

• Chapter Review

This is one of the most important and most difficult of the macroeconomic chapters. While not much new material is introduced, the chapter summarizes and synthesizes many of the concepts presented in preceding chapters concerning the theory of income determination as it discusses a number of thorny issues that policymakers must confront.

Earlier chapters presented an essentially Keynesian model of income determination with its focus on the categories of aggregate demand. The monetarist viewpoint is a modern manifestation of an even older tradition known as the quantity theory of money. The concept of velocity is perhaps the most important tool associated with this approach. Velocity is the average number of times per year that a dollar changes hands to accomplish transactions associated with GDP. Velocity is measured

(1) as nominal _____ divided by the stock of _____. Alternative measures of money, for example, M_1 and M_2, give rise to alternative measures of velocity, V_1 and V_2.

Related to the concept of velocity is something called the equation of exchange, which is simply another way of defining and calculating velocity. The equation of exchange says:

(2)   Money × velocity = _____.

In symbols, it is:

$$\underline{\quad} \times \underline{\quad} = \underline{\quad} \times \underline{\quad}.$$

Statisticians and national income accountants measure the stock of money and nominal GDP. Economists then calculate velocity by dividing nominal GDP by the stock of money. As a result, the equation of exchange is always true.

The quantity theory asserts that there is a close link between changes in nominal GDP and changes

(3) in the stock of _____. This link comes about because the quantity theory assumes that velocity (<u>does/does not</u>) change very much. If velocity is constant, then a change in the money stock translates directly into a change in _____ _____. If velocity is 8 and the money stock increases by $25 billion, then nominal GDP will rise by $ _____ billion.

An analysis of the determinants of velocity as well as the study of historical data suggest that one

(4) (<u>should/should not</u>) expect velocity to be constant. Velocity reflects how much money people hold to make transactions, which in turn reflects such institutional factors as the efficiency of the payments mechanism—the frequency of paychecks and how easy it is to move funds between checking accounts and savings accounts. The amount of money people want to hold, and hence velocity, is also affected by the interest rate as a measure of the opportunity cost of holding money. For example, an increase

in expected inflation is likely to (decrease/increase) nominal interest rates and _____ the amount of money people want to hold.

Monetarism, like the quantity theory, starts with the equation of exchange. But rather than assuming that velocity does not change, monetarists try to predict how velocity will change. From a monetarist perspective, determinants of nominal GDP are broken down into implications for the stock of money and implications for _____. After accounting for appropriate changes,   (5) simple multiplication can be used to predict nominal GDP. The effectiveness of a monetarist approach depends upon how easy it is to predict changes in velocity.

At first glance it may appear that a Keynesian approach to income determination cannot analyze changes in monetary policy whereas a monetarist approach ignores fiscal policy. Such a conclusion would be oversimplified and misleading. In formal theory the two viewpoints are closer than is commonly recognized. Keynesian theory implies that monetary policy can have important impacts on aggregate demand through its impact on interest rates and investment spending. An expansionary change in monetary policy will lead to a(n) (decline/increase) in interest rates. The change in   (6) interest rates will (increase/decrease) investment spending. As we have seen, an increase in investment spending shifts both the expenditure schedule and the aggregate demand curve. Putting all the pieces together we can see that expansionary monetary policy will tend to (increase/decrease) GDP. Restrictive monetary policy would work in exactly the opposite way.

Monetarists are able to analyze the impact of changes in fiscal policy as follows: Expansionary fiscal policy will tend to be associated with (higher/lower) interest rates. As a result, velocity will   (7) (increase/decrease) and a monetarist would forecast a (higher/lower) value for nominal GDP. Neither alone nor together are Keynesian and monetarist theories sufficient to determine output and prices as both are theories of the demand side of the economy and ignore the supply side.

The impact of changes in fiscal policy on interest rates is not only important to a monetarist analysis of changes in fiscal policy. It is also one of the reasons why the multiplier formula of $1/(1 - \text{MPC})$ is oversimplified; increases in autonomous spending will tend to increase interest rates, which in turn induce partially offsetting changes in investment spending.[1]

The choice between monetary and fiscal policy is often influenced by how quickly changes in policy can occur and how long it takes for changes, once made, to affect the behavior of firms and consumers. In general, lags in formulating policy are shorter for (fiscal/monetary) policy, whereas   (8) spending responses of households are typically shorter for _____ policy.

---

[1]Other factors that mean the formula $1/(1 - \text{MPC})$ is oversimplified include the change in imports that normally accompany a change in GDP; the effect of higher prices on consumption spending, net exports, and the demand for money when a shift in the aggregate demand curve leads to a movement along the aggregate supply curve; and income taxes that reduce the change in disposable income for a given change in GDP. In later chapters we will also see how the impact of changes in the exchange rate affect the multiplier.

A major controversy in monetary policy is whether, when formulating monetary policy decisions, the Federal Reserve should pay greater attention to the money supply or to the interest rates. Imagine, for instance, that the Fed is happy with the stock of money and the interest rate given in **Figure 14-1.** Suddenly the demand-for-money schedule shifts to the right because of an increase in the demand for money from some factor other than interest rates. Draw in the new schedule. If the Fed did nothing, then, as a result of this shift in the demand

(9) for money, the stock of money would be (higher/lower) and the interest rate would be _____. To maintain the original money supply, M^*, the Fed should shift the supply-of-money schedule to the _____; to maintain the same rate of interest, the Fed should shift the supply curve to the _____. It should be obvious that the Fed cannot do both at the same time.

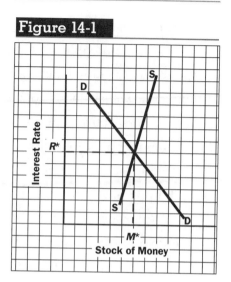

Figure 14-1

Decisions to stick to original monetary targets are likely to mean greater changes in interest rates, while decisions to stabilize interest rates will mean greater changes in the stock of money. The appropriate choice will depend upon the state of the economy and the source of the unexpected changes in interest rates and the stock of money.

Stabilization policy affects the economy primarily by shifting the aggregate demand curve. The final result, however, in terms of changes in output and prices, also depends upon the slope of the aggregate supply curve. A flat aggregate supply curve means that shifts in the aggregate demand curve

(10) will have large effects on (output/price) with only a small change in _____. On the other hand, shifts of the aggregate demand curve will have big effects on prices without much change in output if the aggregate supply curve is (steep/flat). While some argue that the aggregate supply curve is flat and others that it is steep, an emerging consensus sees the slope of the aggregate supply curve as depending upon the period of analysis. The aggregate supply curve is likely to be flatter in the (long/short) run and steeper in the _____ run.

Some economists favor an activist-oriented approach to stabilization policy with significant latitude for discretionary policy. Others favor less activism and a greater reliance on rules. Beyond views about the slope of the aggregate supply curve, these differences also reflect differing political philosophies and judgments concerning the importance of such factors as the speed of the economy's self-correcting mechanisms, the length of various policy lags, and the accuracy of economic forecasting.

It takes time before someone notices that the economy is not operating as hoped for and before the appropriate part of the government can decide what policy measures should be adopted. Once a particular policy is decided upon, there may not be much impact on output and prices until the buying habits of households and firms adjust to the new policy. Because of lags, policy changes today are likely to have their greatest impact in the future. For policy to be effective, economists must be able to anticipate future events. The more accurate the economic forecasts, the more demanding the standards we can set for stabilization policy.

Some argue that stable government policies are best for private spending while others argue that if stable policies mean instability in the economy that would be even worse for firms and households. The flexibility to use changes in spending, taxes, and monetary policy means that activist policy (does/does not) imply that government spending must take an ever larger proportion of the   (11) economic pie.

Important Terms and Concepts Quiz

Choose the best definition for each of the following terms.

1. _____ Quantity theory of money

2. _____ Velocity

3. _____ Equation of exchange

4. _____ Monetarism

a. Variables that normally turn down prior to recessions and turn up prior to expansions

b. Mode of analysis that uses the equation of exchange to organize and analyze macroeconomic data

c. Average number of times a dollar is spent in a year

d. Formula that states that nominal GDP equals the product of money stock and velocity

e. Theory of aggregate demand stating that nominal GDP is proportional to the money stock

Table 14-1

GDP, Money, and Velocity

	Nominal GDP ($ billions)	M_1 ($ billions)	M_2 ($ billions)	V_1	V_2
1995	7,397.7	1,138.8	3,569.3		
1996	7,816.9	1,103.2	3,729.0		
1997	8,304.3	1,075.9	3,924.2		
1998	8,747.0	1,084.3	4,207.8		
1999	9,268.4	1,110.1	4,516.3		
2000	9,817.0	1,106.0	4,790.6		
2001	10,128.0	1,133.6	5,190.4		
2002	10,487.0	1,198.3	5,621.3		
2003	11,004.0	1,255.3	5,928.4		
2004	11,728.0	1,328.3	6,230.1		

SOURCE: GDP: *Economic Report of the President*, 2005, Tables B-1 and B-69.

● Basic Exercises

This exercise is designed to give you practice computing and using velocity.

1. **Table 14-1** contains historical data for nominal GDP, M1, and M2.
   a. Use this data to compute V_1, velocity based on M_1; and V_2, velocity based on M_2. Be sure to round your answers for velocity to two decimal places.
   b. Assume you are a monetarist working for the Federal Reserve and are asked to predict nominal GDP one year in advance. Even if you knew the money supply, M, you would still need an estimate of V. One way to estimate velocity is to use data from the previous year. The idea is that, since you can't know velocity for 2000 until you know nominal GDP and M_1 or M_2 for 2000, you might use velocity for 1999 to predict GDP for 2000. **Table 14-2** assumes that the Federal Reserve can control the money supply exactly. Use your numbers for velocity from

Table 14-2

Money, Velocity, and GDP

	Actual M_1 ($ billions)	V_1 from Previous Year	Estimated Income ($ billions)	Actual Income ($ billions)	Estimated Income ($ billions)	V_2 from Previous Year	Actual M_2 ($ billions)
1996	1,103.2			7,816.9			3,729.0
1997	1,075.9			8,304.3			3,924.2
1998	1,084.3			8,747.0			4,207.8
1999	1,110.1			9,268.4			4,516.3
2000	1,106.0			9,817.0			4,790.6
2001	1,133.6			10,128.0			5,190.4
2002	1,198.3			10,487.0			5,621.3
2003	1,255.3			11,004.0			5,928.4
2004	1,328.3			11,728.0			6,230.1

*Express estimate for Nominal GDP to one decimal point.

the previous year to fill in the blank columns in Table 14-2 to see how well velocity and money predict income.

c. Which years show the largest prediction errors? Why?

2. For this exercise you are asked to assume the role of adviser to the Federal Reserve's Open Market Committee. **Figure 14-2** uses the demand and supply of bank reserves to show the quantity of bank reserves and the rate of interest when the committee last met. Assume that the economy was then at full employment with price stability. The next meeting of the Open Market Committee begins with a report detailing the unexpected increase in the stock of money and interest rates since the last meeting. What to do is not so obvious, however, as suggested by the following arguments offered by two different members of the committee:

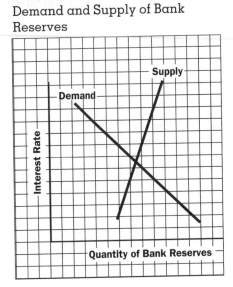

Figure 14-2

Demand and Supply of Bank Reserves

A: This report confirms my fear that aggregate demand is expanding too rapidly. The resulting increase in nominal GDP is increasing the demand for money and hence the demand for bank reserves. We risk unnecessary inflation and should move to reduce aggregate demand by an appropriate change in monetary policy.

B: This report confirms my concern that there has been an increase in the demand for bank reserves that is unrelated to GDP. Businesses and individuals have been harmed buying esoteric and risky financial securities. As a result of these losses, there has been a general increase in the demand for safer bank deposits and hence an increase in the demand for bank reserves. If we do not take appropriate action the increase in interest rates since our last meeting will reduce aggregate demand and threaten recession.

Use Figure 14-2 to illustrate what each speaker is arguing and what actions each is suggesting. Each is arguing for a particular policy to shift the supply-of-reserves schedule. What is that shift and how is it consistent with each speaker's analysis? What is likely to happen if the Fed implements A's desired policy when B's analysis is correct? What is likely to happen if the Fed implements B's desired policy when A's analysis is correct?

Self-Tests for Understanding

Test A

Circle the most appropriate answer.

1. Velocity is measured by
   a. dividing the money stock by nominal GDP.
   b. computing the percentage change in nominal GDP from year to year.
   c. dividing nominal GDP by the stock of money.
   d. subtracting the rate of inflation from nominal interest rates.

2. The equation of exchange says that
   a. for every buyer there is a seller.
   b. $M \times V$ = nominal GDP.
   c. demand equals supply.
   d. P. T. Barnum was right when he said, "There is a sucker born every minute."

3. According to the equation of exchange, an increase in M may lead to (There may be more than one correct answer.)
   a. an increase in Y (real GDP).
   b. an increase in P.
   c. a reduction in V.
   d. an increase in nominal GDP.

4. According to the quantity theory, an increase in M will lead to a(n) _____. (There may be more than one correct answer.)
   a. increase in Y (real GDP).
   b. increase in P.
   c. reduction in V.
   d. increase in nominal GDP.

5. Between 1996 and 1997 the money supply (M_1) decreased by 3.3 percent and yet nominal GDP rose by 5.8 percent. It must be that velocity
   a. decreased.
   b. was unchanged.
   c. increased.

6. From 2001 to 2002 M_1 increased by 5.7 percent and V_1 declined from 8.93 to 8.75. It must be that nominal GDP increased by _____ 5.7 percent.
   a. less than
   b. exactly
   c. more than

7. The historical record shows
   a. that both V_1 and V_2 have been stable.
   b. continual decrease in V_2.
   c. continual increases in V_1.
   d. that V_2 has shown less variation than V_1.

8. Assume that velocity is 7. If one can be sure that velocity will not change, what increase in M will be required to increase real GDP by $140 billion?
   a. $7 billion
   b. $20 billion
   c. $140 billion
   d. insufficient information

9. Because M_2 is _____ than M_1, V_2 should be _____ than V_1.
   a. larger; larger
   b. larger; smaller
   c. smaller; smaller
   d. smaller; larger

10. In recent years the Fed has formulated monetary policy in terms of targets for
    a. growth in M_1 and M_2.
    b. inflation.
    c. interest rates.
    d. unemployment.

11. According to a monetarist analysis of income determination all but which one of the following is likely to increase nominal GDP?
    a. an open market purchase that increases the stock of money
    b. an increase in government spending
    c. a technological change in banking practices that increases velocity
    d. an increase in income taxes

12. A change in interest rates that accompanies an open market purchase is likely to
    a. increase velocity.
    b. have no effect on velocity.
    c. reduce velocity.

13. Which of the following make the value of the multiplier less than $1/(1 - MPC)$? (There may be more than one correct answer.)
    a. increases in interest rates that accompany an increase in the demand for bank reserves as nominal GDP increases
    b. income taxes
    c. an increase in imports that normally accompanies an increase in GDP
    d. the impact of higher prices on consumption spending

14. Which of the following is an example of a lag in policymaking as opposed to a lag in spending by firms and households?
    a. The construction of a new plant, induced by lower interest rates, cannot start for nine months, because it takes that long to prepare architectural drawings and contractors' bids.
    b. Congress takes five months to consider a presidential tax proposal.
    c. Through multiplier impacts, a $3 billion increase in defense spending eventually raises GDP by $5 billion.
    d. Refrigerator sales rise in the month following receipt of a $300 tax rebate.

15. The time it takes to make a change is probably shorter for _____ policy while lags affecting private spending are probably shorter for _____ policy.
    a. fiscal; monetary
    b. monetary; fiscal
    c. fiscal; fiscal
    d. monetary; monetary

16. Assume that the stock of money and interest rates are both at levels desired by the Federal Reserve. Following a shift in the demand for money, the Fed can control _____. (There may be more than one correct answer.)
    a. M but not r
    b. r but not M
    c. both M and r

17. Stabilization policy will be effective in combating recession if the aggregate supply curve is _____ and effective in combating inflation if the aggregate supply curve is _____.
    a. flat; steep
    b. steep; flat
    c. flat; flat
    d. steep; steep

18. If the aggregate supply curve is relatively flat, then
    a. velocity will be constant.
    b. both monetary and fiscal policy will have relatively large effects on output without much effect on prices.
    c. a change in interest rates will have little impact on investment.
    d. monetary policy will be effective while fiscal policy will not.

19. The Federal Reserve cannot control both r and M because its policy actions affect
    a. the demand for money curve but not the supply of money curve.
    b. events in the short run but not the long run.
    c. investment spending but not consumption spending.
    d. the supply of money curve but not the demand for money curve.

20. Active stabilization policy
    a. must increase the size of government.
    b. will only be successful if the size of government declines.
    c. need not imply any tendency toward big government.
    d. will only mean larger and larger government deficits.

Test B

Circle T or F for true or false.

T F 1. If the stock of money is $1 trillion and nominal GDP is $8 trillion, then velocity is 8.

T F 2. Velocity is determined by how often people are paid and is unaffected by the rate of interest.

T F 3. The quantity theory is not really a theory because velocity, by definition, is equal to the ratio of nominal GDP divided by the money stock.

T F 4. If the Fed formulates monetary policy in terms of targets for the size of the stock of money, it must be willing to accept greater variability in interest rates.

T F 5. The lag between a change in fiscal policy and its effects on aggregate demand is probably shorter than the lag between a change in monetary policy and its effects on aggregate demand.

T F 6. The lag in adopting an appropriate policy is probably shorter for monetary policy than for fiscal policy.

T F 7. By simultaneously using open market operations and making changes in minimum reserve requirements, the Fed would be able to achieve any desired combination of the money stock and the interest rate.

T F 8. The shape of the aggregate supply curve is likely to be relatively flat in the short run and steeper in the long run.

T   F   9. If the aggregate supply curve is steep, then changes in fiscal and monetary policy will have major impacts on prices with little impact on output.

T   F   10. Long lags will help make for better stabilization policy because there is more time for a complete analysis of possible actions.

Supplementary Exercises

Leading Indicators

Is the stock market a good leading indicator of overall economic conditions? **Figure 14-3** shows stock prices from January 1950 through December 2004 as measured by Standard and Poor's 500 stock price index. Using just Figure 14-3, make an estimate of how many recessions there have been since 1950. Try to date each one approximately. The National Bureau of Economic Research (NBER) is the organization that dates business cycles. Check their Web site http://www.nber.org to see how your business cycles compare with theirs. How many recessions does the NBER identify? How many did you identify? How many false indications of recession were there? What about the forecasting record of other leading indicators? What are the stock market and other leading indicators saying about the state of the economy over the next six to twelve months?

In addition to the problem of false turning points, there are two other limitations to a purely mechanical use of leading indicators that you should be aware of:

Figure 14-3

Is the Stock Market a Leading Indicator?

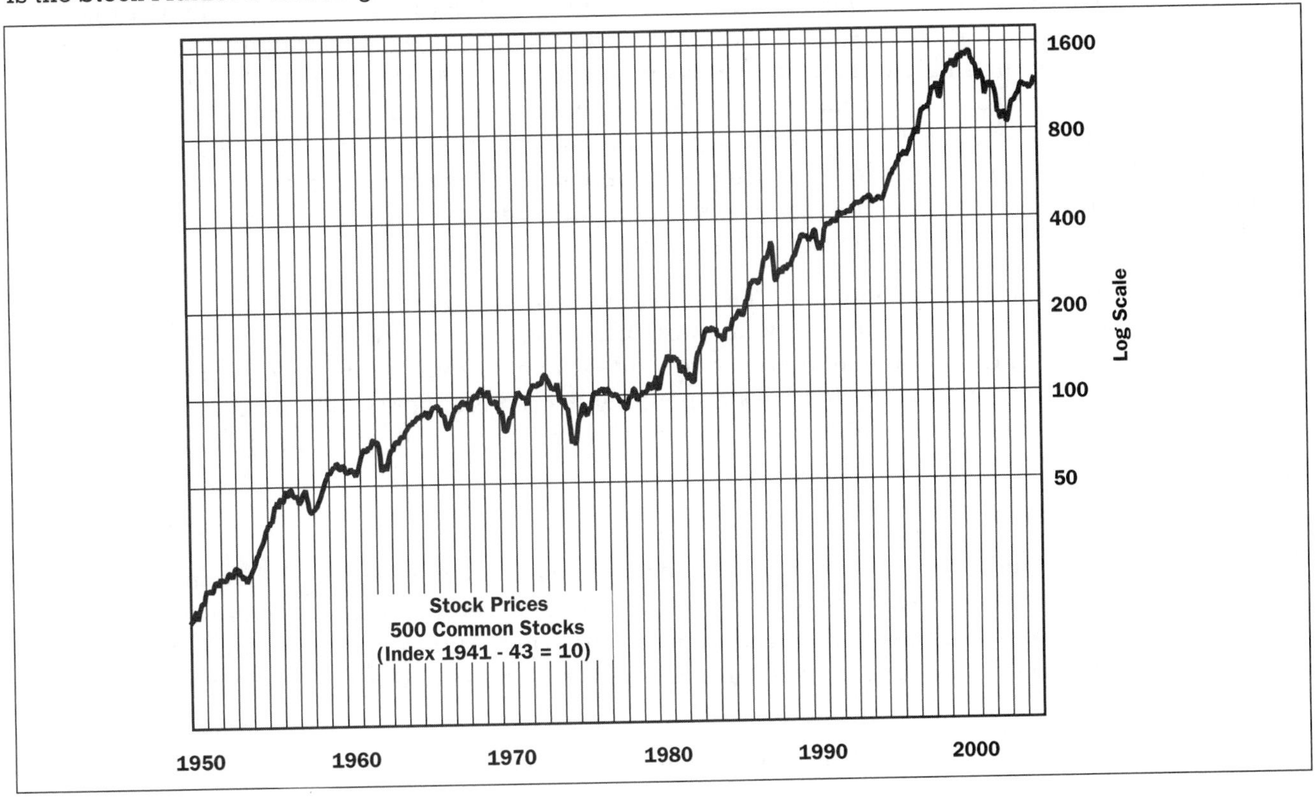

Stock Prices
500 Common Stocks
(Index 1941 - 43 = 10)

a. Most large declines in a leading indicator are the result of not one large decline, but rather a series of consecutive small declines. At the same time, each series has so many ups and downs that most small declines are followed by a small increase. One needs some way of separating those small declines that signal the start of a major slump from those that are quickly reversed.

b. A leading indicator that always changes direction a fixed amount of time before the economy does would be extremely useful. However, the length of time between movements in most leading indicators and the economy is quite variable.

• Economics in Action

What to Do?

What indicators should the Federal Reserve use when formulating monetary policy? General agreement exists that monetary policy should contribute to broad macroeconomic objectives—price stability, full employment, economic growth—although different observers would argue that greater weight should be placed on different objectives, e.g., price stability or full employment. However, the Fed does not control the rate of inflation or the rate of unemployment. A related problem is that observations on different macroeconomic variables are available at different times. Estimates of GDP come only every three months. Unemployment and inflation are measured monthly. Data on M1 and M2 are announced every week while interest rates are available at a moment's notice.

At times the Fed has put more emphasis on interest rates and at others on M1, M2, or bank reserves as indicators of monetary policy. When testifying before Congress in July of 1993, and reporting on growth ranges expected for M1 and M2 for 1994, Alan Greenspan, chairman of the Board of Governors of the Federal Reserve System, made the following argument:

The historical relationships between money and income, and between money and the price level, have largely broken down, depriving the aggregates of much of their usefulness as guides to policy. At least for the time being, M2 has been downgraded as a reliable indicator of financial conditions in the economy, and no single variable has yet been identified to take its place. . . . In the meantime, the process of probing a variety of data to ascertain underlying economic and financial conditions has become even more essential to formulating sound monetary policy. . . . In these circumstances it is especially prudent to focus on longer-term policy guides. One important guidepost is real interest rates, which have a key bearing on longer-run spending decisions and inflation prospects.

Greenspan emphasized what he called the equilibrium real rate of interest:

. . . specifically the real rate level that, if maintained, would keep the economy at its production potential over time. . . . Real rates, of course, are not directly observable, but must be inferred from nominal interest rates and estimates of inflation expectations. The most important real rates for private spending decisions almost surely are the longer maturities. Moreover, the equilibrium rate structure responds to the ebb and flow of underlying forces affecting spending.

Greenspan concluded:

While the guides we have for policy may have changed recently, our goals have not. As I have indicated many times to this Committee, the Federal Reserve seeks to foster maximum sustainable economic growth and rising standards of living. And in that endeavor, the most productive function the central bank can perform is to achieve and maintain price stability.

1. What indicators of monetary policy would you favor if you were a member of the Federal Open Market Committee?

2. When is it appropriate to emphasize measures of the stock of money and when is it appropriate to emphasize interest rates?

3. While one can observe nominal interest rates, how does one measure the equilibrium real rate of interest in a way that makes it operational for the conduct of monetary policy?

Source: Testimony by Alan Greenspan, Chairman of the Board of Governors of the Federal Reserve System, before the Subcommittee on Economic Growth and Credit Formation of the Committee on Banking, Finance, and Urban Affairs, U.S. House of Representatives, July 20, 1993.

Study Questions

1. What is the difference between the equation of exchange, the quantity theory, and monetarism?

2. What do you think explains the different historical experience of V_1 and V_2?

3. Why can't one use monetarism to determine nominal GDP, Keynesian analysis to determine real GDP, and then compute the price level by dividing the one by the other?

4. What is the difference between policy lags and expenditure lags? Which are likely to be more important for fiscal policy? For monetary policy?

5. What's wrong with the following? "Long lags make for better policy as they provide more time for determining the best policy."

6. Why can't the Fed control both M and r?

7. Do you think monetary policy should focus on stabilizing interest rates or stabilizing the growth in the stock of money? Why?

8. Why are concerns about excessive levels of government spending not a legitimate reason to oppose active stabilization policy?

9. Do you favor a more or less activist stabilization policy? Why?

Economics Online

The Fed's latest release on interest rates and the money supply along with a number of other data series can be found here.

http://www.federalreserve.gov/releases

The Federal Reserve Bank of St. Louis offers electronic access to lots of historical data about the economy at its Web site FRED, Federal Reserve Economic Data. FRED will graph data for you.

http://research.stlouisfed.org/fred2

Budget Deficits in the Short and Long Run

Important Terms and Concepts

Mix of monetary and fiscal policy

Budget deficit

Budget surplus

National debt

Structural deficit or surplus

Monetization of deficits

Crowding out

Crowding in

Burden of the national debt

Learning Objectives

After completing this chapter, you should be able to:

- explain how measures to balance the budget may unbalance the economy.

- explain how appropriate fiscal policy depends on the strength of private demand and the conduct of monetary policy.

- explain the implications of changing the mix of monetary and fiscal policy while leaving GDP and prices unchanged.

- explain the difference between the government's budget deficit and the national debt.

- discuss some facts about budget deficits and the national debt: When have budget deficits been largest? What has happened to the national debt as a proportion of GDP?

- describe how the concept of structural deficits or surpluses differs from officially reported deficits or surpluses.

- distinguish between real and fallacious arguments about the burden of the national debt.

- describe the inflationary consequences of a budget deficit and explain why deficits will be more inflationary if they are monetized.

- explain why a debt held by foreigners imposes a larger burden than a debt held by domestic citizens.

- explain why most economists measure the true burden of deficits by their impact on the capital stock.

- evaluate arguments supporting the crowding-out and crowding-in properties of government deficit spending.

Chapter Review

By itself this chapter cannot make government deficits larger or smaller, but it can help to increase your understanding of the impacts of both government deficits and the national debt.

(1)   The government runs a deficit when its (spending/revenue) exceeds its _____. There is a surplus when _____ is greater than _____. The national debt measures the government's total indebtedness. The national debt will increase if the government budget shows a (deficit/surplus). The national debt will decrease if the government budget shows a(n) _____.

What is appropriate deficit policy? Earlier chapters discussed the use of fiscal and monetary policy to strike an appropriate balance between aggregate demand and aggregate supply in order to choose between inflation and unemployment. Considerations of balanced budgets, per se, were absent from that discussion. The conclusion that budget policy should adapt to the requirements of the economy is shared by many economists. Note that this conclusion implies that appropriate fiscal policy depends upon the stance of monetary policy and the strength of private demand.

Some have advocated a policy of strict budget balance. There is good reason to expect that such a policy would balance the budget at the risk of unbalancing the economy. Consider an economy in an initial equilibrium at full employment with a balanced budget. An autonomous decline in private

(2) spending would shift the expenditure schedule (down/up), resulting in a shift of the aggregate demand schedule to the (right/left). In the absence of any further policy action, the result would be a(n) (decline/increase) in GDP. The change in GDP will also mean a(n) (decline/increase) in tax revenues. The government's budget will move from its initial position of balance to one of (deficit/surplus). At this point, deliberate policy actions to reestablish budget balance would call for either a(n) (decrease/increase) in taxes or a(n) (decrease/increase) in government spending. In either case the result would be an additional shift in the expenditure schedule and aggregate demand curve that would (accentuate/counteract) the original shift that was due to the autonomous decline in private spending.

The fact that tax revenues depend on the state of the economy is important to understanding many complicated issues about the impact of deficits. As seen above, it helps to explain why a policy of budget balancing can unbalance the economy in the face of changes in private spending. It helps to explain why deficits can sometimes be associated with a booming economy and at other times with a sagging economy. It also helps to explain interest in alternative measures of the deficit. The concept of the structural deficit/surplus attempts to control for the effects of the economy on the deficit. It does so by looking at spending and revenues at a specified high-employment level of income.

(3) Changes in tax revenues due to changes in GDP (will/will not) affect the actual deficit or surplus but

(will/will not) affect the structural deficit or surplus. For this reason, many analysts prefer to use the structural budget as a measure of the stance of fiscal policy.

Are deficits inflationary? Note that a deficit that arises when the economy slips into recession due to a decline in private spending is likely to be correlated with a reduction, not an increase, in interest rates and the rate of inflation.[1] An increase in the structural deficit—that is, a deliberate (increase/reduction) in spending or _____ in taxes—would shift the aggregate demand   (4) curve to the right and increase both interest rates and prices. Exactly how much inflation would occur will depend upon the slope of the aggregate supply curve, whether the economy is close to or far away from full employment, and the conduct of monetary policy.

Concerns about the impact of the deficit on interest rates may lead a central bank to engage in an open market purchase to increase bank reserves. If the central bank acts to increase bank reserves by buying government securities, one says it has _____ the deficit. Deficit-   (5) induced open market purchases would reduce interest rates from what they would have been, result in a further expansionary shift in the aggregate demand curve and mean even higher prices. Thus monetization of the deficit could lead to (greater/less) inflation. While a problem in some countries, monetization of the deficit has not been a problem in the United States.

Many feelings about the burden of the national debt may be as deeply ingrained and just as irrational as a Victorian's ideas about sex or a football coach's ideas about winning. Many fallacious arguments about the burden of the debt do, however, contain some elements of truth. Arguments about the burden of future interest payments or the cost of repaying the national debt are not relevant when considering debts held by domestic citizens but are relevant when considering debts held by _____. To the extent that debt is held by domestic citizens, interest payments and   (6) debt repayments impose little burden on the nation as a whole; they are only transfers from taxpayers to bondholders, who may even be the same individuals. However, the impact on incentives from higher taxes to accomplish these transfers should not be ignored. A real burden of the debt would arise from a deficit in a high-employment economy that crowded out private (consumption/investment) spending and left a smaller capital stock to future generations.

There will continue to be arguments as to whether U.S. deficits have entailed such a burden. Until 1980, the federal government's deficit had shown its largest increases during periods of _____ (7) and _____. Government deficits during periods of slack may actually result in a benefit rather than a burden if, as a result of increased demand, they lead to (crowding in/crowding out) rather than _____ _____. Major concerns about deficits during the late

---

[1]By assumption, this deficit arose as the aggregate demand curve shifts to the left. It is inflationary only in the sense that a move to balance the budget would mean a further shift of the aggregate demand curve to the left and a larger reduction in the rate of inflation.

1980s and the early part of the 21st century were that they occurred during a period of (high/low) employment and that they were thus likely to have led to crowding _____.

Changes in the mix of fiscal and monetary policy may leave real GDP and the price level unaffected but there will be important effects on the budget deficit, the composition of output, and economic growth. Consider an economy at full employment with a government budget that is in

(8)   balance. A reduction in tax rates would shift the aggregate demand curve to the (right/left). The impact on aggregate demand could be offset by a move to (restrictive/expansionary) monetary policy. The reduction in tax rates will mean that the government is now running a (deficit/surplus). This change in the government budget together with the change in monetary policy will mean (higher/lower) interest rates and a(n) _____ level of investment spending. Because of the change in investment spending, over time this economy is likely to grow (faster/more slowly) that it would have before the change in the mix of fiscal and monetary policy.

Important Terms and Concepts Quiz

Choose the best definition for each of the following terms.

1. _____ Budget deficit

2. _____ Budget surplus

3. _____ National debt

4. _____ Structural budget

5. _____ Monetization of deficits

6. _____ Crowding out

7. _____ Crowding in

a. Amount by which governmental revenue exceeds spending

b. Ratio of government debt to GDP

c. State of budget under current fiscal policy if the economy was at full employment

d. Amount by which government spending exceeds revenue

e. Increase in private investment spending induced by deficit spending

f. Purchases of government bonds by central bank to finance deficit

g. Contraction of private investment spending induced by deficit spending

h. Federal government's total indebtedness

Basic Exercises

This exercise is designed to show how a rigid policy of balanced budgets may unbalance the economy. To simplify the calculations, the exercise focuses on the income-expenditure diagram.

1. a. Fill in the last column of **Table 15-1** to determine the initial equilibrium level of income.

   The equilibrium level of income is $_____.

Table 15-1

Income (Output) Y	Taxes T	Disposable Income DI	Consumption Spending C	Investment Spending I	Government Purchases G	Exports X	Imports IM	Total Spending C + I + G + (X – IM)
10,000	1,800	8,200	6,860	1,625	1,900	1,150	1,335	_____
10,100	1,825	8,275	6,920	1,625	1,900	1,150	1,345	_____
10,200	1,850	8,350	6,980	1,625	1,900	1,150	1,355	_____
10,300	1,875	8,425	7,040	1,625	1,900	1,150	1,365	_____
10,400	1,900	8,500	7,100	1,625	1,900	1,150	1,375	_____
10,500	1,925	8,575	7,160	1,625	1,900	1,150	1,385	_____
10,600	1,950	8,650	7,220	1,625	1,900	1,150	1,395	_____
10,700	1,975	8,725	7,280	1,625	1,900	1,150	1,405	_____
10,800	2,000	8,800	7,340	1,625	1,900	1,150	1,415	_____

Table 15-2

Income (Output) Y	Taxes T	Disposable Income DI	Consumption Spending C	Investment Spending I	Government Purchases G	Exports X	Imports IM	Total Spending C + I + G + (X – IM)
10,000	1,800	8,200	6,860	1,525	1,900	1,150	1,335	_____
10,100	1,825	8,275	6,920	1,525	1,900	1,150	1,345	_____
10,200	1,850	8,350	6,980	1,525	1,900	1,150	1,355	_____
10,300	1,875	8,425	7,040	1,525	1,900	1,150	1,365	_____
10,400	1,900	8,500	7,100	1,525	1,900	1,150	1,375	_____
10,500	1,925	8,575	7,160	1,525	1,900	1,150	1,385	_____
10,600	1,950	8,650	7,220	1,525	1,900	1,150	1,395	_____
10,700	1,975	8,725	7,280	1,525	1,900	1,150	1,405	_____
10,800	2,000	8,800	7,340	1,525	1,900	1,150	1,415	_____

b. At the initial equilibrium level of income, what is the government's actual deficit or surplus?

_____

c. The high-employment level of income is $10,700. What is the structural deficit/surplus?

_____

d. Investment spending now declines by $100 billion. Use **Table 15-2** to compute the new equilibrium level of income. _____

How has the actual government deficit/surplus changed, if at all? _____

How has the structural deficit/surplus changed, if at all? _____

Table 15-3

Income (Output) Y	Taxes T	Disposable Income DI	Consumption Spending C	Investment Spending I	Government Purchases G	Exports X	Imports IM	Total Spending C + I + G + (X − IM)
10,000	1,800	8,200	6,860	1,525	1,850	1,150	1,335	_____
10,100	1,825	8,275	6,920	1,525	1,850	1,150	1,345	_____
10,200	1,850	8,350	6,980	1,525	1,850	1,150	1,355	_____
10,300	1,875	8,425	7,040	1,525	1,850	1,150	1,365	_____
10,400	1,900	8,500	7,100	1,525	1,850	1,150	1,375	_____
10,500	1,925	8,575	7,160	1,525	1,850	1,150	1,385	_____
10,600	1,950	8,650	7,220	1,525	1,850	1,150	1,395	_____
10,700	1,975	8,725	7,280	1,525	1,850	1,150	1,405	_____
10,800	2,000	8,800	7,340	1,525	1,850	1,150	1,415	_____

e. The government is contemplating a reduction in spending of $50 billion, an amount that should balance the government's budget if income does not change. Use **Table 15-3** to see if reducing government spending by $50 billion will balance the budget. What is the new equilibrium level of income? Did the reduction in government spending balance the budget? If not, why not?

2. This problem is meant to illustrate how the effects of changes in fiscal policy depend upon what happens to monetary policy. The solid lines in **Figure 15-1** show an economy in an initial position of equilibrium at full employment with a balanced budget, low interest rates, and no trade deficit, i.e., exports equal imports. The dashed line shows the same economy following a decrease in personal income taxes. Assume the decrease in taxes is equal to $100 billion at the full-employment level of income.

Figure 15-1

Aggregate Demand and Aggregate Supply

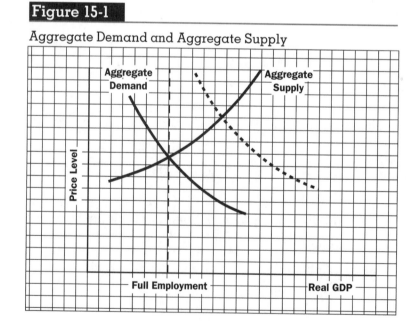

a. Assume the monetary authority wants to avoid the inflation that would be associated with the increase in the structural deficit. Should the monetary authority engage in an open market purchase or sale? Why?

b. Assume the monetary authority is successful in offsetting the expansionary impact of the increase in the structural deficit. That is, open market operations are successful in shifting the aggregate demand curve back to its initial position. Initially the economy was at full employment with no inflation, a balanced budget, low interest rates, and no trade deficit. Call this outcome Option A. Now the economy is again at full employment with no inflation, but with a structural deficit and high interest rates. Call this outcome Option B. What difference does it make whether the economy is at full employment under Option A or Option B?

Self-Tests for Understanding

Test A

Circle the most appropriate answer.

1. The federal government deficit is
   a. the excess of tax revenues over transfer payments.
   b. another term for political gridlock.
   c. total indebtedness of the government.
   d. the difference between government spending and the government's revenue for a given year.

2. The federal government runs a surplus when
   a. spending is greater than tax receipts.
   b. interest payments on the national debt are less than 5 percent.
   c. Social Security payments are balanced by Social Security taxes.
   d. revenues exceed spending.

3. The national debt is
   a. equal to the cumulation of past federal government deficits and surpluses.
   b. another term for the federal government's deficit.
   c. what the U.S. government and private businesses owe foreigners.
   d. the excess of spending over revenue for a given year.

4. The structural deficit (surplus) is
   a. equal to interest payments on the national debt.
   b. equal to zero by definition.
   c. defined as the deficit (surplus) the government would run if the economy were at full employment.
   d. the excess of government investment spending over allocations for these projects.

5. At high levels of unemployment, the government's actual deficit will be _____ the structural deficit.
   a. smaller than
   b. the same as
   c. larger than

6. Many observers argue that the structural deficit is a better measure of the stance of fiscal policy than the actual deficit because the
   a. actual deficit can be larger or smaller depending upon the impact of changes in private demand on GDP.
   b. actual deficit does not include the impact of automatic stabilizers.
   c. structural deficit is based on real rather than nominal interest rates.
   d. structural deficit represents what the president proposes rather than what is enacted by Congress.

7. Which mix of fiscal and monetary policy is likely to lead to a higher rate of economic growth? (Assume that either mix of policies achieves the same level of real GDP.)
   a. a small structural deficit and low interest rates
   b. a large structural deficit and high interest rates
   c. Both a and b have the same implications for economic growth.

8. Which of the following is likely to increase the government's structural deficit?
   a. open market purchase
   b. decline in private investment spending
   c. reduction in personal income tax rates
   d. increase in exports from strong economic expansion in Europe

9. Which of the following is likely to increase the government's actual deficit? (There may be more than one correct answer.)
   a. open market purchase
   b. decline in private investment spending
   c. reduction in personal income tax rates
   d. increase in exports from strong economic expansion in Europe

10. Until the 1980s, large government deficits had been primarily associated with periods of _____. (There may be more than one correct answer.)
    a. high inflation
    b. war
    c. recession
    d. low unemployment

11. An autonomous decline in private spending will lead to all but which one of the following?
    a. a downward shift in the expenditure schedule
    b. a decline in the equilibrium level of GDP
    c. an increase in the government deficit or a reduction in the surplus
    d. a decline in the structural budget deficit or surplus

12. Rigid adherence to budget balancing will
    a. help the economy adjust to shifts in private spending.
    b. have little impact on business cycles.
    c. accentuate swings in GDP from autonomous changes in private spending.
    d. help maintain full employment.

13. The inflationary consequences of a budget deficit are likely to be greatest when
    a. the deficit is the result of a decline in private spending.
    b. the Fed conducts monetary policy to offset the impact of the deficit.
    c. the aggregate supply curve is flat.
    d. there is an increase in the structural deficit at a time of full employment.

14. If the Federal Reserve monetizes a budget deficit, there will be a(n)
    a. smaller inflationary impact.
    b. unchanged inflationary impact.
    c. larger inflationary impact.

15. An increase in the deficit is likely to be correlated with which of the following? (There may be more than one correct answer.)
    a. faster growth in GDP
    b. lower interest rates
    c. a reduction in the rate of inflation
    d. higher interest rates
    e. greater inflation
    f. a slowing of the rate of growth of GDP

16. The macroeconomic impact of a decrease in taxes that increases the structural deficit could be offset by a(n)
    a. equal increase in transfer payments.
    b. open market purchase.
    c. equal increase in government spending.
    d. change in monetary policy that increases interest rates.

17. Which of the following is a valid argument about the burden of the national debt for an economy whose debt is held entirely by its own citizens?
    a. Future generations will find interest payments a heavy burden.
    b. When the debt is due, future generations will be burdened with an enormous repayment.
    c. The debt will bankrupt future generations.
    d. If the deficits causing the debt reduced private investment spending, then future generations would be left with a smaller capital stock.

18. "Crowding out" refers to
    a. increased population pressures and arguments for zero population growth.
    b. the effects of government deficits on private investment spending.
    c. what happens at the start of the New York City marathon.
    d. the impact of higher prices on the multiplier.

19. Crowding out is likely to occur if the _____. (There may be more than one correct answer.)
    a. amount of private savings is unchanged
    b. economy is operating near full employment
    c. rate of unemployment is high
    d. aggregate supply curve is flat

20. Crowding in is more likely to occur when
    a. the economy is operating near full employment.
    b. prices are rising.
    c. the government lowers expenditures.
    d. there is substantial slack in the economy.

Test B

Circle T or F for true or false.

T F 1. A policy calling for continuous balance in the government's budget will help offset shifts in autonomous private demand.

T F 2. A structural deficit of zero is necessary if the equilibrium level of GDP is to equal the full-employment level of GDP.

T F 3. The "mix" of fiscal and monetary policy is of little importance for the composition of output.

T F 4. When the economy is in a recession, the structural deficit will be smaller than the actual deficit.

T F 5. The inflationary impact of any budget deficit depends on the conduct of monetary policy.

T F 6. Government deficits since 1980 mean that the ratio of national debt to GDP has never been higher than it is today.

T F 7. Interest payments on the national debt, whether to domestic citizens or foreigners, are not really a burden on future generations.

T F 8. A major limitation of the simple crowding-out argument is the assumption that the economy's total pool of savings is fixed.

T F 9. Crowding in is likely to occur when the economy is operating with slack employment, whereas crowding out is likely to occur at full employment.

T F 10. Government deficits may impose a real burden on future generations if, as a result of crowding out, there is less private investment and a smaller capital stock in the future.

Supplementary Exercises

1. Government Deficits and Interest Rates

Between 1957 and 1958, the federal government's budget shifted from a surplus of $2.3 billion to a deficit of $10.3 billion. This was the largest deficit since World War II and in dollar terms was bigger than any deficit during the Great Depression. At the same time, interest rates declined. The rate on three-month Treasury bills declined from an average of 3.267 percent in 1957 to 1.839 percent in 1958. The rate on three- to five-year securities fell from 3.62 percent to 2.90 percent.

Between 1974 and 1975, the federal government's budget deficit increased from $11.6 billion to $69.4 billion. Interest rates again declined. The rate on three-month Treasury bills declined from 7.886 percent to 5.838 percent, while the rate on three- to five-year securities declined more modestly from 7.81 percent to 7.55 percent.

Between 1981 and 1982, the federal government deficit increased dramatically from $58.8 billion to $135.5 billion. Again, interest rates declined. The rate on three-month Treasury bills declined from 14.029 percent to 10.686 percent. Interest rates on longer term government securities also declined.

Between 1991 and 1992, the federal government's deficit went from $210.4 billion to $298 billion, the largest year-to-year increase to date. Interest rates on long-term government bonds declined from 7.86 percent to 7.01 percent while rates on short-term government borrowing declined almost two percentage points from 5.42 percent to 3.45 percent.

How do you explain the seemingly contradictory results that larger deficits are associated with lower, not higher, interest rates? Do these observations prove that larger deficits will always be associated with lower interest rates?

2. **Repudiate the National Debt?**

If the national debt is so onerous, we could solve the problem by simply repudiating the debt; that is, we would make no more interest or principal payments on the outstanding debt.

Imagine that in keeping with democratic principles such a proposition were put to American voters. Who do you think would vote pro and who would vote con? Which side would win? Would the outcome of the vote be different if the debt were held entirely by foreigners? By banks and other financial institutions? (The Treasury publishes data on who holds the national debt in the *Treasury Bulletin*. These data are also published in the annual *Economic Report of the President*. You might want to look at these data and consider what would happen to depositors, shareholders, and pensioners, both current and prospective, if the national debt held by banks, corporations, and pension funds was suddenly worthless.)

Would repudiating the national debt make it easier or harder to sell government securities in the future?

Economics in Action

How Should One Project the State of the Federal Budget?

The Congressional Budget Office (CBO) was established to provide non-partisan, technical assistance to Congress as it wrestles with spending and tax proposals. In addition to background papers that examine the microeconomic implications of various programs, CBO also publishes regular macroeconomic analysis of the overall federal budget.

To help lawmakers, CBO publishes baseline budget projections of deficits and surpluses over a ten-year horizon. These baseline projections draw a lot of attention and play an important role in congressional policy debates. For example, the ten-year budget projections figured prominently in debate over the President Bush's tax cut proposals in the spring of 2001.

While considering the long-run implications of budget proposals is clearly a good thing, the way that CBO projects deficits and surpluses in the baseline budget projections is not above criticism. One should note that the construction of the baseline projections is constrained by law. In particular CBO has been instructed to assume that current laws continue without change. The result is that for many programs, the CBO projections assume that spending only increases to match inflation.

Economists Alan Auerbach and William Gale criticize these ten-year projections, arguing that they are "not always consistent with responsible budgeting practices" and often employ "a series of unrealistic assumption regarding future taxes and spending." While the CBO forecasts may accurately project current law, Auerbach and Gale argue that they are not a good "forecast of what is most likely to occur."

For example, with regard to annual discretionary spending, CBO procedures hold real spending constant at its current level. Auerbach and Gale argue that a more realistic approach would assume that inflation-adjusted spending grows in proportion to either GDP or population. Similarly CBO projections model tax receipts under current law. A number of recent tax cuts are scheduled to expire in the near future. The CBO procedure counts the increased tax revenue following the expiration of the tax cuts while most analysts assume that the tax cuts will be extended in some form. The CBO includes tax revenues under something called the Alternative Minimum Tax (AMT) while most analysts believe that Congress will modify the AMT as it begins to affect large numbers of taxpayers who were not intended to pay the AMT.

In addition Auerbach and Gale argue that a ten-year forecast is inherently arbitrary and policymakers should be concerned about trends over an even longer time horizon. Projections for Social Security and Medicare are relatively benign over the next ten years, as it is not until sometime between 2010 and 2020 that baby boomers will start to retire in significant numbers. Restricting one's view to ten years may obscure significant fiscal problems that lie just beyond the ten-year horizon.

1. What do you think is a good way to project the state of the federal budget?

2. How long a time horizon should be used for projections?

3. How would you project discretionary programs, the funding for which is determined as part of the annual federal budget process? Is projecting current law sufficient or do you think it more realistic to assume that spending is either a constant proportion of GDP or grows in proportion to population?

Sources: William G. Gale and Peter R. Orszag, "The Budget Outlook: Projections and Implications," *The Economists' Voice*. Vol. 1: No. 2, Article 6, 2004. This article is available online at http://www.bepress.com/ev/vol1/iss2/art6

To learn more about the Alternative Minimum Tax see Leonard E. Burman, William G. Gale, and Jeffrey Rohaly, "Unintended Consequences Run Amok—The Individual Alternative Minimum Tax," *Journal of Economic Perspectives, Spring 2003*, and Leonard E. Burman, William G. Gale, Matthew Hall, Jeff Rohaly, and Mohammed Adeel Saleem, "The Individual Alternative Minimum Tax: A Data Update," August 31, 2004, available online at http://www.taxpolicycenter.org/publications/template.cfm?PubID=411051.

Study Questions

1. What is the difference between the government's deficit and its debt? What is the link between the two?

2. What does the historical record show about when the federal government has run large deficits?

3. What does the historical record show about the ratio of federal government debt to GDP?

4. Why are policies to stabilize the deficit likely to destabilize the economy?

5. When is a budget deficit appropriate and why? When is it inappropriate?

6. What is the difference between the structural deficit and the actual deficit? Which is usually larger and why? Which is a more accurate measure of the stance of fiscal policy?

7. Does an increase in the deficit always indicate a move to expansionary fiscal policy? Why?

8. Does an increase in the deficit always lead to higher interest rates and more inflation? Why?

9. Why do economists argue that foreign-held debt imposes more of a burden than government debt held by Americans?

10. What is crowding out and crowding in? When is one more likely than the other and why?

11. Since deficits are a result of fiscal policy decisions, why does the impact of deficits depend upon the conduct of monetary policy?

Economics Online

Find out more about the magnitude of the national debt and how you can own a part of it from the Bureau of the Public Debt in the U.S. Treasury Department.

http://www.publicdebt.treas.gov/

The Congressional Budget Office posts all of its reports including historical data and periodic projections of the federal government budget on its Web site:

http://www.cbo.gov

The Trade-Off between Inflation and Unemployment

16

Important Terms and Concepts

Demand-side inflation

Supply-side inflation

Phillips curve

Stagflation caused by supply shocks

Self-correcting mechanism

Natural rate of unemployment

Vertical (long-run) Phillips curve

Trade-off between inflation and unemployment in the short run and in the long run

Rational expectations

Indexing (escalator clauses)

Real versus nominal interest rates

Learning Objectives
After completing this chapter, you should be able to:

- explain how prices can rise following either the rapid growth of aggregate demand or the sluggish growth of aggregate supply.

- explain what the Phillips curve is and what it is not.

- explain why the economy's self-correcting mechanism means that the economy's long-run choices lie along a vertical Phillips curve.

- explain how the accuracy of expectations about inflation can affect the slope of both the aggregate supply curve and the Phillips curve.

- discuss the implications of and evidence for the hypotheses of rational expectations.

- explain how and why one's views on appropriate aggregate demand policy are likely to depend upon one's views on

  ○ the social costs of inflation vs. unemployment.

  ○ the slope of the short-run Phillips curve.

  ○ how quickly inflationary expectations adjust.

  ○ the efficiency of the economy's self-correcting mechanism.

- discuss measures that have been advocated to reduce the natural rate of unemployment.

- discuss the advantages and disadvantages of universal indexing.

• Chapter Review

This chapter discusses the hard choices that policymakers must make when deciding how to respond to inflation or unemployment. Previous chapters discussed how changes in various tools of fiscal and monetary policy can be used to influence aggregate demand. This chapter uses that material to study the policy implications for fighting unemployment and inflation.

Here, as in many other areas of life, one cannot have one's cake and eat it too. Actions taken to reduce unemployment will often lead to higher rates of inflation, while actions to reduce inflation will often lead to higher rates of unemployment. Economists can help to define the nature of this trade-off, examine the factors that are responsible for it, and clarify the implications of different choices, but they cannot tell anyone which choice to make. In a democratic society, this decision is left to the political process.

Any shift in the aggregate demand or aggregate supply curve, whether induced by policy or not, is likely to affect both prices and output. The nature of the association between changes in prices and changes in output will depend upon which curve shifts. If fluctuations in economic activity are predominantly the result of shifts in the aggregate demand curve, then higher output will be

(1) associated with (higher/lower) levels of prices. The transition to higher prices is a period of inflation. A higher level of output means more employment and a (higher/lower) rate of unemployment. Hence, shifts in the aggregate demand curve imply that inflation and unemployment are (negatively/positively) correlated. That is, if you plotted the rate of unemployment on the horizontal axis and the rate of inflation on the vertical axis, the resulting curve, called the _____ curve, would have a (positive/negative) slope.

Data for the 1950s and 1960s are consistent with the view sketched above and seemed to imply that policymakers could choose between inflation and unemployment. In particular, it used to be thought that the Phillips curve implied that policymakers could permanently increase output beyond the level of full employment, or potential output, at the cost of only a small increase in the rate of inflation.

(2) Subsequent experience has shown that this view is (correct/incorrect). The Phillips curve represents the statistical correlation between inflation and unemployment. It ignores the implications of the economy's self-correcting mechanisms.

As we have seen, output beyond the level of potential output results in

(3) a(n) (inflationary/recessionary) gap. The economy's self-correcting mechanism will shift the aggregate supply curve to reestablish long-run equilibrium at the _____ rate of unemployment. The economy's long-run choices lie along a(n) _____ Phillips curve.

In the short run, shifts in the aggregate demand curve will move the economy up or down the short-run Phillips curve, but the economy's self-correcting mechanism implies that this trade-off is only temporary. How long this trade-off lasts depends upon the speed of the economy's self-correcting mechanism. Differing views about the relative costs of inflation and unemployment, the slope of the short-run Phillips curve, and the speed of the economy's self-correcting mechanism are an important part of differences in Keynesian and monetarist policy prescriptions.

Changes in money wages are an important determinant of shifts in the aggregate supply curve that lead an inflationary gap to self-destruct. It is the original increase in prices while wages are unchanged that induces firms to expand output. As workers recognize that the purchasing power of their money wages has declined, the subsequent increases in wages to restore real wages will lead to shifts in the aggregate supply curve. Rather than always being a step behind, workers can try to protect their real wages by anticipating the increase in prices. In this case the expectation of higher prices will lead to higher wages and a shift in the aggregate supply curve in anticipation of inflation.[1] Compared with cases where the aggregate supply curve did not shift, a shift in the aggregate demand curve accompanied by an expectations-induced shift in the aggregate supply curve will have a (larger/smaller) impact on output and a(n) _____ impact on prices. The result will be a (higher/lower) rate of inflation and the slope of the short-run Phillips curve will be (steeper/flatter).   (4)

Economists associated with the hypothesis of *rational expectations* have focused special attention on the formation of expectations. While much remains to be learned, these economists argue that errors in predicting inflation should not be systematic. An implication of this view is that, except for random elements, both the aggregate supply curve and the short-run Phillips curve will be vertical. Not only is there no long-run trade-off between inflation and unemployment, but, according to this view, there is also no systematic short-run trade-off.

Others are less convinced that expectations are rational in the sense of no systematic errors. These economists believe that people tend to underpredict inflation when it is rising and overpredict it when it is falling. Long-term contracts also make it difficult to adjust to changing expectations of inflation. These economists argue that policy measures to shift the aggregate demand curve can affect output and employment in the short run. But remember that these short-run impacts will eventually be constrained by the long-run Phillips curve, which is _____.   (5)

Most economists believe that aggregate demand policy will affect employment and inflation in the short run and will also affect the place where the economy ends up on the long-run Phillips curve. Thus, to fight a recession rather than to wait for the economy's self-correcting mechanism will mean more employment in the short run and is likely to mean more inflation in the long run as compared to a status quo policy that waits on the economy's self-correcting mechanisms. (See Figure 16-9 in the text.) Whether one wants to use aggregate demand policy or wait for natural processes depends on one's assessment of the costs of inflation and unemployment, the slope of the short-run Phillips curve,

---

[1]The story of workers trying to protect themselves against inflation seems to imply that labor is responsible for inflation. When the economy is booming, workers will be concerned about inflation, but firms will willingly pay higher wages to attract workers in a tight labor market. The real cause of inflation is not workers or firms but rather excessive aggregate demand.

the quickness with which inflationary expectations adjust, and the efficiency of the economy's self-correcting mechanisms.

A number of policies have been advocated in the hope that they will improve the inflation-unemployment trade-off. Increased efforts at education and job retraining are seen as efforts to reduce frictional unemployment and lower the natural rate of unemployment.

A number of individuals have argued that rather than trying to reduce the rate of inflation, we should simply learn to live with it and rely on automatic adjustments of monetary payments to reflect changes in prices, a process known as indexing. Inflation-linked adjustments of tax brackets, Social Security benefits, as well as other government transfer programs, and escalator clauses in wage

(6)   contracts are examples of _____. A number of observers also advocate this mechanism for interest rates.

Indexing does seem to offer some relief from many of the social costs of inflation. As workers, firms, and lenders scramble to protect themselves against anticipated future increases in prices,

(7)   current prices and interest rates will (increase/decrease) to reflect the expectation of inflation. If actual inflation turns out to be greater or less than expected, there will be a redistribution of wealth that many feel is essentially arbitrary. Uncertainty over future prices may make individuals and businesses extremely reluctant to enter into long-term contracts. Indexing appears to offer relief from these problems. Labor contracts and other agreements could be written in real rather than nominal terms, and arbitrary redistributions would be avoided because money payments would reflect actual, not expected, inflation. At the same time, there is concern that learning to live with inflation may make the economy (more/less) inflation prone.

Important Terms and Concepts Quiz

Choose the best definition for each of the following terms.

1. _____ Phillips curve
2. _____ Self-correcting mechanism
3. _____ Natural rate of unemployment
4. _____ Long-run Phillips curve
5. _____ Rational expectations
6. _____ Indexing

a. Graph depicting unemployment rate on horizontal axis and inflation rate on vertical axis
b. Vertical line at the natural rate of unemployment
c. Unemployment rate at full employment
d. Vertical line at natural rate of inflation
e. Forecasts that make optimal use of available and relevant data
f. Adjustments of monetary payments whenever a specified price index changes
g. The economy's way of curing inflationary and recessionary gaps

• Basic Exercises

This exercise is designed to illustrate the nature of the inflation-unemployment trade-off that policymakers must face when planning aggregate demand policy.

1. **Figure 16-1** shows an economy with a recessionary gap. Which of the following monetary and fiscal policies could be used to help eliminate this gap?

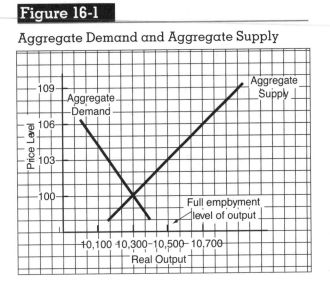

Figure 16-1

Aggregate Demand and Aggregate Supply

❏ open market (<u>purchase/sale</u>)

❏ (<u>increase/decrease</u>) in taxes

❏ (<u>increase/decrease</u>) in government transfer payments to individuals

❏ (<u>increase/decrease</u>) in government purchases of goods and services

2. Assume the full-employment level of income is $10,500 billion. Draw a new aggregate demand curve, representing one or more of the appropriate policies you identified in question 1 that will restore full employment for this economy. Following a shift in the aggregate demand curve, prices will rise to _____.

3. Consider the following statement:

"The increase in prices that resulted when we restored full employment was a small price to pay for the increased output. Why not try moving even farther along the aggregate supply curve? If we further stimulate the economy to lower unemployment we can increase output to, say, $10,700 billion and prices will only rise to 106. We can thus have a permanent increase in output of $200 billion every year in return for a one-time increase in prices of just under 3 percent. That's a pretty favorable trade-off." What is wrong with the reasoning of this argument?

4. **Figure 16-2** shows an economy following an adverse shift in the aggregate supply curve. Equilibrium used to be an output of $10,500 and a price level of 103. Answer the following questions to see how stabilization policy that shifts the aggregate demand curve is constrained in efforts to offset the adverse impact of the shift in the aggregate supply curve.

Figure 16-2

Aggregate Demand and Aggregate Supply

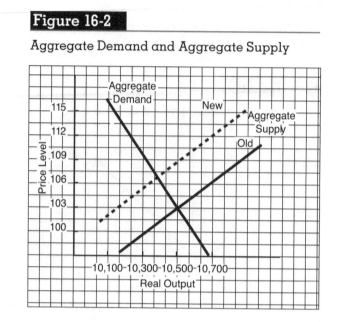

a. If there is to be no decline in employment, the government will need to implement (expansionary/restrictive) policies to shift the aggregate demand curve. The government could maintain employment, but at the cost of an increase in prices to _____.

b. Alternatively, the government could avoid any increase in prices. Such a decision would require (expansionary/restrictive) policies and would result in a new equilibrium level of output of _____.

• Self-Tests for Understanding

Test A

Circle the most appropriate answer.

1. If fluctuations in economic activity are caused by shifts in the aggregate demand curve, then
   a. prices and output will be negatively correlated.
   b. the short-run Phillips curve will be vertical.
   c. the long-run Phillips curve will have a negative slope.
   d. the rates of inflation and unemployment will tend to be negatively correlated.

2. If fluctuations in economic activity are the result of shifts in the aggregate supply curve, then
   a. prices and output will be positively correlated.
   b. the short-run Phillips curve will have a negative slope.
   c. the long-run Phillips curve will be horizontal.
   d. the rate of inflation and rate of unemployment will tend to be positively correlated.

3. The Phillips curve
   a. is a statistical relationship between unemployment and inflation when economic fluctuations are dominated by changes in the growth of aggregate demand.
   b. is the set of long-term equilibrium relationships between the rate of unemployment and the rate of inflation.
   c. is the third turn at the Indianapolis 500 Speedway.
   d. shows how nominal interest rate changes when expectations of inflation change.

4. The economy's self-correcting mechanisms mean that in the long run the Phillips curve is likely to
   a. have a negative slope.
   b. have a positive slope.
   c. be horizontal.
   d. be vertical.

5. The long-run Phillips curve will be vertical
   a. at the natural rate of inflation.
   b. at the point where real and nominal interest rates are equal.
   c. at the natural rate of unemployment.
   d. wherever the aggregate demand and aggregate supply curves intersect.

6. The positively sloped aggregate supply curve is drawn on the assumption that
   a. the cost of productive inputs remains unchanged in the short run as output changes.
   b. wages are fully indexed.
   c. the Phillips curve is never vertical.
   d. wage and price controls limit the impact of inflation.

7. An increase in wages, due either to inflation that has occurred in the past or inflation that is expected to occur in the future, can be modeled as a(n)
   a. upward shift in the aggregate supply curve.
   b. inward shift in the production possibilities frontier.
   c. downward shift in the aggregate demand curve.
   d. leftward shift in the long-run Phillips curve.

8. An increased emphasis on expectations of future inflation in wage settlements will lead to a _____ aggregate supply curve and a _____ Phillips curve.
   a. flatter; flatter
   b. flatter; steeper
   c. steeper; steeper
   d. steeper; flatter

9. Consider a shift to the right of the aggregate demand curve due to expansionary monetary and fiscal policy. Assume that the adoption of expansionary policies leads to expectations of inflation that induce a simultaneous shift in the aggregate supply curve. The resulting change in output will be _____ if there were no shift in the aggregate supply curve.
   a. smaller than
   b. the same as
   c. larger than

10. Under the same conditions as question 9, the resulting change in prices will be _____ if there were no shift in the aggregate supply curve.
    a. smaller than
    b. the same as
    c. larger than

11. Stabilization policy faces a trade-off between inflation and unemployment in the short run because changes in monetary and fiscal policy have their most immediate impact on the
    a. aggregate supply curve.
    b. Phillips curve.
    c. production possibilities frontier.
    d. aggregate demand curve.

12. Which of the following are necessary for expectations to meet the economist's definition of rational expectations? (There may be more than one correct answer.)
    a. They are based on relevant and available information.
    b. They can only be made by economists and statisticians.
    c. There are no systematic errors.
    d. They are always correct.

13. A strong believer in rational expectations would be surprised by which one of the following occurrences?
    a. An announcement by the Fed that it will increase the rate of growth of the money supply leads to expectations of higher inflation.
    b. Plans to lower taxes give rise to expectations of higher prices.
    c. Plans to fight inflation by restrictive policy succeed in reducing the rate of inflation with no increase in unemployment.
    d. An examination of the record shows that people consistently underestimate the rate of inflation during periods when it is increasing.

14. The hypothesis of rational expectations implies that increases in output beyond the level of potential output can be produced by
    a. expected increases in prices.
    b. unexpected increases in prices only.
    c. any increase in prices whether expected or not.
    d. preannounced increases in the money supply or reductions in taxes.

15. Which of the following is not a feasible alternative for aggregate demand policy following an adverse shift of the supply curve to the left?
    a. Do nothing and initially experience both higher prices and lower output.
    b. Avoid the reduction in output at the cost of even higher prices.
    c. Avoid the increase in prices at the cost of an even greater decline in output.
    d. Avoid both the reduction in output and increase in prices by using fiscal policy to shift the aggregate demand curve and monetary policy to shift the aggregate supply curve.

16. Restrictive monetary and fiscal policy adopted to reduce the rate of inflation will work quicker and have a smaller impact on unemployment when
    a. changes in inflationary expectations take a long time.
    b. the long-run Phillips curve is vertical.
    c. expectations of inflation adjust quickly to the change in macro policy.
    d. the natural rate of unemployment equals the natural rate of inflation.

17. Who is most likely to advocate government action to eliminate a recessionary gap? The economist who believes
    a. the short-run Phillips curve is quite steep.
    b. expectations of inflation will adjust rapidly to lower rates of inflation.
    c. we should pay any price to avoid higher inflation.
    d. the short-run Phillips curve is fairly flat.

18. If job retraining or other measures are successful in reducing the natural rate of unemployment, then the
    a. long-run Phillips curve will shift to the left.
    b. aggregate demand curve will become less steep.
    c. short-run Phillips curve will become vertical.
    d. natural rate of inflation will increase.

19. A general policy of indexing
    a. is an attempt to shift the aggregate supply curve downward and to the right.
    b. would help to balance the federal government's budget.
    c. is an attempt to ease the social cost of inflation.
    d. runs little risk of accelerating the rate of inflation.

20. Which of the following is an example of indexing?
    a. tax penalties on firms that grant excessive wage increases
    b. the adjustment of nominal interest rates in response to expectations of inflation
    c. the average change in prices on the New York Stock Exchange
    d. increases in Social Security checks computed on the basis of changes in the consumer price index

Test B

Circle T or F for true or false.

T   F   1. Inflation occurs only as a result of shifts in the aggregate demand curve.

T   F   2. In contrast to expansionary monetary or fiscal policy, an autonomous increase in private spending will increase output without increasing prices.

T F 3. If fluctuations in economic activity are predominantly the result of shifts in the aggregate supply curve, the rate of unemployment and the rate of inflation will tend to be positively correlated.

T F 4. The economy's self-correcting mechanism implies that the only long-run policy choices for the economy lie along a vertical Phillips curve.

T F 5. The natural rate of unemployment is given by the position of the long-run Phillips curve.

T F 6. A belief that the economy's self-correcting mechanism works quickly is an argument in favor of activist demand-management policy.

T F 7. Expectations of inflation that lead to higher wages will be somewhat self-fulfilling as the increase in wages shifts the aggregate supply curve.

T F 8. One can minimize the inflationary effects of fighting a recession by using fiscal policy rather than monetary policy.

T F 9. Following an adverse shift in the aggregate supply curve, aggregate demand policies can stop the rise in prices with no increase in unemployment.

T F 10. The economy's self-correcting mechanism means that, in the face of a recessionary gap, output and prices will eventually be the same with or without expansionary stabilization policy.

● Economics in Action

How Natural Is the Natural Rate?

The experience of the 1990s has led a number of economists to refine their views of the natural rate of unemployment. Based on estimates from the late 1980s or early 1990s, many would have expected that an unemployment rate of under 5 percent would have been accompanied by significant inflation. Instead, as the rate of unemployment fell from 7.5 percent in 1992 to under 4 percent by late 2000, the rate of inflation decreased rather than increased. For much of 1998, inflation as measured by the CPI was only 1.5 percent. Although inflation rose somewhat in 1999 and 2000, it was still quite low by historical standards, especially when viewed in light of the low rate of unemployment.

What happened? Has the trade-off between unemployment and inflation vanished? As the economy recovers from the 2001 recession, should policy again aim for a rate of unemployment of 4 percent or even lower?

Some argued that while there may still be a trade-off between unemployment and inflation, the "new economy" meant a dramatic decline in the natural rate of unemployment. Advocates of this view argue that new information technologies lowered the natural rate of unemployment as they increased growth in productivity. In addition, increased international competition weakened the resolve of unions while stiffening the spine of management engaged in wage negotiations.

Economist Robert J. Gordon believes that much of the experience of the 1990s was related to good luck, fortuitous events that are unlikely to be as favorable over the long run. According to Gordon, falling food prices, reductions in the rate of increase of the cost of medical care, and cheap imports were an important part of the good inflation news in the 1990s but are not likely to be factors that one can count on continuing forever.

Economist Robert Hall argues that our good fortune reflects well-executed monetary policy. He believes that the best policy for central bankers is "to set clear targets for inflation and stick by them . . . If the [Federal Reserve] convinces traders in financial markets that inflation will be low and steady, the economy will gravitate toward the lowest possible unemployment rate."

Economists Lawrence Katz and Alan Kreuger have suggested that 4 to 4.5 percent may be as low as one should aim for. They argue that the decline from 7.5 percent to under 4.5 percent was relatively easy as employers could hire from students, spouses, and laid-off workers. Katz and Kreuger point to the increasing proportion of long-term unemployment as the rate of unemployment fell and argue that once the rate of unemployment is at 4 to 4.5 percent, many people who are still unemployed will have a hard time meeting labor force needs as they may have obsolete skills and suffer from physical or mental limitations.

Some, like economist James Stock, argue that while there is a link between inflation and overall economic activity, one needs broader measures than just unemployment. Stock points out that in the late 1990s while the rate of unemployment was low suggesting possible inflationary pressures, other indicators such as plant utilization still showed significant capacity.

1. What has happened to the rate of inflation recently?

2. What do you think the value of the natural rate of unemployment is?

3. If you were responsible for macroeconomic policy, what if anything should policy do to move the economy toward the natural rate of unemployment?

SOURCE: Michael M. Weinstein, "Unemployment's Natural Rate May Have a Mind of Its Own," *New York Times*, April 22, 1999; Stuart Silverstein, "Some Economists Question Link Between Wages and Inflation," *Los Angeles Times*, January 14, 2001.

Study Questions

1. Why does the correlation between inflation and unemployment depend upon the source of macroeconomic fluctuations?

2. Does the Phillips curve offer macroeconomic policymakers a menu of choices between the rate of unemployment and inflation? Why or why not?

3. What is meant by the statement that the economy's self-correcting mechanisms mean that in the long run, the Phillips curve is vertical?

4. What is the natural rate of unemployment?

5. How does the expectation of future inflation and the expectations-related shifts in the aggregate supply curve affect the Phillips curve?

6. How can expectations of inflation be rational if they are never accurate?

7. What sort of policies might reduce the natural rate of unemployment?

8. Should wages and interest rates be fully indexed?

9. Should stabilization policy aim to reduce inflation to zero? Why or why not?

10. Has the natural rate of unemployment changed in recent years? If so, how and why?

● Economics Online

How accurate are expectations of inflation? Are there systematic errors when inflation is rising or falling? You can access two surveys of expectations of inflation online.

The Livingston Survey, begun by Joseph Livingston in 1946, summarizes the inflation forecasts of economists from industry, government, banking, and academia. The Livingston Survey data are available online from the Federal Reserve Bank of Philadelphia:

http://www.phil.frb.org/econ/liv/index.html

The Federal Reserve Bank of St. Louis posts data on inflation expectations from the University of Michigan survey of consumers. Data on consumer inflation expectations is found under the "Business/Fiscal" heading at:

http://research.stlouisfed.org/fred2/categories/98

The U.S. government now issues inflation-indexed bonds. Find out more about inflation-indexed bonds from the Bureau of the Public Debt, U.S. Treasury.

http://www.treasurydirect.gov/instit/annceresult/tipscpi/tipscpi.htm

International Trade and Comparative Advantage

17

Important Terms and Concepts

"Cheap foreign labor" argument

Imports

Exports

Specialization

Mutual gains from trade

Absolute advantage

Comparative advantage

Mercantilism

Tariff

Quota

Export subsidy

Trade adjustment assistance

Infant-industry argument

Strategic trade protection

Dumping

Learning Objectives
After completing this chapter, you should be able to:

- list the important factors that lead countries to trade with one another.

- explain how voluntary trade, even if it does not increase total production, can be mutually beneficial to the trading partners.

- explain in what ways international and intranational trade are similar and dissimilar.

- distinguish between absolute and comparative advantage.

- explain how absolute advantage and comparative advantage are related to the location and slope of a country's per capita production possibilities frontier.

- explain how trade means that a country's consumption possibilities can exceed its production possibilities.

- compare the advantages and disadvantages of tariffs and quotas.

- analyze the arguments used to advocate trade restrictions.

- explain the role of adjustment assistance in a country favoring free trade.

- explain the fallacy in the "cheap foreign labor" argument.

• Chapter Review

The material in this chapter discusses the basic economic forces that influence the international division of labor in the production of goods and services and the resulting pattern of international trade. Trade between cities or states within a single country is, in principle, no different than trade between nations. Economists and others spend more time studying international trade rather than intranational trade for several reasons: International trade involves more than one government with a resulting host of political concerns; it usually involves more than one currency; and the mobility of labor and capital between nations is typically more difficult than within nations.

Exchange rates—that is, how much of one country's currency it takes to buy one unit of another country's currency—are an important determinant of international trade and will be discussed in the next chapter. However, the real terms of trade—how many import goods a country can get indirectly through export production rather than through direct domestic production—are the important measure of the benefits of trade, and they are considered here in some detail.

Individual countries can try to meet the consumption needs of their citizens without trade by producing everything their populations need. Alternatively, they can specialize in the production of fewer commodities and trade for commodities they do not produce. Even if there were no differences between countries, specializing and trading would still make sense if there were important economies

(1) of _____— in production.

An important reason for trade is that differences in climate, oil deposits, minerals, and other natural resources, as well as differences in labor inputs and productive capital, will affect the efficiency

(2) with which countries can produce different goods. It is the law of (absolute/comparative) advantage that then indicates where countries should concentrate their production to maximize the potential gains from trade.

Assume country A can produce 80,000 bushels of wheat if it produces one less car, while country B can produce only 70,000 bushels of wheat. For the same world production of cars, world production

(3) of wheat will increase if country (A/B) produced ten fewer cars and country _____ produced ten more cars. (World wheat production would increase by _____ bushels.) In this case country A has a comparative advantage in the production of _____.[1]

Looking only at its own domestic production, the opportunity cost of one more car in country A is

(4) _____ bushels of wheat. Country B can produce one more car by giving up only _____ bushels of wheat. Thus it should not be surprising if country B concentrates on the production of _____ and trades with country A, which concentrates on the production of _____.[2]

---

[1]Note that we have said nothing so far about absolute advantage. For example, if it takes 300 labor hours to produce one car or 70,000 bushels of wheat in country B and 600 labor hours to produce 1 car or 80,000 bushels of wheat in country A, country B has an absolute advantage in the production of both goods while country A still has a comparative advantage in the production of wheat.
[2]Does the law of comparative advantage imply that all countries should specialize in the production of just a few commodities? No, it does not, for several reasons. One important reason is that production possibilities frontiers are likely to be curved rather than straight lines. The implica-

It is also important to realize that comparative advantage is not a static concept. The mix of industries that maximizes a country's comparative advantage is not something that can be determined once for all time. Rather, there will need to be continual adjustments in response to innovations and competition, both domestically and abroad. Countries that try to isolate themselves from foreign competition have usually ended up with stagnating industries and incomes.

As countries concentrate production on those goods in which they have a comparative advantage, equilibrium world prices and trade flows—that is, exports and imports—will be determined at the point where world demand equals world supply, not at the intersection of domestic demand and supply curves. Advanced courses in international trade show how prices derived under conditions of free trade will lead competitive, profit-maximizing firms to exploit the comparative advantage of individual countries and help to achieve an efficient allocation of resources.

Most countries do not have unrestricted free trade. Rather, imports are often restricted by the use of _____ and _____, and exports are often promoted through the use (5) of export _____. Tariffs reduce the quantity of imports by raising their _____ while quotas raise the price of imports by restricting _____. Either a tariff or a quota could be used to achieve the same reduction in imports, but the choice between the two has other consequences.

Tariff revenues accrue directly to the _____ while the benefits of higher prices (6) under a quota are likely to accrue to private producers, both foreign and domestic. (The government might be able to capture some of these profits by auctioning import licenses, but this is not usually done.)

Tariffs still require foreign suppliers to compete among themselves. This competition will favor the survival of (high/low) -cost foreign suppliers. What about domestic firms? They (do/do not) have to (7) pay the tariff, so high-cost domestic suppliers (can/cannot) continue in business. Quotas are apt to be distributed on almost any grounds except economic efficiency and thus have no automatic mechanism that works in favor of low-cost foreign suppliers.

Why do countries impose tariffs and quotas? Many trade restrictions reflect the successful pleadings of high-cost domestic suppliers. Free trade and the associated reallocation of productive resources in line with the law of comparative advantage would call for the elimination of these firms in their traditional lines of business. It is not surprising that managers and workers resist these changes. If everyone is to benefit from the increased output opportunities offered by free trade, then a program of trade _____ assistance will be necessary to help those most affected by the (8) realignment of productive activities.

---

tion of the curved frontier is that the opportunity cost of cars in terms of wheat for country B will rise as B produces more cars. Simultaneously, the opportunity cost of cars in terms of wheat for country A will fall as A concentrates on wheat. In equilibrium, the opportunity cost, or slope of the production possibilities frontier, in both countries will be equal. At this point neither country has an incentive for further specialization. Exactly where this point will occur will be determined by world demand and supply for cars and wheat.

(9) Other traditional justifications for trade restrictions include the national _____
argument and the _____ -industries argument. In both cases it is extremely difficult to
separate firms with legitimate claims from those looking for a public handout. In recent years some
have argued that the threat of trade restrictions should be used in a strategic manner to convince
others not to impose restrictions.

Much of the free trade fuss in the United States is concerned about competing with low-cost
foreign producers who pay workers lower wages. Concerns about wages need to be joined with
measures of productivity. A clear understanding of comparative advantages shows that the standard

(10) of living of workers in (<u>the exporting/the importing/both</u>) country(ies) can rise as a result of
specialization and trade. Even countries with high wages can benefit from trade when high wages
are associated with high productivity and trade induces adjustments in the structure of worldwide
production consistent with the principle of _____ advantage.

Important Terms and Concepts Quiz

Choose the most appropriate definition for each of the following terms.

1. _____ Imports
2. _____ Exports
3. _____ Specialization
4. _____ Absolute advantage
5. _____ Comparative advantage
6. _____ Mercantilism
7. _____ Tariff
8. _____ Quota
9. _____ Export subsidy
10. _____ Trade adjustment assistance
11. _____ Infant-industry argument
12. _____ Strategic trade policy
13. _____ Dumping

a. Maximum quantity that can be imported per unit of time
b. Threats to implement protectionist policies designed to promote free trade
c. Selling goods in a foreign market at higher prices than those charged at home
d. Domestically produced goods sold abroad
e. Selling goods in a foreign market at lower prices than those charged at home
f. Tax on imports
g. Decision by a country to emphasize production of particular commodities
h. Provision of special aid to those workers and firms harmed by foreign competition
i. Ability of one country to produce a good less inefficiently (relative to other goods) than another country
j. Foreign-produced goods purchased domestically
k. Tariff protection for new industries, giving them time to mature
l. Payment by the government that enables domestic firms to lower prices to foreign buyers
m. Ability of one country to produce a good using fewer resources than another country requires
n. Doctrine arguing that exports are good while imports are bad

• Basic Exercises

This exercise is designed to review the law of comparative advantage.

1. Assume that the hours of labor shown below are the only input necessary to produce calculators and backpacks in Canada and Japan.

	Calculators	Backpacks
Canada	4	5
Japan	2	3

   Which country has an absolute advantage in the production of calculators? _____

   Which country has an absolute advantage in the production of backpacks? _____

2. If labor in Canada is reallocated from the production of calculators to the production of backpacks, how many calculators must be given up in order to produce one more backpack? _____ What about Japan? How many calculators must it give up in order to produce one more backpack? _____ Which country has a comparative advantage in the production of backpacks? _____ Which country has a comparative advantage in the production of calculators? _____ According to the law of comparative advantage, _____ should concentrate on the production of backpacks while _____ concentrates on the production of calculators.

3. Assume each country has 12 million hours of labor input that initially is evenly distributed in both countries between the production of backpacks and calculators: 6 million for each. Fill in the following table of outputs.

	Output of Calculators	Output of Backpacks
Canada	_____	_____
Japan	_____	_____
Total	_____	_____

4. Assume that Canada now reallocates 2.4 million labor hours away from the production of calculators and into backpacks. The change in Canadian calculator output is –_____. The change in Canadian backpack output is +_____.

5. What reallocation of labor in Japan is necessary to be sure that world output of calculators (Japan plus Canada) remains unchanged? _____ labor hours. What are the changes in Japanese output from this reallocation? The change in Japanese calculator output is +_____. The change in Japanese backpack output is –_____.

6. By assumption, the world output of calculators has not changed, but the net change in the world output of backpacks is a(n) (increase/decrease) of _____ backpacks.

7. Questions 3 through 6 showed how specialization according to the law of comparative advantage could increase the output of backpacks without decreasing the output of calculators. This is just one possibility. Adjustments in line with the law of comparative advantage could increase the output of both goods. Suppose Japan had reallocated 1,350,000 labor hours to the production of calculators. Fill in the following table and compare total outputs with your answers to question 3.

Calculators

	Labor Input (millions of hours)	Output
Canada	3.60	_____
Japan	7.35	_____
Total		_____

Backpacks

	Labor Input (millions of hours)	Output
Canada	8.40	_____
Japan	4.65	_____
Total		_____

8. Work through questions 4 and 5 again, but assume this time that the initial reallocation of 2.4 million labor hours in Canada is away from backpacks and to the production of calculators. Calculate the reallocation in Japan necessary to maintain world backpack output. What happens to the total output of calculators? Why?

9. Assume that the production of backpacks in Canada requires 6 hours rather than 5 hours. Work through the original output levels in question 3 and the reallocation of labor in questions 4 and 5 to see what now happens to total output of calculators and backpacks. Does your answer to question 6 differ from your original answer? Why or why not??

● Self-Tests for Understanding

Test A

Circle the most appropriate answer.

1. Even if there were no differences in natural resources, climate, labor skills, etc., nations would still find it advantageous to specialize production and trade
   a. because of differences in absolute advantage.
   b. to take advantage of economies of scale.
   c. to take advantage of differences in national currencies.
   d. when inflation rates differ.

2. International trade is different from intranational trade because of
   a. political issues that arise from different governments.
   b. limitations of the ability of labor and capital to move between countries compared to their ability to move within countries.
   c. the use of different currencies.
   d. all of the above.

3. Economists argue that
   a. efficiency in international trade requires countries to produce those goods in which they have an absolute advantage.
   b. efficiency in international trade requires countries to produce those goods in which they have a comparative advantage.
   c. efficiency in international trade requires countries that have an absolute advantage in the production of all goods to become self-sufficient.
   d. countries with export surpluses will have a comparative advantage in the production of all goods.

4. Using per capita production possibilities frontiers showing the production of clothes on the vertical axis and cars on the horizontal axis, the absolute advantage in the production of clothes would be determined by comparing
   a. the slope of the per capita production possibilities frontiers.
   b. where the per capita production possibilities frontiers cut the horizontal axis.
   c. the area under the per capita production possibilities frontiers.
   d. where the per capita production possibilities frontiers cut the vertical axis.

5. Using per capita production possibilities frontiers described above, the comparative advantage in the production of clothes would be determined by comparing
   a. the slope of the per capita production possibilities frontiers.
   b. where the per capita production possibilities frontiers cut the horizontal axis.
   c. the area under the per capita production possibilities frontiers.
   d. where the per capita production possibilities frontiers cut the vertical axis.

6. Which of the following is an example of comparative advantage?
   a. Wages of textile workers are lower in India than in America.
   b. The slope of the production possibilities frontier between tomatoes and airplanes differs for Mexico and the United States.
   c. American workers must work an average of only 500 hours to purchase a car, while Russian workers must work 4,000 hours.
   d. In recent years, Swedish income per capita has exceeded that of the United States.

7. Specialization and free trade consistent with the law of comparative advantage will enable
   a. increased world production of all traded goods.
   b. increases in the standard of living for workers in both exporting and importing countries.
   c. countries to consume at some point outside their production possibilities frontier.
   d. all of the above.

8. From a worldwide perspective, economic efficiency is enhanced if production and trade is organized according to the law of comparative advantage. Economic efficiency within a single country is enhanced if regional production and trade are organized according to
   a. absolute advantage.
   b. the political power of particular states or regions.
   c. which regions have the highest unemployment.
   d. comparative advantage.

9. If shoes can be produced with two hours of labor input in Italy and three hours of labor input in the United States, then it is correct to say that
   a. Italy has an absolute advantage in the production of shoes.
   b. Italy has a comparative advantage in the production of shoes.
   c. the United States has an absolute advantage in the production of shoes.
   d. the United States has a comparative advantage in the production of shoes.

10. Assuming that shoes are produced as in question 9 and shirts can be produced with four hours of labor in both countries, then it is correct to say that
   a. the United States has a comparative advantage in the production of shirts.
   b. Italy has a comparative advantage in the production of shirts.
   c. Italy has an absolute advantage in the production of shirts.
   d. the United States has an absolute advantage in the production of shirts.

11. Under free trade, world prices for exports and imports would be such that
   a. countries would specialize production along lines of absolute advantage.
   b. all countries would show a slight export surplus.
   c. the quantity supplied by exporters would just equal the quantity demanded by importers.
   d. every country would be self-sufficient in all goods.

12. Which one of the following is not intended to restrict trade?
   a. export subsidies
   b. tariffs
   c. quotas

13. A tariff affects trade by
   a. imposing a tax on imported goods.
   b. limiting the quantity of goods that can be imported.
   c. offering a subsidy to producers who export for foreign sales.
   d. the voluntary actions of foreign manufacturers to limit their exports.

14. A quota affects trade by
   a. imposing a tax on imported goods.
   b. limiting the quantity of goods that can be imported.
   c. offering a subsidy to producers who export for foreign sales.
   d. the voluntary action of foreign manufacturers to limit their exports.

15. Which of the following is an example of a tariff?
    a. Japanese car manufacturers agree to limit exports to the United States.
    b. U.S. law limits the imports of cotton shirts to 20 million.
    c. Television manufacturers outside Great Britain must pay a 10 percent duty on each set they ship to Great Britain.
    d. Foreign bicycle manufacturers receive a rebate of taxes from their own government for each bicycle they export.

16. One economic advantage of tariffs over quotas is that tariffs
    a. typically give preferential treatment to long-term suppliers.
    b. expose high-cost domestic producers to competition.
    c. force foreign suppliers to compete.
    d. help avoid destructive price wars.

17. The imposition of a tariff on steel will lead to all but which one of the following?
    a. a lower volume of steel imports
    b. higher domestic steel prices
    c. reduced domestic demand for steel
    d. a smaller market share for domestic producers

18. The imposition of a quota on steel will lead to all but which one of the following?
    a. a lower volume of steel imports
    b. increased domestic production of steel
    c. lower domestic steel prices
    d. reduced domestic demand for steel

19. A quota that limits the importation of foreign computer chips is likely to be in the interest of all but which of the following? (There may be more than one correct answer.)
    a. domestic chip manufacturers
    b. domestic computer manufacturers
    c. labor employed domestically in the production of computer chips
    d. consumers interested in buying computers

20. Which one of the following is a justification for fewer trade restrictions?
    a. Some industries would be so vital in times of war that we cannot rely on foreign suppliers.
    b. A temporary period of protection is necessary until an industry matures and is able to compete with foreign suppliers.
    c. Competition from foreign suppliers will help keep prices to consumers low.
    d. The threat of trade restrictions may prevent the adoption of restrictions by others.

Test B

Circle T or F for true or false.

T   F   1. A country with an absolute advantage in producing all goods is better off being self-sufficient than engaging in trade.

T   F   2. A country with an absolute advantage in the production of all goods should only export commodities.

T F 3. The unequal distribution of natural resources among countries is one important reason why countries trade.

T F 4. Which of two countries has a comparative advantage in the production of wine rather than cloth can be determined by comparing the slopes of the production possibilities frontiers of both countries.

T F 5. It is possible for all countries to simultaneously expand exports and reduce imports.

T F 6. Tariffs act like a tax on imported goods and have no impact on the price of similar goods that are produced by domestic firms.

T F 7. A quota on shirts would reduce the volume of imported shirts by specifying the maximum quantity of shirts that can be imported.

T F 8. The infant-industry argument is used to justify protection for industries that are vital in times of war.

T F 9. Dumping of goods by the United States on Japanese markets would necessarily harm Japanese consumers.

T F 10. If foreign labor is paid less, foreign producers will always be able to undersell American producers.

| Appendix | *Supply, Demand, and Pricing in World Trade*

This exercise is designed to illustrate the material in the Appendix to Chapter 17 and give you practice in understanding how world prices are determined and in analyzing the impact of quotas and tariffs. To simplify the analysis, the question assumes that the world is composed of only two countries, the United States and India.

1. **Figure 17-1** shows the demand and supply for shirts in the United States and India. Prices in India are expressed in terms of American dollars. In the absence of international trade, what are the domestic price and quantity of shirts in India and the United States?

	Price	Quantity
India	_____	_____
United States	_____	_____

2. Assume now that India and the United States are free to trade without restrictions. What is the world price of shirts? _____. At this price what happens to domestic demand, production, exports, and imports?

	Price	Domestic Demand	Domestic Production	Exports	Imports
India	_____	_____	_____	_____	_____
United States	_____	_____	_____	_____	_____

Figure 17-1

Demand and Supply: Shirts

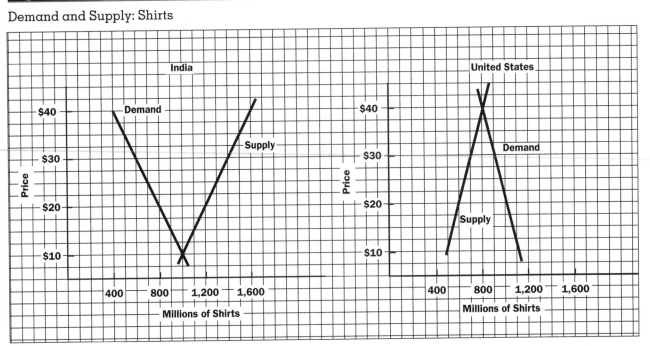

3. Assume that American producers are able to persuade the government to impose a quota limiting shirt imports to 200 million. Following imposition of the quota, what happens to prices, demand, production, and trade?

	Price	Domestic Demand	Domestic Production	Exports	Imports
India	_____	_____	_____	_____	_____
United States	_____	_____	_____	_____	_____

Compared to the free trade equilibrium described in question 2, shirt prices have increased in (India/the United States) and decreased in _____. The production of shirts has increased in _____ and decreased in _____.

4. What tariff would have yielded the same results as the quota of 200 million shirts? _____.

5. Discuss the reasons for choosing between a tariff and a quota.

• Supplementary Exercises

1. Demand and supply for widgets in Baulmovia and Bilandia are as follows:

Baulmovia
   Demand: $Q = 156 - 7P$
   Supply: $Q = -44 + 18P$

Bilandia
   Demand: $Q = 320 - 10P$
   Supply: $Q = -20 + 10P$

   a. In the absence of trade, what are the price and quantity of widgets in Baulmovia? In Bilandia?

   b. With free trade, what is the one common world price for widgets? Which country exports widgets? Which country imports widgets? What is the volume of exports and imports?

   c. Manufacturers in the importing country have convinced the government to impose a tariff on widget imports of $4.50 a widget. What will happen to trade and the price of widgets in the two countries?

   d. What quota would have the same impact on trade?

   e. What factors might lead one to prefer a tariff over a quota?

2. This exercise offers another review of the law of comparative advantage.

Figure 17-2

Arcadia and Ricardia: Production Possibilities Frontiers

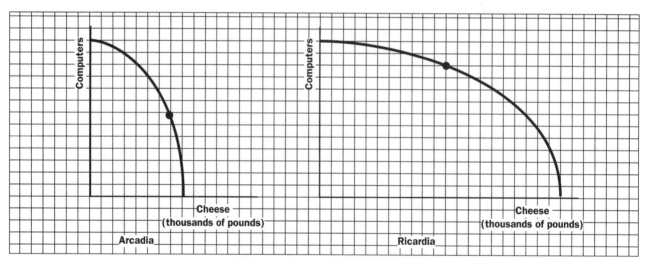

Figure 17-2 shows the production possibilities frontier for Arcadia and Ricardia. For every computer they buy, citizens of each country want to consume 1,000 pounds of cheese. As a result production and consumption in each country takes place at the dot on the frontier. Some have argued that citizens in both countries could consume more of both goods if each country concentrated production on the good in which it has a comparative advantage and traded for the other good.

In order to construct a numerical example, assume that at the dot the slope of the PPF for Arcadia is –2 while the slope of the PPF for Ricardia is –1/2. (Arcadia must give up two computers for an additional 1,000 pounds of cheese, while Ricardia can increase the production of cheese by 2,000 pounds at the cost of only one less computer.)

a. Which country has a comparative advantage in the production of computers? _____

b. Which country has a comparative advantage in the production of cheese? _____

c. Construct a numerical example that shows how what changes in production and what pattern of trade would allow both countries to consume outside their PPF.

3. Cimonoce is a small country that produces wine and cloth. The production possibilities frontier for Cimonoce is

$$W = 324 - C^2$$

where W = millions of barrels of wine and C = millions of bolts of cloth.

a. Use a piece of graph paper. Label the vertical axis "wine" and the horizontal axis "cloth." Draw the production possibilities frontier.

b. Since Cimonoce is a small country, it can export or import cloth or wine without affecting world prices. World prices are such that Cimonoce can export one million barrels of wine for 750,000 bolts of cloth or it can export 750,000 bolts of cloth for one million barrels of wine. The government's chief economist argues that regardless of consumption preferences, Cimonoce should produce 14.4 million bolts of cloth and 10.8 million barrels of wine. Do you agree? Why? (Hint: Consider what a graph of consumption possibilities looks like. For any production combination of wine and cloth, Cimonoce's consumption possibilities are given by a negatively sloped straight line through the production point. The slope of the consumption possibilities line reflects world prices. A movement up the straight line to the left of the production point would imply exporting cloth in order to import and consume more wine. A movement down the straight line to the right would reflect exporting wine in order to import and consume more cloth. Exactly where Cimonoce chooses to consume is a matter of preferences, but its choice is constrained by its consumption possibilities line, which in turn is determined by Cimonoce's production choice and world prices for cloth and wine. Why does the production point 10.8 million barrels of wine and 14.4 million bolts of cloth offer the greatest consumption possibilities?)

Economics in Action

Trade in Textiles

Since the end of World War II there has been a conscious effort to lower barriers to international trade. Part of this effort has been driven by the intellectual arguments in favor of the benefits of free trade and part has been driven by a strong feeling that protectionist pressures in the 1930s added to the depth and severity of the Great Depression. Much of the advance to date has come in the form of reduced tariff barriers resulting from complicated, multinational negotiations and treaties.

Sensitive areas where tariff reductions have been more difficult include textiles and clothing along with trade in agricultural products. Other areas of concern include trade in steel, services, and intellectual property like books and movies. With tariffs in many developed countries now eliminated or very low, increasing attention is being paid to nontariff barriers that limit trade. Nontariff barriers include policies like quotas, excessively detailed and time-consuming processing at ports of entry, and the strict adherence to rules and regulations that serve only to protect domestic producers.

Reaching an agreement on freer trade in textiles in the mid-1990s was only possible when it was proposed that changes be made over a 10-year period of adjustment. Thus, a complicated system of tariffs and quotas that had evolved since 1950 was scheduled for elimination at the beginning of 2005. The production of textiles has been important to many developing countries and full implementation of the 1995 Multi-Fibre Agreement was seen as a major concession that would aid economic development. One estimate projected a gain of 27 million jobs in developing countries from the elimination of tariffs and quotas on textiles.

As January 2005 approached, a number of countries were having second thoughts. Developing countries that had secured preferential quota arrangements were now facing international competition. The big new competitor was China, which would be able to export textiles without limit. The rules allowed for "safeguard" tariffs against Chinese textile exports that would permit an additional three years of adjustment. At the end of 2004, there were cries in the United States and Europe to adopt safeguard tariffs to resist an expected surge in textile exports from China.

Other voices argued for restraint, pointing out that the magnitude of expected adjustments in 2005 was due in part to most countries waiting to the last moment to eliminate quotas. While it appears that bulk production of basic clothes may concentrate in Asia, primarily China, India, and Pakistan, there were those who expected production for the fashion industry to concentrate in Turkey and Latin America.

Textile production in Africa was of special concern as it did not appear that African producers had the efficiency of Asian production or the proximity of Turkey and Latin America to markets in Europe and the United States. The economic literature on international trade argues that benefits within a country should be sufficient to provide trade adjustment help to workers in industries that cannot compete following a move to freer trade. The same principle ought to apply internationally, but it is not clear how such help might be organized.

1. What has happened to trade in textiles? Who have been the winners and losers from the elimination of tariffs and quotas? How large is the increase in textile exports from China? What about exports from other countries? Have any countries adopted safeguard tariffs and if so, under what conditions?

Sources: "Textile and China," *The Washington Post*, December 16, 2004; "Textile producers weave a web to restrict China: Less efficient poor nations fear they will lose rich-world trade when the global quota system ends this year," *Financial Times of London*, October 22, 2004. "Textile and Clothing Summary," Global Trade Negotiations Home Page, Center for International Development, Harvard University, May 2004.

Trade data on U.S. imports of textiles and apparel are available online from the Office of Textiles and Apparel, U.S. Department of Commerce, International Trade Administration: http://otexa.ita.doc.gov/mrspoint.htm and from the U.S. Census Bureau: http://www.census.gov/foreign-trade/statistics/index.html. Data on exports and imports from different countries is available from the World Trade Organization at http://www.wto.org/english/res_e/statis_e/its2002_e/its02_bysector_e.htm.

● Study Questions

1. Why do countries trade with each other? Why don't they try to be self-sufficient in the production of all goods?

2. What is the difference between absolute advantage and comparative advantage? (Use a per capita production possibilities frontier to illustrate your answer.)

3. Why do economists argue that a country with an absolute advantage in the production of all goods can still gain from trade if it specializes in a manner consistent with the law of comparative advantage? (Consider a two-good, two-country example.)

4. Why isn't it possible for all countries to improve their balance of trade by simultaneously increasing exports and decreasing imports?

5. Why aren't a country's consumption possibilities limited by its production possibilities?

6. It is often asserted that for every tariff there is a corresponding quota in the sense of having the same impact on prices and production. Is this statement correct and if so what difference(s) would one policy make over the other?

7. Since higher prices following the imposition of a tariff or a quota will reduce domestic demand, how can these policies ever be in the interest of domestic producers?

8. How do you evaluate the arguments supporting strategic trade policies?

9. What is the role of trade adjustment assistance and why do many think it a necessary element of a policy that favors free trade?

10. What is the infant-industry argument? Do you believe it is ever a compelling argument? Why or why not?

11. Some industries argue for trade protection on the grounds of national defense. Do you believe this is ever a compelling argument? Why or why not?

12. "In order to increase the consumption possibilities of Americans, the United States should never prohibit dumping by foreign manufacturers." Do you agree? Why or why not?

13. Why isn't it obvious to many economists that the United States should enact tariffs to level the playing field and protect American workers from unfair competition from low-wage foreign workers?

Economics Online

Data on American international trade is reported by several U.S. government offices.

U.S. Census Bureau

http://www.census.gov/ftp/pub/foreign-trade/www

Office of Trade and Economic Analysis, International Trade Administration

http://www.ita.doc.gov/

Data on American international accounts is available online from the Bureau of Economic Analysis, U.S. Department of Commerce

http://www.bea.gov/

Information on international trade from the World Trade Organization can be found through the WTO homepage.

http://www.wto.org

The International Monetary System: Order or Disorder?

18

Important Terms and Concepts

Exchange rate

Appreciation

Depreciation

Devaluation

Revaluation

Floating exchange rates

Purchasing-power parity theory

Fixed exchange rates

Balance of payments deficit and surplus

Current account

Capital account

Gold standard

Bretton Woods system

International Monetary Fund (IMF)

"Dirty" or "managed" float

Learning Objectives
After completing this chapter, you should be able to:

- identify the factors that help determine a country's exchange rate under a system of floating exchange rates.

- explain why an appreciation of the dollar against any other currency is simultaneously a depreciation of that currency against the dollar.

- distinguish between long-, medium-, and short-run factors that help determine the demand and supply of currencies.

- use a demand and supply diagram to show how changes in GDP, inflation, or interest rates can lead to appreciation or depreciation of the dollar under a system of floating exchange rates.

- show, on a supply-demand graph, how fixed exchange rates can lead to a balance of payments deficit or surplus.

- explain the difference between the current and capital accounts.

- explain why under a system of floating exchange rates a deficit on the current account will be accompanied by a surplus on the capital account.

- explain why, under the gold standard, countries lost control of their domestic money stock.

- describe the options, other than changing the exchange rate, that were available under the Bretton Woods system to a country wanting to eliminate a balance of payments deficit or surplus.

- explain why, under a system of fixed exchange rates, there was very little risk in speculating against an overvalued currency.

- explain how speculators can reduce the uncertainty exporters and importers face under a system of floating exchange rates.

● Chapter Review

Meeting: President Richard M. Nixon and H. R. Haldeman, Oval Office, June 23, 1972
(10:04–11:39 a.m.)

Haldeman: Bums is concerned about speculation against the lira.

Nixon: Well, I don't give a (expletive deleted) about the lira . . . There ain't a vote in it.

Source: Statement of Information: Appendix III, *Hearings before the Committee on the Judiciary*, House of Representatives, Ninety-third Congress, Second Session, May–June 1974, page 50.

Even American presidents now pay attention to exchange rates. So should you. Even if you are never president, exchange rates are important for all Americans. Consumers are affected by the price of imports, and jobs for workers can be affected by the price of exports and imports. This chapter discusses exchange rates, that is, the price of one currency in terms of another. The discussion in the text covers the economic factors that determine exchange rates, the implications of attempts by governments to fix exchange rates, and a review of recent history focusing on the evolution of the world's current mixed international monetary system.

Discussions of international monetary arrangements involve a whole new vocabulary of fixed and floating exchange rates, current and capital accounts, appreciating and depreciating currencies, and devaluations and revaluations. It may help you to keep the vocabulary straight if you remember that most of the analysis of international monetary arrangements is merely an application of the supply-demand analysis originally introduced in Chapter 4.

Find out how much it would cost, in American dollars, to buy one Canadian dollar. This figure

(1) is the current _____ rate, expressed in American dollars. Many newspapers now publish exchange rates on a daily basis. A student in Canada could do the same thing and get a price for American dollars in terms of Canadian dollar. If you both call on the same day you should both get the same price (ignoring sales commissions).[1] If the American dollar price of one Canadian dollar increases, so that it takes more American dollars to buy one Canadian dollar, we say that the Canadian dollar has _____ relative to the American dollar. When it takes more American dollars to buy a Canadian dollar, it will take (<u>fewer/more</u>) Canadian dollars to buy one American dollar and we would say that the American dollar has _____ relative to the Canadian dollar.

Under a system of floating exchange rates, exchange rates will be determined by market forces

(2) of _____ and _____. Consider an example that consists of just two

---

[1]If in the United States, you get a price of 80 cents for one Canadian dollar. The Canadian student would get a price of 1.25 Canadian dollar for one American dollar. If x is the American dollar price of one Canadian, then $1/x$ is the Canadian dollar price of one American dollar.

currencies, the Japanese yen and the American dollar. The demand for yen comes from holders of American dollars who are interested in

(a) Japanese exports, such as cars, cameras, and televisions;

(b) Japanese physical assets, such as factories, office buildings, and land;

(c) Japanese financial assets, such as stocks and bonds; and

the supply of Japanese yen also has three sources: the demand by Japanese for American (exports/imports), American _____ assets, and American _____ assets. (Note that the demand and supply of yen has an interpretation in terms of the demand and supply of dollars. The demand for yen by holders of dollars is simultaneously a(n) _____ of dollars. Understanding this mirror-image aspect of exchange rates should help keep the vocabulary and analysis straight.)

Under a system of floating rates, the equilibrium exchange rate will be at a level where demand equals supply. A change in any factor that affects demand or supply will change the exchange rate. For example, a sudden increase in demand for British wool on the part of Americans would shift the (demand/supply) curve for pounds. The dollar price of pounds will (increase/decrease), a result (3) economists call a(n) (appreciation/depreciation) of the pound in terms of the dollar. Conversely, a sudden increase in demand for California wines on the part of the English would shift the _____ curve of pounds and would mean a(n) (appreciation/depreciation) of the pound in terms of the dollar.

In the long run, the exchange rate between two currencies should be influenced by the prices of traded goods according to the theory of _____ _____ _____. In order that its goods remain competitive on world markets, a country with a (4) very high rate of inflation will see its exchange rate (appreciate/depreciate). In the medium run, a country that experiences an economic boom is likely to find its imports rising, a development that by itself should lead to a(n) _____ of its exchange rate. But if the economic boom means higher interest rates and strong investment opportunities that attract foreign investment, the result may be a(n) _____ of the exchange rate. Exchange rates, especially in the short run, will be affected by the movement of large pools of investment funds that are sensitive to international differences in interest rates. An increase in interest rates should attract funds, (appreciating/depreciating) the exchange rate.

Governments may try to peg the exchange rate. In fact, from the end of World War II until 1973, the world operated on a system of fixed exchange rates, established at the _____ (5) Woods conference. At the time, it was thought that fixed exchange rates were necessary to stimulate the growth of international trade, so countries could reap the benefits of specialization according to the law of comparative advantage. Pegging an exchange rate is very similar to any other sort of price control and is subject to similar problems.

(6)
If, say, the Japanese government pegs the exchange rate at too high a level, the supply of Japanese yen will exceed the demand for yen, and Japan will experience a balance of payments (deficit/surplus) If the government pegs the rate too low, then (demand/supply) will exceed _____ and the result will be a balance of payments _____.

It is traditional to measure the demand and supply of currencies as either current or capital transactions. The current account includes private transactions for exports, imports, cross-border payments of interest, dividends, unilateral transfer, and gifts. The capital account includes private payments for financial investments and physical assets. Under a system of floating exchange rates,

(7)
we know that any current account deficit must be offset by a capital account _____ as total demand equals total supply. Adjustments in the _____ _____ ensure the equality of the quantity demanded and supplied. Under a system of fixed exchange rates there may be an imbalance in private demand and supply requiring government intervention to maintain the exchange rate.

A government pegging its exchange rate and faced with a balance of payments deficit will need

(8)
to use its holdings of international reserves, that is, foreign currencies, in order to (buy/sell) its own currency. A country faced with a balance of payments surplus will need to supply its currency to satisfy the demand of foreigners offering their currencies. As a result, it will find its international reserves (increasing/decreasing).

Under fixed exchange rates, most of the pressure for adjustment is placed on countries

(9)
experiencing a balance of payments (deficit/surplus). If nothing else, such a country will eventually run out of international reserves. If a country does not want to change its exchange rate, other adjustment options include monetary and fiscal policies that (increase/decrease) interest rates, (increase/decrease) the rate of inflation, or induce a general (contraction/expansion) in the level of economic activity. Many of these adjustments occurred automatically under the gold standard as a balance of payments deficit led to an outflow of gold and an automatic (increase/reduction) in the stock of money.

A major weakness of the Bretton Woods system of fixed exchange rates was that deficit countries disliked adjusting their domestic economies for balance of payments reasons rather than for domestic political and economic reasons. Another weakness was the special role accorded the U.S. dollar.[2]

In recent years many of the world's major industrialized countries have operated under a mixed system of fixed and floating rates. Some exchange rates are allowed to change on a daily basis in response to market forces. At the same time, many governments intervene by buying or selling currencies, hoping to influence the exchange rate to their advantage. Some have worried that floating exchange rates would be so volatile as to destroy world trade. However, market-determined prices need not be volatile, and importers and exporters can often relieve the business risk of changes in exchange rate by dealing with _____. (10)

In January 1999, members of the European Union agreed to link their currencies at fixed exchange rates and, in January 2002 replaced their own currencies with the _____. While the (11) common currency implies a system of fixed exchange rates among the euro countries, remember that there is a floating exchange rate between the euro and other currencies like there is between the dollar and yen.

The International Monetary Fund, or IMF, was established to oversee the fixed exchange rates established as part of the Bretton Woods agreement. Now the IMF provides loans to countries with significant balance of payments problems. These loans usually come with significant restrictions and conditions. Some critics have argued that IMF conditions only help to ensure that international investors from rich countries are protected while the contractionary macroeconomic policies bring hardship for local citizens.

---

[2]The United States has run a deficit on its current and capital account in recent years without seeming to be subject to the problems discussed in the text. Rather than the United States government having to buy dollars, foreign governments have been willing to buy dollars. See Economics in Action in the next chapter for additional discussion of this issue.

Important Terms and Concepts Quiz

Choose the best definition for each of the following terms.

1. _____ Exchange rate
2. _____ Appreciation
3. _____ Depreciation
4. _____ Devaluation
5. _____ Revaluation
6. _____ Floating exchange rates
7. _____ Purchasing-power parity theory
8. _____ Fixed exchange rates
9. _____ Balance of payments deficit
10. _____ Balance of payments surplus
11. _____ Current account balance
12. _____ Capital account balance
13. _____ Gold standard
14. _____ Bretton Woods system
15. _____ International Monetary Fund
16. _____ Dirty float

a. Decrease in the amount of foreign currency a unit of domestic currency can buy
b. Price of one currency in terms of another
c. Exchange rates determined in free market by supply and demand
d. Increase in official value of a currency
e. Value of currencies linked to the dollar whose value was linked to gold
f. System where exchange rates change in response to market forces, but with intervention by central banks
g. International agency that extends loans for infrastructure to developing countries
h. Amount by which quantity supplied of a country's currency exceeds quantity demanded
i. Balance of trade involving purchases and sales of financial and real assets
j. International agency that monitors exchange rate policies of member countries
k. Reduction in official value of a currency
l. Balance of trade in goods and services plus cross-border payments for interest, dividends, gifts, and unilateral transfers
m. System where currencies are defined in terms of gold
n. Increase in the amount of foreign currency a unit of domestic currency can buy
o. Exchange rates set by the government
p. Amount by which quantity demanded of a country's currency exceeds quantity supplied
q. Idea that exchange rates adjust to reflect differences in the prices of traded goods

● Basic Exercises

1. Purchasing-Power Parity

This exercise is designed to illustrate the theory of purchasing-power parity.

Assume that the United States and France are the only suppliers of wine on the world market. Consumers of wine are indifferent between French and California wines and buy whichever is cheaper. Initially, the dollar-euro exchange rate is assumed to be $1.20 to the euro and California wine sells for $12 a bottle.

Ignoring transportation costs, the initial dollar price of French wines must be $12. Accordingly, we know that the initial franc price of French wine is 10 euros a bottle.

Assume now that inflation in the United States has raised the price of California wine to $15.60 a bottle, while inflation in France has raised the price of French wine to 12 euros. Based on this data, answer each of the following:

a. If the exchange rate is fixed at $1.20 to the euro, what is the new dollar price of French wine? $_____. What would happen to the sales of French and California wines? If wine is the only good traded between France and the United States, what happens to the U.S. balance of payments?

b. If the dollar-euro exchange rate is free to adjust, what dollar price of a euro is necessary to equalize the dollar (or euro) price of both wines? _____ This change in the dollar price of a euro is a(n) (appreciation/depreciation) of the euro and a(n) _____ of the dollar.

c. Assuming that the change in the price of wine is typical of the change in other prices, who had the higher rate of inflation? _____

d. From questions a and c, it is seen that the purchasing-power parity theory implies that under fixed exchange rates a currency with more inflation will experience a balance of payments (deficit/surplus).

e. From questions b and c, it is seen that the purchasing-power parity theory implies that under floating exchange rates a currency with more inflation will (appreciate/depreciate).

2. **The Risks of Speculation against Fixed Exchange Rates**

Assume that in the fall of 1967 you are treasurer for a large multinational corporation with 10 million British pounds to invest. The fixed official exchange rate vis-à-vis the U.S. dollar has been $2.80. At this exchange rate Britain has been experiencing large and growing deficits in its balance of payments and has been financing this deficit by buying pounds with foreign currencies. Britain's holdings of foreign currencies are running low, and there is a general feeling that Britain will have to devalue the pound. Exactly how large the devaluation will be and exactly when it will occur are uncertain, but given the history of chronic deficits, there is absolutely no chance that the pound will be revalued.

Complete **Table 18-1** to measure the risks of speculating against the pound. (Changing from pounds to dollars and back again will involve transaction costs. Table 18-1 abstracts from these costs, which are apt to be small.)

Table 18-1

Speculation Against the Pound

	(1)	(2)	(3)
Initial holdings of pounds	£10,000,000	£10,000,000	£10,000,000
Current exchange rate	$2.80	$2.80	$2.80
Number of dollars if you sell pounds for dollars	_____	_____	_____
Possible new exchange rate	$2.80*	$2.60	$2.40
Number of pounds following reconversion to pounds after devaluation	_____	_____	_____

*This exchange rate assumes Britain takes other steps and does not devalue the pound.

What is the worst outcome?

As the talk of devaluation heats up, what are you apt to do? How will your actions affect the British balance of payments deficit and the pressures for devaluation?

3. **Determination of Exchange Rates**

This exercise is designed to contrast the impact of similar events under systems of fixed and floating exchange rates.

Assume that the world is divided into two countries, the United States and Japan. **Table 18-2** lists a number of events. Fill in the squares in the table to analyze the impact of these events on the dollar–yen exchange rate under a system of floating rates, and the Japanese balance of payments under a system of fixed exchange rates. Assume that each event takes place from an initial equilibrium that under fixed exchange rates entails neither a deficit nor a surplus. **Figure 18-1** illustrates such an equilibrium at an initial exchange rate of 110 yen per dollar.

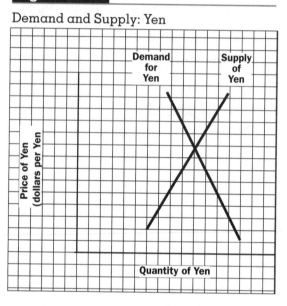

Figure 18-1

Demand and Supply: Yen

Table 18-2

Dollar–Yen Exchange Rates/Balance of Payments

Event	Shift in Demand Curve for Yen (left, right, no shift)	Shift in Supply Curve for Yen (left, right, no shift)	Floating Rates Appreciation or Depreciation of Yen	Fixed Rates Change in Japanese Balance of Payments*
a. Federal Reserve policy raises interest rates in the United States.				
b. A change in tastes increases American demand for Japanese electronics.				
c. The U.S. economy enters a recession.				
d. Major labor strikes in Japan have resulted in a sudden increase in the (yen) price of Japanese goods.				
e. A terrible typhoon destroys the Japanese rice crop and increases the demand for American rice.				

*Appropriate answers would be deficit, surplus, or no change.

• Self-Tests for Understanding

Test A

Circle the most appropriate answer.

1. The exchange rate between the American dollar and the Mexican peso tells us
   a. how much gold each currency is worth.
   b. the dollar price of a peso and the peso price of a dollar.
   c. whether the Mexicans are running a balance of payments deficit.
   d. how many pounds each currency will purchase.

2. If an American can buy a Polish zloty for 40 cents, how many zloty must a Pole spend to buy a dollar?
   a. 0.4 zloty
   b. 4 zloty
   c. 2.5 zloty
   d. 40 zloty

3. If the euro appreciates relative to the British pound, then a euro will buy
   a. fewer pounds than before.
   b. the same number of pounds as before.
   c. more pounds than before.

4. If under a system of floating exchange rates the Mexican peso used to cost 20 cents and now costs 10 cents, one would say that the _____. (There may be more than one correct answer.)
   a. peso has appreciated relative to the dollar
   b. peso has depreciated relative to the dollar
   c. dollar has appreciated relative to the peso
   d. dollar has depreciated relative to the peso

5. If it used to take one euro to buy one dollar and now it takes 0.80 euros, one would say that the _____. (There may be more than one correct answer.)
   a. euro has appreciated against the dollar
   b. dollar has appreciated against the euro
   c. dollar has depreciated against the euro
   d. euro has depreciated against the dollar

6. If the yen appreciates against the euro, then we know that the
   a. dollar has also appreciated against the yen.
   b. euro has appreciated against the dollar.
   c. euro has depreciated against the yen.
   d. yen has appreciated against the dollar.

7. Under a system of floating exchange rates, an increase in the demand for dollars by foreigners will cause a(n) _____ of the dollar.
   a. devaluation
   b. appreciation
   c. revaluation
   d. depreciation

8. Which of the following, by itself, would cause an appreciation of the dollar? (There may be more than one correct answer.)
   a. an increase in American GDP
   b. an increase in foreign GDP
   c. a decrease in American interest rates
   d. a decrease in foreign interest rates
   e. an increase in inflation in the United States
   f. an increase in inflation in the rest of the world

9. Which of the following, by itself, would cause a depreciation of the dollar?
   a. a decrease in American GDP
   b. an increase in foreign GDP
   c. an increase in American interest rates
   d. a decrease in foreign interest rates
   e. a decrease in inflation in the United States
   f. a decrease in inflation in the rest of the world

10. Under a system of floating exchange rates, which one of the following conditions will tend to depreciate the Japanese yen relative to the British pound?
    a. an economic boom in Britain
    b. a higher level of inflation in Japan than in Britain
    c. an increase in interest rates in Japan
    d. a sudden increase in British demand for imports from Japan

11. Which of the following would lead to an appreciation of the peso relative to the dollar?
    a. a recession in America
    b. less inflation in America than in Mexico
    c. an increase in Mexican interest rates
    d. a boom in Mexico

12. Purchasing-power parity theory says that
    a. only the volume of exports and imports determines exchange rates; interest rates have nothing to do with exchange rates.
    b. all countries are better off with a system of fixed exchange rates.
    c. adjustment of fixed exchange rates should be symmetrical between deficit and surplus countries.
    d. in the long run, exchange rates adjust to reflect differences in price levels between countries.

13. If inflation in United States is at an annual rate of 2 percent and inflation in Brazil is at 8 percent, then the purchasing-power parity theory suggests that in the long run the dollar price of one Brazilian real will
    a. increase at an annual rate of 8 percent.
    b. decrease at an annual rate of 6 percent.
    c. increase at an annual rate of 6 percent.
    d. increase at an annual rate of 2 percent.

14. In question 13, one would say that the higher rate of inflation in Brazil results in a(n)
    a. depreciation of the real relative to the dollar.
    b. appreciation of the real relative to the dollar.
    c. depreciation of the dollar relative to the real.
    d. cross-subsidy of the real by the dollar.

15. Assume that the real–dollar exchange rate is fixed, that Brazil and the United States are the only two countries in the world, and that inflation rates differ as described in question 13. Which country will have a balance of payments deficit?
    a. the United States
    b. Brazil

16. When accounting for American international transactions, which of the following would be counted in the current account?
    a. Karen and David buy a case of French wine.
    b. Jared buys shares on the Italian stock market.
    c. The Japanese government buys a ten-year U.S. government security.
    d. Northwest Airlines buys an airport hanger in Tokyo.

17. From an initial position of equilibrium under a system of fixed exchange rates, which of the following would lead to a balance of payments deficit? (There may be more than one correct answer.)
    a. a reduction in foreign interest rates
    b. an increase in domestic interest rates
    c. domestic inflation in excess of inflation in the rest of the world
    d. a devaluation by a country's major trading partner

18. If the country of Zenon tries to fix its exchange rate at a level above that determined by demand and supply, it will likely _____. (There may be more than one correct answer.)
    a. run a balance of payments deficit
    b. run a balance of payments surplus
    c. find its exports being priced out of world markets
    d. see reduced interest by foreigners in investing in Zenon

19. Which one of the following policies would not help to eliminate a deficit under a system of fixed exchange rates?
    a. monetary and fiscal policies to raise the level of unemployment
    b. a devaluation of the exchange rate
    c. monetary and fiscal policies that increase the rate of inflation
    d. a change in monetary policy that increases interest rates

20. If it takes 9 cents to buy one Swedish kronor and $0.90 to buy one euro, then how many kronor should it take to buy one euro?
    a. $(0.09 \div 0.90) = .10$
    b. $(0.90 \div 0.09) = 10$
    c. $(1.0 \div 0.09) = 11.111$
    d. $(1.0 \div 0.90) = 1.111$

Test B

Circle T or F for true or false.

T   F   1. If one dollar previously cost 120 yen and now costs 100 yen, the dollar has appreciated relative to the yen.

T   F   2. A pure system of floating exchange rates requires government intervention—purchases and sales of its own currency—in order to work properly.

T   F   3. Under a system of floating exchange rates, a sudden increase in the demand for U.S. exports will lead to appreciation of the dollar relative to other currencies.

T   F   4. Under a system of fixed exchange rates, a sudden increase in the demand for imports by Americans would increase the U.S. balance of payments deficit (or reduce the size of the surplus).

T   F   5. Purchasing-power parity is a theory of the long-run determination of exchange rates.

T   F   6. Under a system of fixed exchange rates, a country that attempts to peg its exchange rate at an artificially low level will end up with a balance of payments surplus.

T   F   7. Today, world international monetary relations are based on the gold standard.

T   F   8. A major advantage of the gold standard was that countries could control their own domestic money stock.

T   F   9. The Bretton Woods gold-exchange system established a system of fixed exchange rates based on the convertibility of dollars into gold.

T   F   10. Under the Bretton Woods system of fixed exchange rates, both surplus and deficit countries felt the same pressure to correct any imbalance in their balance of payments.

● Supplementary Exercise

World Trade under Fixed and Flexible Exchange Rates

Some observers worried that the introduction of a system of floating exchange rates would have adverse effects on the volume of world trade, as exporters and importers would have trouble coping with short-run fluctuations in exchange rates. You might compare the growth in world trade with the growth in world output. The IMF regularly publishes estimates of world output and world trade as part of its World Economic Outlook. Start at http://www.imf.org/external/index.htm. Click on the link for the latest World Economic Outlook and then click on the link for the WEO database. Has trade grown faster than output or have floating exchange rates held back the growth of world trade?

Economics in Action

Hedging One's International Investments

The movement of exchange rates complicates the lives of companies and individual investors who by choice or necessity have to deal with international investments. Imagine that interest rates in Britain offer a better return than in the United States. Do you want to convert your dollars into pounds, invest in Britain, and then convert back to dollars? The higher interest rate may look tempting, but any advantage of higher interest rates in Britain could be completely offset by an adverse movement in the dollar/pound exchange rate. For example, assume that a pound costs $1.75 when you invest to take advantage of a 10 percent interest rate in Britain compared to a 5 percent interest rate in the United States. What happens if at the end of the year, when you go to convert your pounds back into dollars, the pound has depreciated to $1.55 or appreciated to $1.95? As the example shows, changes in exchange rates can have a major impact on international investors and on the dollar value of international earnings of corporations.[3] Economists would say that these changes add to the variability and risk of international investments. If potential returns are sufficiently attractive, there is an incentive to learn how to manage the associated risk.

It is often argued that one should fully hedge international investments. That is, if you make an investment in Britain you should at the same time take other actions that lock in the exchange rate you will use to convert your pounds back into dollars. While such actions mean you would not benefit from an appreciation of the pound, you would also avoid the loss that would accompany a depreciation. The use of futures markets—that is, dealing with speculators in foreign exchange—is one way to lock in a particular exchange rate.

How important is it to hedge one's international investments? Economist Kenneth Froot argues that whether one should hedge international investments depends upon one's time horizon. Using almost 200 years' worth of data on exchange rates between the dollar and the pound along with investment returns in the United States and the United Kingdom, Froot argues that hedging reduced the variance of international investments that were held for short horizons (e.g., one or two years). However, he also found that as one's investment horizon lengthened, there was less need to hedge international investments. How can this be?

Consider the following simple example. Assume that over longer time horizons, exchange rates tend toward levels defined by purchasing-power parity, real interest rates are the same in the United States and Britain, and nominal investment returns reflect any differences in inflation. If inflation is higher in Britain, then nominal interest rates in Britain should be higher than in the United States. Note that nominal interest rates in Britain are measured in terms of pounds while in the United States they are measured in terms of dollars. If exchange rates are determined by purchasing-power parity, the pound will depreciate at a rate that just offsets the difference in nominal interest rates. A U.S. investor would not be disadvantaged by the depreciation in the pound and would receive no benefit from dealing with speculators who would incorporate the difference in rates of inflation into the future exchange rates they offer investors. This view suggests that one should evaluate particular investments in the United States or Britain on their merits and that markets may work to minimize the risks associated with changes in the exchange rates if one is investing for the long term.[4]

---

[3]Changes in exchange rates are not just an issue for a system of flexible exchange rates. The system of fixed rates under the Bretton Woods agreement included long periods of stable exchange rates marked by sudden and often large adjustments of official exchange rates. If one of those large changes occurred when you had made an international investment, you could be much worse or better off.

[4]Froot's argument is controversial. Measures of the returns one might have received in the past are no guarantee of what one will receive in the future. Even if over the long term one need not worry about movements in exchange rates, an investment that does poorly in either country will have been a mistake.

How do businesses respond to the ups and downs of the dollar? A story in *The New York Times* talked about how Eastman Kodak and other companies deal with changes in exchange rates. These changes are of growing importance as American companies increase foreign operations. David Fiedler, director of foreign exchange for Kodak, reported that in the short term he uses financial hedges to protect against changes in exchange rates. Over the longer term he views questions of foreign exchange as a "business problem like any other business problem." That is, exchange rate risk is something that should be given careful consideration from the very beginning, when making decisions about markets, suppliers, and production sites. "Before 1988, Mr. Fiedler . . . often had to respond to currency swings within minutes after a phone call about foreign developments startled him from sleep. 'That's a real motivator to think of another way,' he said."

1. If you were to make a personal financial investment in a foreign stock market, in what market would you invest? How do you evaluate the exchange rate risks of your choice?

2. What strategies might business follow, other than financial hedges, to minimize the risks associated with international operations?

Sources: "Companies Learn to Live with Dollar's Volatility," *The New York Times*, August 31, 1992; Kenneth A. Froot, "Currency Hedging over Long Horizons," Working Paper No. 4355, National Bureau of Economic Research, May 1993.

Study Questions

1. If you know the dollar price of a euro, how can you figure out how many euros it takes to buy a dollar?

2. What is the difference between an appreciation and a depreciation of the dollar? Which is better for American tourists? For American exporters?

3. What factors would cause an appreciation of the dollar? What factors would cause depreciation?

4. Is it possible for the dollar to appreciate against the pound and, at the same time, for the pound to appreciate against the dollar? Why?

5. What is meant by purchasing-power parity? How is it possible for exchange rates to vary from levels determined by purchasing-power parity?

6. How did the gold standard work to maintain fixed exchange rates?

7. What was the difference between the gold standard and the Bretton Woods system?

8. What is a balance of payments deficit? Is it possible to have an overall deficit under a system of floating exchange rates? Fixed exchange rates?

9. What is meant by the current account? The capital account? How are these measures related to a country's balance of payments?

10. Under a system of fixed exchange rates, what policies might a country adopt to eliminate a balance of payments deficit? Surplus?

11. Who bore most of the burden for adjustment under the Bretton Woods system, deficit or surplus countries? Why wasn't the burden of adjustment equal?

12. Under fixed exchange rates, balance of payment deficits reflect an overvalued exchange rate. The overvalued exchange rate increases the price of a country's exports. A devaluation would help to correct the balance of payments deficit by lowering the price of exports, increasing the demand for exports, and increasing employment in export industries. Yet most countries have resisted devaluation even when facing chronic deficits. What do you think explains this reluctance?

13. When would a country prefer a system of fixed exchange rates and when might it prefer a system of floating exchange rates?

14. What steps might exporters and importers take to minimize the risk of currency fluctuations under a system of floating exchange rates?

15. Why is it said that under fixed exchange rates currency speculation was destabilizing, while under floating exchange rates it is likely to be stabilizing?

16. What is meant by the term "dirty" or "managed" float?

17. What is the IMF and how effective have its policies been?

18. What are the advantages/disadvantages for Europe of adopting the euro?

Economics Online

You can get up-to-the-minute and historical information about exchange rates at a number of Web sites.

Current information is available at:

Federal Reserve Bank of New York:

http://www.newyorkfed.org/markets/fxrates/noon.cfm

Bloomberg:

http://www.bloomberg.com/markets/currencies/fxc.html

CNN Financial:

http://money.cnn.com/markets/currencies/

The Federal Reserve Bank of St. Louis posts historical daily and monthly data on exchange rates at

http://research.stlouisfed.org/fred2/categories/15

The Oanda exchange rate converter allows you to find the exchange rate between any of 164 currencies back to January 1, 1990.

http://www.oanda.com/converter/classic

Exchange Rates and the Macroeconomy

19

Important Terms and Concepts

Open economy

Net exports

Exchange rate

Appreciation

Depreciation

International capital flows

Closed economy

Trade deficit

Budget deficits and trade deficits

$(X - IM) = (S - I) - (G - T)$

Learning Objectives

After completing this chapter, you should be able to:

- explain how an appreciation or depreciation of the exchange rate affects net exports.

- show how an appreciation or depreciation of the exchange rate affects real GDP and the price of domestically produced goods by shifting the aggregate demand and aggregate supply curves appropriately.

- describe how changes in interest rates affect international capital flows and the exchange rate.

- explain why the reaction of international capital flows to changes in interest rates works to offset the impact of changes in fiscal policy.

- explain why the reaction of international capital flows to changes in interest rates works to enhance the impact of changes in monetary policy.

- explain in what way government deficits and trade deficits are linked.

- explain how a change in the mix of fiscal and monetary policy affects macroeconomic variables such as GDP, real interest rates, prices, the trade deficit, and the exchange rate.

Chapter Review

This chapter integrates the discussion of international trade and exchange rates of the preceding two chapters with the earlier discussions of income determination and fiscal and monetary policy.

(1)   An economy that did not trade with any other economy would be called a(n) _____ economy. Today all industrial economies and most developing economies have extensive links with other economies through trade in goods and services and financial assets. Such economies are called _____ economies. These international linkages can affect important macroeconomic outcomes such as GDP and prices. While a complete and rigorous examination of these linkages is the stuff of more advanced courses in economics, we can use the model of income determination that we developed in earlier chapters to shed light on a number of important issues.

We start with a review of factors affecting the demand for exports and imports. As we saw earlier, the demand for exports and imports is influenced by income and prices. A decrease in foreign income

(2) will (decrease/increase) the demand for American exports and is an important reason why economic fluctuations abroad (are/are not) felt in the United States.

Exports and imports are also influenced by changes in the exchange rate, as these changes alter the relative price of foreign and domestic goods. An appreciation of the dollar makes foreign goods

(3) (less/more) expensive. The result is likely to be a(n) (decrease/increase) in American imports and a(n) _____ in American exports. Putting these two effects together shows that an appreciation of the exchange rate will lead to a(n) (decrease/increase) in net exports, $(X - IM)$. Similar reasoning shows that a depreciation of the dollar should lead to a(n) _____ in exports, a(n) _____ in imports, and a(n) _____ in net exports.

A change in net exports that comes from a change in exchange rates is analogous to any other autonomous change in spending. It shifts the expenditure schedule and leads to a

(4) (movement along/shift in) the aggregate demand curve. More precisely, following an appreciation of the dollar, net exports decline, the expenditure schedule shifts (down/up), and the aggregate demand curve shifts to the (left/right). Opposite results follow from a depreciation of the dollar.

A change in exchange rates can also lead to a shift in the aggregate supply curve through its impact on the price of imported intermediate goods. An appreciation of the dollar makes imported

(5) inputs (less/more) expensive. This result can be modeled as a(n) (downward/upward) shift in the aggregate supply curve. A depreciation of the dollar makes imported inputs _____ expensive and leads to a(n) _____ shift in the aggregate supply curve.

Once we understand the impact of a change in interest rates on international capital flows and on the exchange rate, we will have all the pieces necessary to examine how fiscal and monetary policy work in an open economy with flexible exchange rates. We saw in the previous chapter that an increase

in interest rates is apt to (<u>decrease/increase</u>) the demand by foreigners for American financial assets. (6)
This change in the demand for dollars should lead to a(n) (<u>appreciation/depreciation</u>) of the dollar.
Tracing through the impact of this capital-flow-induced change in the exchange rate is the key to
understanding how fiscal and monetary policy work in an open economy.

To review, consider a change in fiscal policy. A move to expansionary fiscal policy, say a(n)
(<u>decrease/increase</u>) in taxes, would shift the expenditure schedule (<u>up/down</u>) and shift the (7)
aggregate demand curve to the (<u>right/left</u>). For a closed economy where interest rates do not change,
that would be the end of the story. But, if as is likely, the fiscal stimulus results in higher interest rates,
there is more to the story. The impact of higher interest rates on international capital flows will lead
to a(n) (<u>appreciation/depreciation</u>) in the exchange rate. This change in the exchange rate will shift
the aggregate demand curve to the (<u>left/right</u>) and shift the aggregate supply curve (<u>down/up</u>).
The shift in the aggregate demand curve, induced by the change in the exchange rate, works to
(<u>enhance/offset</u>) the original expansionary change in fiscal policy. The shift in the aggregate supply
curve works to (<u>lower/raise</u>) prices and to (<u>increase/decrease</u>) output. If the shift in the aggregate
supply curve induced by the change in exchange rates were large enough, it could offset the impact on
output from the exchange-rate-induced shift in the aggregate demand curve. Evidence suggests that
for the United States, the shift in the aggregate supply curve is small relative to that of the aggregate
demand curve and that, on net, the shifts in the two curves work to (<u>enhance/offset</u>) the impact of
expansionary fiscal policy on output.

A move to restrictive monetary policy can be analyzed in the same way. The initial effects will
include an increase in interest rates that leads to a(n) (<u>appreciation/depreciation</u>) of the exchange (8)
rate. The impact of the change in the exchange rate will (<u>enhance/offset</u>) the original restrictive
change in monetary policy.

Income and product definition of GDP can be manipulated to illustrate the important link
between government budget deficits and trade deficits.[2]

$$(X - IM) = (S - I) - (G - T).$$

If the government deficit increases, that is, if $(G - T)$ becomes larger, then $(S - I)$ must increase
and/or $(X - IM)$ must decrease. For $(S - I)$ to increase either private savings must increase or private
investment will need to decrease. A decrease in $(X - IM)$ means that either exports decrease or

---

[1]The analysis would also be complete if the Fed conducts monetary policy by fixing interest rates regardless of what happens to fiscal policy.
[2]Remember that on the income side GDP = $Y = DI + T = C + S + T$ while on the product side GDP = $Y = C + I + G + (X - IM)$. Since both expressions equal GDP, we can set $C + S + T = C + I + G + (X - IM)$. Canceling C on both sides of the equal sign and rearranging terms yields the expression above. This expression can also be written as $G + I + X = S + T + IM$. In terms of the circular flow diagram we saw earlier, this formulation says that injections must equal leakages.

imports increase, i.e., a larger trade deficit. As we have seen, in a world of flexible exchange rates, any deficit on the current account must be offset by a surplus on the capital account. Thus a trade deficit will be associated with a net capital inflow, that is, increased indebtedness to foreigners. It is changes in income, interest rates, exchange rates, and prices that enforce the link between savings, investment, budget deficits, trade deficits, and international capital flows. During the 1990s the reduction in the federal government deficit did not result in a smaller trade deficit because domestic savings (<u>decreased/increased</u>) and domestic investment _____.

Is the American trade deficit a problem? The answer to this question depends upon whether capital inflows are a market response to extravagant spending that result in high interest rates in the United States attracts foreign capital or the result of an autonomous increase in foreign demand for investment in the United States. The former suggests an economy spending beyond its means while the latter suggests a strong economy in which people want to invest. More generally, individuals and firms borrow from "foreigners" all the time. If they use these funds wisely, for example to invest future income, financing the borrowing need not be a special burden. On the other hand, if there is nothing to show for the increased debt, the result may be significant financial problems. There is a legitimate concern about how long large trade deficits and capital inflows can continue. Is there a limit to the willingness of foreigners to accumulate American assets and what happens if and when foreigners no longer want to do so?

A number of suggestions have been made to reduce the American trade deficit. For a number of years, many argued for a change in the mix of fiscal and monetary policy. According to this view, the increase in the American trade deficit during the 1980s was the result of expansionary fiscal policy and tight monetary policy. Reversing these actions, could work in reverse and lower the trade deficit as long as other factors, specifically the difference between domestic savings and investments, did not change. Rapid economic growth abroad would increase American (<u>exports/imports</u>). Protectionism would lower imports, but retaliation by foreign governments could (<u>lower/raise</u>) American exports with little change in net exports. For any of these measures to work, the accounting identity of $(X - IM) = (S - I) - (G - T)$ shows that any reduction in the trade deficit will require a combination of lower budget deficits, higher savings, or lower investment.

Important Terms and Concepts Quiz

Choose the best definition for each of the following terms.

1. _____ Net exports
2. _____ Closed economy
3. _____ Open economy
4. _____ Trade deficit
5. _____ International capital flows

a. Balance of payments accounting for exports and imports
b. Graph depicting response of inflation to changes in the exchange rate
c. Economy that trades with other economies
d. Difference between exports and imports
e. Interest-sensitive money flows between countries
f. Economy that does not trade with other economies

● Basic Exercises

This exercise is designed to review how the operation of fiscal and monetary policy is affected by interest-sensitive capital flows in an open economy.

1. **Table 19-1** is designed to help you review the impact of changes in the exchange rate on various macroeconomic variables. First, complete the column for an appreciation of the exchange rate. Then complete the column for a depreciation of the exchange rate. Indicate how each variable changes, i.e., increases or decreases, shifts left, right, up or down, as appropriate. Be sure you can explain why each variable shows the change you have indicated. If the change in GDP and the price level seems ambiguous, see if you can resolve the ambiguity by assuming, as in the text, that any shift in the aggregate demand curve is greater than the shift in the aggregate supply curve.

Table 19-1

Impact of Changes in the Exchange Rate

Macroeconomic Variable	Exchange Rate Appreciation	Exchange Rate Depreciation
Exports	_____	_____
Imports	_____	_____
Net Exports	_____	_____
Expenditure Schedule	_____	_____
Aggregate Demand Curve	_____	_____
Aggregate Supply Curve	_____	_____
Real GDP	_____	_____
Price Level	_____	_____

Table 19-2

Fiscal Policy in an Open Economy

	Decrease In *G*	Decrease In Taxes	Open Market Sale	Open Market Purchase
Aggregate Demand Curve	Left	Right	Left	Right
Real GDP	Down	Up	Down	Up
Price Level	Down	Up	Down	Up
Interest Rate	Down	Up	Up	Down
Exchange Rate	_____	_____	_____	_____
Real GDP	_____	_____	_____	_____
Price Level	_____	_____	_____	_____
Overall Impact	_____	_____	_____	_____
Real GDP	_____	_____	_____	_____
Price Level	_____	_____	_____	_____

2. **Table 19-2** is designed to analyze the impact on GDP and the price level of changes in fiscal and monetary policy. The completed upper portion of the table ignores any impact on exchange rates. Remembering that changes in interest rates are likely to influence the international investment of funds and hence the demand for dollars, complete Table 19-2 to determine whether capital flows offset or enhance these changes in monetary and fiscal policy. You should first determine how the exchange rate is affected and then consider the impact of the change in the exchange rate on GDP and prices. Finally, combine your results from the change in policy and the change in exchange rates to determine the overall impact. **Figure 19-1** may be helpful when completing Table 19-2.

3. What general conclusion can you draw about the effectiveness of monetary and fiscal policy in a world of interest-sensitive capital flows and flexible exchange rates?

Figure 19-1

Aggregate Demand and Aggregate Supply

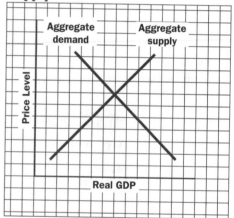

• Self-Tests for Understanding

Test A

Circle the most appropriate answer.

1. An increase in foreign GDP is likely to lead to
   a. a decrease in our exports.
   b. little if any change in our exports.
   c. an increase in our exports.

2. An appreciation of the exchange rate will make
   a. both exports and imports cheaper.
   b. exports more expensive for foreigners but imports cheaper for domestic citizens.
   c. exports cheaper for foreigners but imports more expensive for domestic citizens.
   d. both exports and imports more expensive.

3. An appreciation of the exchange rate will lead to a(n)
   a. increase in exports and imports.
   b. decrease in exports and an increase in imports.
   c. increase in exports and a decrease in imports.
   d. decrease in both exports and imports.

4. An appreciation of the exchange rate will lead to _____ in net exports.
   a. a decrease
   b. no change
   c. an increase

5. A decrease in net exports will
   a. shift the aggregate demand curve to the left.
   b. have no impact on the aggregate demand curve.
   c. shift the aggregate demand curve to the right.

6. An appreciation of the exchange rate will
   a. shift the aggregate supply curve up.
   b. have no impact on the aggregate supply curve.
   c. shift the aggregate supply curve down.

7. Evidence suggests that when the exchange rate changes, shifts in the aggregate demand curve will _____ shifts in the aggregate supply curve.
   a. be smaller than
   b. just offset
   c. be larger than

8. On balance, an appreciation of the exchange rate should tend to
   a. raise real GDP and raise the price of domestically produced goods.
   b. raise real GDP but lower the price of domestically produced goods.
   c. lower real GDP but raise the price of domestically produced goods.
   d. lower real GDP and lower the price of domestically produced goods.

9. A depreciation of the exchange rate tends to
   a. raise real GDP and raise the price of domestically produced goods.
   b. raise real GDP but lower the price of domestically produced goods.
   c. lower real GDP but raise the price of domestically produced goods.
   d. lower real GDP and lower the price of domestically produced goods.

10. Higher foreign interest rates are likely to be followed by an _____. (There may be more than one correct answer.)
    a. inflow of international capital
    b. increase in foreign investments by domestic citizens, i.e., a capital outflow
    c. appreciation of the exchange rate
    d. increase in net exports

11. An increase in domestic interest rates should lead to which one of the following?
    a. capital outflow
    b. appreciation of the dollar
    c. increase in exports
    d. upward shift in the expenditure schedule

12. An appreciation in the dollar vis-à-vis other currencies should lead to all but which one of the following?
    a. a decrease in exports
    b. an increase in imports
    c. a shift of the aggregate demand curve to the right
    d. a downward shift of the aggregate supply curve

13. A move to expansionary fiscal policy will tend to lead to all but which one of the following?
    a. an increase in interest rates
    b. an appreciation of the dollar
    c. a decrease in American imports
    d. an increase in the American trade deficit

14. A move to expansionary monetary policy will tend to lead to all but which one of the following?
    a. a decrease in interest rates
    b. an appreciation of the dollar
    c. an upward shift in the expenditure schedule
    d. an increase in inflationary pressures

15. Taking account of interest-sensitive international capital flows means that in an open economy the impact of fiscal policy is
    a. smaller than in a closed economy.
    b. the same as in a closed economy.
    c. larger than in a closed economy.

16. Taking account of interest-sensitive international capital flows means that in an open economy the impact of monetary policy is
    a. smaller than in a closed economy.
    b. the same as in a closed economy.
    c. larger than in a closed economy.

17. In an open economy that trades with other countries,
    a. $IM - X = (S - I) + (G - T)$.
    b. $X - IM = (S - I) - (G - T)$.
    c. $X - IM = (I - S) - (G - T)$.
    d. $IM - X = (S - I) - (G - T)$.

18. If there is no change in the balance of domestic savings and investment, then any increase in the government deficit must be matched by a(n) _____. (There may be more than one correct answer.)
    a. increase in the trade deficit
    b. reduction in the equilibrium level of output
    c. capital inflow
    d. reduction in interest rates

19. Which one of the following would help to reduce the U.S. trade deficit?
    a. higher government deficits
    b. increased domestic investment
    c. increased domestic savings
    d. a decrease in exports

20. A reduction in the government deficit need not lead to a reduction in the trade deficit if there is an increase in _____. (There may be more than one correct answer.)
    a. private saving
    b. private investment
    c. consumption spending
    d. imports

Test B

Circle T or F for true or false.

T F 1. International trade means that an economic boom in the United States is likely to lead to recession in the rest of the world.

T F 2. A change in net exports has no multiplier impacts.

T F 3. A shift in the expenditure schedule coming from an autonomous change in domestic investment spending would be expected to have no impact on a country's trade deficit.

T F 4. A depreciation in the exchange rate is inflationary.

T F 5. A depreciation in the exchange rate should help to reduce a country's trade deficit.

T F 6. Under floating exchange rates, a country with a trade deficit will also experience a capital inflow.

T F 7. Interest-sensitive international capital flows make monetary policy less effective.

T F 8. International capital flows are unaffected by changes in fiscal policy.

T F 9. Increased protectionism has been shown to be an effective tool for eliminating a trade deficit.

T F 10. The only way to reduce the trade deficit is by reducing the government's budget deficit.

● Economics in Action

Wither the Dollar?

Writing in *The New York Times* in November 2004, Edmund Andrews described three views of the continuing American trade deficit and the associated increases in American international indebtedness.

There were those, including Federal Reserve chairman Alan Greenspan and prominent members of the Bush administration who saw little to worry about. These observers argued that global financial markets were so much larger than they used to be that large borrowing on the part of the United States should not be a problem. Indeed, some in the Bush administration argued that large borrowing was a sign of American strength and indicated the interest of foreigners in investing in the United States.

Others were not as sanguine and worried about a sudden collapse of the value of dollar as the capacity and willingness of international investors to absorb additional dollar denominated debt could reach a limit and quickly reverse. Economist Kenneth Rogoff worried that a large drop in the dollar would drive up interest rates as foreign investors would demand "higher returns to compensate for higher risks." The result could be a dramatic decline in the dollar and American GDP.

Economist Catherine Mann offered a third viewpoint. While concerned that the magnitude of current deficits, both that of the federal government and the trade deficit, seemed unsustainable, Ms. Mann was more optimistic that adjustment to more sustainable levels would be gradual rather than abrupt. She noted that much of the recent capital inflow had come from Asian central banks buying significant quantities of U.S. government securities. Much of this investment seemed aimed at stabilizing exchange rates to keep Asian exports competitive. Mann described these developments as one of "global co-dependency" and argued that a number of countries had a vested interest in preventing a sharp decline in the dollar. While there could easily be a decline in the dollar, Mann expected it to be an orderly decline and not "a panicky flight by foreign investors."

1. As this edition of the Study Guide was being prepared, the dollar had depreciated significantly against the euro, with the dollar price of a euro increasing from $0.90 in early 2002 to $1.30 in early 2005. There had been similar declines in the value of the dollar against the British pound and the Canadian dollar. Over the same period of time the exchange rate between the dollar and the Chinese yen had hardly changed. What has happened to the international value of the dollar since early 2005? Has the dollar continued to depreciate against European currencies? What about the exchange rate between the dollar and Asian currencies? Has any change in the value of the dollar been gradual or abrupt?

2. As noted in Chapter 19, it must always be true that $X - IM = (S - I) - (G - T)$. The implication of this expression is that any reduction in the trade deficit will require a combination of higher levels of domestic savings relative to domestic private investment or a smaller government deficit. What has happened to the trade deficit, domestic savings, domestic investment, and the deficit/surplus position of the federal government along with states and local governments?

The Federal Reserve Bank of St. Louis maintains an extensive online database for many economic time series, including exchange rates. You can access information on exchange rates at http://research.stlouisfed.org/fred2/categories/15 and information on national income accounts at http://research.stlouisfed.org/fred2/categories/18.

Sources: "The Dollar is Down: Is it a Cause for Concern?" Edmund L. Andrews, *The New York Times*, November 16, 2004.

You might also want to look at

- "Managing Exchange Rates: Achievement of Global Re-balancing or Evidence of Global Co-dependency?" Catherine L. Mann, *Business Economics*, July 2004.

- "America's current account deficit is not only sustainable, it is perfectly logical given the world's hunger for investment returns and dollar reserves," Richard Cooper, *The Financial Times*, November 1, 2004.

- "The U.S. deficit problem is not only a domestic issue, but a global concern and neither candidate has the answer," Maurice Obstfeld and Kenneth Rogoff, *The Financial Times*, November 1, 2004.

- "The disappearing dollar: How long can it remain the world's most important reserve currency?, " *The Economist*, December 2, 2004.

- "A Field Guide to the Falling Dollar, " *The New York Times*, December 5, 2004.

Study Questions

1. What is the difference between an open versus a closed economy?

2. How does an appreciation in the exchange rate affect net exports? What about a depreciation? Why?

3. How does a change in the exchange rate affect the aggregate demand curve? The aggregate supply curve? Which effect is likely to be larger?

4. Does an increase in interest rates lead to an appreciation or depreciation of the exchange rate? Why?

5. Consider a move to contractionary fiscal policy that reduces aggregate demand. What is the likely impact on interest rates, international capital flows, the exchange rate, and net exports? Do these changes tend to enhance or offset the original change in fiscal policy?

6. Consider a move to expansionary monetary policy that increases aggregate demand. What is the likely impact on interest rates, international capital flows, the exchange rate, and net exports? Do these changes enhance or offset the original change in monetary policy?

7. What is the link between government deficits and trade deficits? Under what conditions does an increase in the government deficit lead to an increase in the trade deficit?

8. What is your evaluation of the cumulative impact of American trade deficits since 1980?

9. Why isn't increased protectionism a surefire way to reduce the trade deficit?

10. Why didn't the large currency deprecations in Southeast Asia in 1997 and 1998 lead to expansions in output?

• Economics Online

The Organization for Economic Co-operation and Development (OECD) was originally composed of 20 or so European and North American industrialized economies plus Australia, Japan, and New Zealand. With changes in the world economy over the past 20 years, the OECD now describes itself as "30 member countries sharing a commitment to democratic government and the market economy." The OECD monitors economic trends and does comparative analysis of member countries. Its home-page can be found at

http://www.oecd.org

Statistics Netherlands maintains a set of Web links to statistical agencies for a number of countries. These links can be found at

http://www.cbs.nl/en-GB/default.htm?Languageswitch=on

What are current differences in interest rates in different countries? Bloomberg.com posts interest rate data for some of the world's largest economies at

http://www.bloomberg.com/markets/rates/index.html

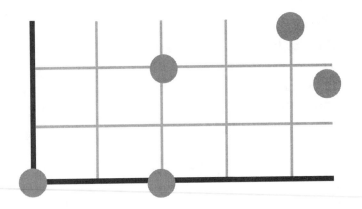

Answer Key

Chapter 1

Chapter Review

(1) information; value

Important Terms and Concepts Quiz

1. e
2. a
3. d
4. b
5. f

Basic Exercises

1. C
2. G
3. B
4. E
5. A
6. I
7. H
8. J
9. D
10. F

Self-Tests for Understanding

Test A

1. c
2. b
3. d
4. a
5. c
6. a
7. b
8. d
9. c
10. b

Test B

1. F
2. F
3. T
4. T
5. F
6. F
7. F
8. F
9. F
10. F
11. F
12. F
13. F
14. F
15. F
16. F
17. F
18. F

Appendix

Chapter Review

(1) horizontal; vertical; origin

(2) vertical; horizontal; constant; positive; up; negative; no

(3) ray; 45-degree

(4) tangent

(5) contour; production indifference

Important Terms and Concepts Quiz

1. d
2. h
3. g
4. b
5. f
6. c
7. e
8. i

Basic Exercises

1. a. 400
   b. increase; 800
   c. 600
   d. −50
   e. Slope equals vertical change divided by horizontal change or the change in salary divided by the change in the quantity demanded. The change in the number of new Ph.D. economists demanded as salary changes is equal to the reciprocal of the slope: The demand curve implies that a $1,000 increase in salary will reduce the quantity demanded by 20.

2. a. 4
   b. 5
   c. above
   d. non-economics

Self-Tests for Understanding: Appendix

Test A

1. b
2. b
3. c
4. d
5. a
6. a
7. c; a; b; d
8. A&E; C; B&D; none
9. d   slope = vertical change/ horizontal change; (16-10)/(5-8) = 6/-3 = -2
10. c
11. b
12. b
13. b
14. d
15. c
16. a
17. d
18. a   slope = 2/5 = 0.4
19. b
20. b

Test B

1. F
2. F
3. T
4. T
5. F
6. T
7. F
8. T
9. T
10. F

Chapter 2

Chapter Review

(1) domestic product; GDP; productivity

(2) inputs; outputs; free; private

(3) open; closed; closed

(4) recessions

(5) factors

(6) labor; 15 cents; service

(7) small

Important Terms and Concepts Quiz

1. h
2. i
3. a
4. f
5. e
6. g
7. d
8. j
9. b

Basic Exercises

1960: 13.1%; 46.1%; 40.9%

2007: 11.1%; 29.1%; 59.8%

1960: 52.2%; 0.9%; 20.6%; 7.5%; 18.9%

2007: 18.9%; 21.6%; 31.2%; 8.0%; 19.4%

Men: 29.1%; 55.2%; 78.7%; 92.2%; 92.3%; 88.2%; 69.6%; 20.5%

Women: 31.0%; 54.1%; 70.1%; 74.5%; 75.5%; 76.0%; 58.3%; 12.6%

Self-Tests for Understanding

Test A

1. a, d
2. c.
3. b, c
4. d
5. a
6. c
7. a
8. d

---

9. d
10. c
11. d
12. d
13. b
14. d
15. d
16. a
17. c
18. d
19. c
20. a

Test B

1. T
2. F
3. F
4. T
5. T
6. F
7. F
8. F
9. F
10. T

Chapter 3

Chapter Review

(1) scarce

(2) opportunity cost

(3) scarce; specialized; slope

(4) increase; increasing; specialized

(5) inside; inefficient,

(6) will

Important Terms and Concepts Quiz

1. f
2. k
3. m
4. h
5. a
6. g
7. l
8. j

---

9. e
10. c
11. d
12. i

Basic Exercise

1. 560,000; 40,000; rises; 120,000; continue to rise; specialized

2. Point A is not attainable; point B is attainable; point C is attainable; on and inside; on

3. Point B is inefficient. You should be able to shade a small triangular area above and to the right of point B out to and including a small segment of the PPF.

4. Without additional information about the preferences of the citizens of Adirondack one cannot determine which point on the production possibilities frontier is best for a country.

Self-Tests for Understanding

Test A

1. c
2. c
3. d
4. d
5. a
6. b
7. c
8. b
9. d
10. d
11. b
12. c
13. c
14. a
15. b
16. c
17. c
18. a
19. b
20. d

Test B

1. F
2. F
3. T
4. F
5. F
6. F
7. T
8. T
9. F
10. F

Supplementary Exercises

2. a. 300,000 cars (set T = 0); 1,000 tanks (set C = 0)

   c. Yes, it bows out.

   d. $1/2C^*$, $1/2T^*$ should be on straight line connecting C^* and T^*. Combination is attainable, lies inside frontier; inefficient, not on frontier as frontier bows out.

   e. 6 cars; 30 cars; 120 cars

   f. Opportunity cost = $(0.6)\,T$ cars; yes, opportunity cost increases as the production of tanks increases.

Chapter 4

Chapter Review

(1) price; negative; more; movement along; shift in

(2) price; positive; more; shift in

(3) demand

(4) $300; 4,000; less; 6,000; 2,000; surplus; reduction; shortage; demanded; supplied; increase

(5) intersection; equilibrium

(6) demand; supply; movement along; supply; demand; demand

(7) maximum; minimum; above

(8) hard; auxiliary restrictions

(9) shortages; decrease

(10) high

Important Terms and Concepts Quiz

1. f
2. e
3. g
4. c
5. m
6. k
7. i
8. q
9. o
10. p
11. n
12. h
13. a
14. j
15. b

Basic Exercises

1.

   b. 60; 1,100

   c. increased; 70; increased; 1,200; less

The impact of the change in price following the shift of the demand curve means that the change in the equilibrium quantity will be less than the horizontal shift in the demand curve.

   d. increase; decrease; 75; 1,100; less than

2. a. demand; right; rise; rise

   b. supply; right; fall; rise

   c. supply; left; rise; fall

   d. demand; left; fall; fall

3. a. 100; 100; neither, as ceiling exceeds equilibrium price

   b. 110; 80; shortage

Price ceilings lead to shortages when they are less than the free market equilibrium price.

   c. 90; 120; surplus

Price floors lead to surpluses when they are greater than the free market equilibrium price.

   d. 100; 100; neither, as floor is less than equilibrium price

Self-Tests for Understanding

Test A

1. c
2. a
3. d
4. c
5. c
6. b
7. a
8. a
9. d
10. b
11. c
12. a
13. b, d
14. b
15. b
16. c
17. b
18. a
19. d
20. b

Test B

1. F
2. T
3. T
4. F
5. F
6. T
7. T
8. F
9. F
10. F
11. T
12. F
13. T
14. F
15. F

Chapter 5

Chapter Review

(1) microeconomics; macroeconomics

(2) price; quantity; domestic product

(3) inflation; deflation; recessions; higher; higher; left; decrease; stagflation

(4) money; final; excludes; includes; are not

(5) nominal; real; Real; nominal; real

(6) is not; increase; decreasing; larger; lower

(7) up; depends; risen

(8) inflation; stabilization; recessions; inflation

Important Terms and Concepts Quiz

1. p
2. h
3. i
4. m
5. o
6. q
7. l
8. b
9. n
10. d
11. j
12. g
13. k
14. r
15. c
16. s
17. e
18. f

Basic Exercises

1. a. Panels c and d
   b. Panel b; yes, most notably 1929-1933, see Figure 22-6 in the text.
   c. Panel a
   d. Panel c
2. a. shift aggregate demand curve to left
   b. shift aggregate demand curve to right
   c. Real GDP will fall as aggregate demand curve is shifted to the left; prices will rise as aggregate demand curve is shifted to the right.
3. a. col (3) : $600; $300; $225; $1,125 col (6): $868; $416; $297; $1,581
   b. 40.5 percent
   c. $620; $320; $247.50; $1,187.50
   d. 5.56 percent
   e. The increase in real GDP is less than the increase in nominal GDP as the increase in nominal GDP includes both the increase in production and the increase in prices. The increase in real GDP is the better measure of the change in output.

Self-Tests for Understanding

Test A

1. b
2. d
3. a
4. c
5. a
6. b
7. a
8. a
9. c
10. d
11. d
12. b
13. a
14. d
15. d
16. b
17. d
18. c
19. c
20. b

Test B

1. F
2. T
3. F
4. T
5. F
6. F
7. T
8. T
9. T
10. T

Economics in Action

1. The NBER committee dated the end of the 1990's expansion, or the business cycle peak, as March 2001. The committee dated the end of the recession as November 2001.

Chapter 6

Chapter Review

(1) productivity

(2) more; more; demand; supply; right; increase

(3) is; 200

(4) potential; actual

(5) discouraged; decrease; understate; understate; overstate

(6) frictional; cyclical; structural

(7) frictional; increased; lower

(8) cannot; partial; some

(9) real; the same; as; were unchanged

(10)   different; less; more

(11)   higher; nominal; real

(12)   will; be unchanged; small; large; nominal

Important Terms and Concepts Quiz

1. a
2. t

3. r

4. k

5. c

6. q

7. b

8. v

9. e

10. h

11. j

12. n

13. i

14. d

15. p

16. m

17. o

18. l

19. f

20. s

Basic Exercises

1. a. $250,000; $5,250,000; $4,772,727; $5,750,000; $5,227,273. Borrowers gain at expense of lenders.

   b. $775,000; $5,775,000; $5,250,000; $5,225,000; $4,750,000. Both are treated equally.

   c. $1,000,000; $6,000,000; $5,454,545; $5,000,000; $4,545,455. Lenders gain at expense of borrowers.

2. a. 1.70; –1.81; –2.04; –3.00; –0.52; 5.98; 9.05; 5.11; 6.21; 5.53; 6.57; 1.47; 2.77; 4.39; 1.62; 3.95; 1.48; 1.01; 0.91; 4.64; 2.01; 3.77; 3.93; 1.82; 2.44; 4.00; –0.18; –0.45; –1.99

   c. When actual inflation turns out to be greater than expected, the difference between nominal interest rates that were set at the beginning of the period and the actual rate of

inflation may be negative.

3. 1.07; 1.09; 1.03; 1.24; 1.52; 1.52; 1.35; 1.24; 1.16; 1.12; 0.85; 0.84; 0.80; 0.82; 0.89; 0.84; 0.81; 0.77; 0.75; 0.75; 0.78; 0.77; 0.65; 0.70; 0.88; 0.82; 0.75; 0.86; 1.00 After adjusting for inflation unleaded gas prices were highest in 1980 and 1981.

Self-Tests for Understanding

Test A

1. d

2. a

3. c

4. c

5. b, a, d, c

6. a, b, d

7. a

8. c

9. b

10. b

11. a, d

12. c

13. b

14. b

15. c

16. b

17. b

18. a

19. a

20. c

Test B

1. F

2. T

3. F

4. F

5. F

6. F

7. F

8. F

9. F

10. T

Appendix

Important Terms and Concepts Quiz: Appendix

1. b

2. f

3. d

4. a Don't forget to multiply by 100.

5. c

Basic Exercises: Appendix

1. a. 2,500; 400

   b. $16,500 = 2,500 × $2.36 + 400 × $26.50

   c. 110 = (16,500/15,000) × 100

   e. 10 percent

   f. $15,771 ; 5.1 percent

2. 2004 index, using 2005 base, 91.1. 2005 base implies inflation of 9.8 percent. The slightly lower rate of inflation reflects a larger weight on more slowly rising clothing prices when using the 2005 expenditure pattern.

Supplementary Exercise

1. a and b. Insufficient information; for example, the value of the price index for Canada for 2004 shows how 2004 Canadian prices compare to Canadian prices in the base period, 1982–1984, not how Canadian prices compare to those in other countries.

   c. Inflation within a country can be measured by the percentage change in that country's price index. Italy had the most inflation; Germany had the least inflation.

2. 69,905; 119,246; 250,760

Chapter 7

Chapter Review

(1) growth; stabilization

(2) investment (or capital formation); innovation; invention; human

(3) convergence; innovate; imitate; rights

(4) low; are not; decrease

(5) investment

(6) goods; services

(7) cost disease

Important Terms and Concepts

1. h
2. a
3. b
4. e
5. k
6. l
7. d
8. m
9. j
10. i
11. g
12. c
13. n

Basic Exercises

1. a. 24.52
   b. 33.30
   c. No. labor productivity grows more slowly, but it continues to grow.
2. 1.4%: 200.4; 401.6
   2.5%: 343.7; 1,181.4
   2.9%: 438.4; 1,921.9

Test A

1. c
2. a
3. b, c
4. a, b, d
5. c
6. a

7. b
8. d
9. c
10. c
11. b
12. a
13. b, c
14. c
15. b
16. a
17. c
18. a, b
19. a
20. a, b, c

Test B

1. F
2. F
3. F
4. T
5. T
6. T
7. F
8. F
9. F
10. F

Supplementary exercise

6.211%; 4.084%; 36 years

Chapter 8

Chapter Review

(1) demand; consumption; investment; government; exports; imports; net exports

(2) before; taxes; transfer

(3) disposable; more; movement along; shift in

(4) *C*; *I*; *G*; *X*; *IM*; less; decrease

(5) increase; larger; more; smaller

Important Terms and Concepts Quiz

1. g
2. d
3. h

4. c
5. k
6. l
7. b
8. n
9. a
10. i
11. e
12. m
13. j

Basic Exercises

1. a. consumption spending; disposable income; .75;.75;.75;.75
   b. .9; .825; .8; .7875; .78
   c. No they are not. The MPC is the same at all levels of income. The APC falls as income rises.
   d. See diagram below
   e. slope of consumption function
   f. rays become less steep, that is their slope decreases. For a straight line consumption function with a positive Y intercept the APC will be greater than the MPC although the difference will get smaller as income increases.
2. a. $18,000; $78,000; $9,600,000
   b. .78; .9
   c. $21,750; $74,250; $9,600,000
   d. In this example, MPC is the same for the rich and poor. The rich reduce their consumption by the same amount that the poor increase their consumption.
3. *C* = 3,000 +.75 *DI*
4. a. 0.55/0.50 = 1.1
   b. The estimate in a is greater than the slope of the

consumption function. It overestimates the MPC because it includes the effect of the shift of the consumption function.

Self-Tests for Understanding

Test A

1. b
2. b
3. d
4. b
5. b
6. d
7. c
8. a
9. c
10. b
11. c
12. c
13. a
14. d
15. d
16. d
17. c
18. c
19. a
20. b

Test B

1. F
2. F
3. F
4. T
5. T
6. T
7. F
8. T
9. T
10. T

Appendix

Appendix Review

(1) final; produced

(2) exports; imports; produced

(3) income

(4) depreciation

(5) value added

Important Terms and Concepts Quiz: Appendix

1. a
2. b
3. c

Basic Exercises: Appendix

1. a. $2,200
   b. $1,700
   c. $1,700; wages = $1,200; profits $500
   d. $500
   e. $1,200 ($1,700 - $500)
   f. $1,700
   g. $1,700
   h. $1,700
2. a. $1,000; $2,100; $1,600; $4,700
   b. The $200 addition to inventories.

Self-Tests for Understanding: Appendix

Test A

1. c
2. c
3. b
4. c
5. a
6. d
7. d
8. b
9. c
10. d
11. b
12. d
13. c
14. c
15. a
16. d
17. c
18. c

Test B

1. F
2. T
3. F
4. F
5. F
6. T
7. F
8. F
9. F
10. T

Supplementary Exercise

1. MPC = $60/DI^{1/2}$; MPC declines as income rises. Consumption spending rises following redistribution from rich to poor as increase in consumption by poor is greater than decline in consumption by rich.

Chapter 9

Chapter Review

(1) increase; increasing; decrease

(2) equal to

(3) horizontal; vertical

(4) intersection

(5) less; reduce; increase; less; downward; lower; increase; increase; higher

(6) price level

(7) less; recessionary; inflationary

(8) autonomous; induced

(9) MPC

(10) income; MPC

(11) smaller; inflation; trade; income; financial

(12) do not; shift in; horizontal

Important Terms and Concepts Quiz

1. f
2. b
3. g
4. j
5. a
6. i
7. e
8. c
9. k
10. h
11. l
12. d

Basic Exercises

1. e. $10,000
   f. 9,600; 9,800; 10,000; 10,200; 10,400; 10,600; 10,800
   g. Spending would be greater than output, inventories would decline, firms would increase output.
   h. recessionary gap, 250; inflationary gap, $200

2. a. 9,700; 9,900; 10,100; 10,300; 10,500; 10,700; 10,900; equilibrium = 10,500
   b. 5; equilibrium level; GDP; autonomous spending
   c. 0.80
   d. 5 = 1/(1-0.8)
   e. 0.80; yes

3. b. 9,500
   c. 10,500
   d. aggregate demand curve
   e. negative

4. The increase in investment spending shifts the aggregate demand curve to the right. Points on the new aggregate demand curve include P = 90, Y = 11,000; P = 100, Y = 10,500; P = 110; Y = 10,000

Self-Tests for Understanding

Test A

1. c
2. c
3. a, c, d, e, g
4. c
5. d
6. c
7. a
8. b
9. c
10. a
11. a
12. c
13. b
14. a, b, c
15. c
16. b
17. d
18. c
19. a, c, e, g
20. c

21. c

22. b

23. b

24. a

Test B

1. T

2. F

3. F

4. T

5. T

6. F

7. T

8. F

9. F

10. F

11. T

12. T

13. T

14. T

Appendix A

Basic Exercise: Appendix A

1. $C = 340 + 0.8 (Y - T) = -1100 + 0.8 Y$

2. $C + I + G + (X - IM) = 2000 + 0.8 Y$

3. $Y = 2,000 + 0.8 Y$; $Y(1 - 0.8) = 2000$; $Y = 2000/(1-(1-0.8)) = 10,000$

4. $Y = 2,100 + .8 Y = 10,500$; Increase in $Y = 500$; Multiplier = 5 = 500/100

Appendix B

Basic Exercise: Appendix B

1. Total spending: 9,625; 9,812; 10,000; 10,287; 10,375; 10,562; 10,750; equilibrium = 10,000

2. Total spending: 9,750; 9,937; 10,125; 10,312; 10,500; 10,687; 10,875; equilibrium = 10,500

3. multiplier = 500/125 = 4

4. The multiplier is smaller because imports increase with income. The slope of the expenditure schedule = 375/500 = 0.75. Multiplier = 1/(1 - 0.75) = 1/0.25 = 4. Alternatively, MPC = 0.8 and the marginal propensity to import, MPI = 0.05. Multiplier = 1/(1 - MPC - MPI) = 1/(1 - 0.8 - 0.05) = 1/(1 – 0.75) = 1/(0.25) = 4.

Supplementary Exercises

1. a. $Y = C + I + G + (X - IM)$

   $Y = 340 + 0.8DI(-1) + 1,500 + 1,750 + (1,200 - 1,350)$

   $Y = 0.8Y[(-1) - 1,800] + 3,400$

   $Y = 0.8Y(-1) + 2,000$

   At equilibrium $Y = Y(-1)$:

   $Y = 0.75Y + 2,000$

   $0.25Y = 2,000$

   $Y = 10,000$

   b. Yes, the economy converges to a new equilibrium value of 10,500. The multiplier is 5 (= 500/100), the same multiplier we get from using the simple multiplier formula.

   c. The effects of changes in government spending and net exports will be similar to results in 1b, that is, the multiplier is 4, so for every dollar change in autonomous spending, equilibrium income will change by four dollars.

   d. If the MPC changes, the slope of the consumption function, and therefore the slope of the expenditure function, will change. If the MPC increases, then the consumption function and the expenditure schedule will be steeper.

An increase in the MPC will lead to an increase in the size of the multiplier.

Chapter 10

Chapter Review

(1) increase; movement along; shift in; right

(2) intersection; decrease; increases

(3) inflationary; inward; movement along; higher; lower

(4) recessionary

(5) inflationary; supply; falling; rising

Important Terms and Concepts Quiz

1. f

2. c

3. b

4. d

5. a

6. e

Basic Exercises

1. a. increases; increases; $10,250

   e. 95; $10,125

   f. Inflationary gap; increasing wages and other business costs will shift the aggregate supply curve up; 100 and $10,000

   g. no gaps

   h. recessionary gap; elimination of gap likely to be very slow; 90; $10,250

2. horizontal

   a. no

   b. Output and prices increase as the economy moves along the aggregate supply curve. The increase in prices reduces net exports and the purchasing power of money-fixed assets. The reduction in net exports and the resulting shift in the consumption function means a downward shift in the expenditure schedule (not drawn) that partially offsets the expansionary impact of the original increase in investment spending and reconciles equilibrium in the income-expenditure diagram with that of the aggregate demand-aggregate supply diagram (Y_2, P_2). That is, to complete the analysis one would need to draw a third expenditure schedule between the solid and dashed ones already shown in Figure 27-4. We know from the equilibrium determined in the aggregate demand-aggregate supply diagram that this final expenditure schedule will intersect the 45-degree line at a real GDP level of Y_2.

3. s to left, m, -, -; m, s up, -, +; s to right, m, +, +; m, s down, +, -; s to left, m, -, -; m, s up, -, +

Self-Tests for Understanding

Test A

1. b
2. b
3. a
4. d
5. a
6. c
7. a, b, c, d, e
8. a
9. d
10. c
11. d
12. a
13. c
14. b, d
15. a, b, d
16. c

17. c
18. c
19. d
20. c

Test B

1. T
2. T
3. T
4. T
5. T
6. F
7. T
8. T
9. F
10. F

Supplementary Exercises

1. $C + I + G + (X - IM) = 2,500 + .8Y - 5P$

2. $P = 500 - .04Y$ or $Y = 12,500 - 25P$

3. Solve the ADC and the ASC for the equilibrium levels of Y and P

    $12,500 - 25P = 7,750 + 25P$; $P=95$; $Y = 10,125$; $C = 7,022.5$; $I = 1,500$; $G = 1,800$; $X - IM = -197.5$

4. $P = 90$; $Y = 10,000$; $C = 6,945$; $I = 1,450$; $G = 1,800$; $X - IM = -195$

    New expenditure schedule:
    $C + I + G + (X - IM) = 2,450 + .8Y - 5P$

    New aggregate demand curve:
    $P = 490 - .04Y$

Chapter 11

Chapter Review

(1) fiscal; expenditure; demand; supply

(2) up; 1; 1

(3) are not; higher; permanent; less than; investment

(4) income; consumption; minus; plus; up; down

(5) less; smaller

(6) smaller

(7) MPC, smaller; smaller; flatter

(8) less than

(9) increase; decrease; decrease; increase

(10) supply; increase

Important Terms and Concepts Quiz

1. c
2. e
3. b
4. d

Basic Exercises

1. Total spending: 9,700; 9,850; 10,000; 10,150; 10,300; 10,450; 10,600; equilibrium = 10,000

2. Total spending: 9,500; 9,650; 9,800; 9,950; 10,100; 10,250; 10,400; equilibrium = 9,500

3. 2.5 = 500/200; in Chapter 26 the multiplier = 5. Multiplier is lower here because income taxes mean that each round of induced spending in the multiplier chain is smaller, hence the change in the equilibrium level of income is less.

4. 300 = 750/2.5

5. 9,500; the multipliers are the same.

Self-Tests for Understanding

Test A

1. c
2. d
3. b
4. c

5. c

6. c

7. c

8. b

9. a

10. d

11. a

12. b

13. a

14. a

15. c

16. b

17. c

18. c

19. c

20. b

Test B

1. F

2. T

3. F

4. F

5. F

6. F

7. F

8. T

9. F

10. F

Appendix A

1. $200; yes $\Delta C = 200 = 0.8 \times 250$

2. Total spending: 9,700; 9,850; 10,000; 10,150; 10,300; 10,450; 10,600; equilibrium = 10,000

3. No. The increase in GDP from the multiplier process increased tax revenues by $125, an amount less than the $250 reduction in taxes that initiated the multiplier process.

4. 11,000; 10,500; variable taxes reduce the slope of the expenditure schedule and hence the value of the multiplier for the economy.

Appendix B

1. $Y = 340 + 0.8 [Y – (–700 + 0.25) Y] + 1,500 + 1,750 – 150$

$Y = [1- 0.8 (1 - 0.25)] = 340 + 560 + 1,500 + 1,800 - 200$

$Y = 4,000 / 0.4 = 10,000$

2. No; Y = 3,990/0.4 = 9,975, the value of the expenditure multiplier is higher than the value of the tax multiplier.

3. 2.5; 2.5; 2.5; 2.0

4. Simultaneous reduction in G and T reduces Y to 9,950; multipliers = 5;5;5;and 4; with fixed taxes the slope of the expenditure schedule is steeper and multipliers are larger.

Supplementary Exercises

1. Income taxes are an important reason why Okun's multiplier is less than the oversimplified formula.

2. The multiplier for a change in taxes is less than the multiplier for changes in autonomous spending.

Chapter 12

Chapter Review

(1) barter; more difficult

(2) money; commodity; fiat

(3) M1; M2

(4) 1,338.8; 6,283.3

(5) lending; 900; reserve requirement

(6) 1/(reserve requirement)

(7) smaller; excess; smaller

(8) contraction; no

Important Terms and Concepts Quiz

1. c

2. j

3. g

4. m

5. m

6. d

7. t

8. n

9. s

10. k

11. o

12. e

13. f

14. p

15. w

16. v

17. u

18. b

19. r

20. l

21. h

22. q

23. a

24. i

Basic Exercises

1. $10,000; col. 1: $1,000; $9,000

2. col. 2: $1,000; $9,000; $10,000; $1,000; 0

3. col. 3: $9,000; 0; $9,000; $900; $8,100; $19,000

4. col. 4: $900; $8,100; $9,000; $900; 0

5. col. 5: $8,100; 0; $8,100; $810; $7,290; $27,100

6. B: $9,000; C: $8,100; D: $7,290; E: $6,561; 0.1; $100,000; required reserve ratio.

Self-Tests for Understanding

Test A

1. b
2. c
3. a
4. c
5. b, d
6. b
7. c
8. d
9. c
10. d
11. d
12. b
13. d
14. c
15. d
16. a
17. a
18. d
19. a
20. b

Test B

1. T
2. F
3. T
4. F
5. F
6. T
7. T
8. F

9. F
10. T

Supplementary Exercises

1. 2,500; 1,500
2. Change in deposits = (change in reserves) x $[1/(M + E + C)]$

Chapter 13

Chapter Review

(1) central; 12; Board; Governors; Federal Open Market; fiscal; monetary

(2) excess

(3) increase; discount rate

(4) securities; buys; increase; reduction; destruction

(5) federal funds; right; lower

(6) decrease

(7) supply; demand; shift in; shift in; demand; supply

Important Terms and Concepts Quiz

1. g
2. b
3. h
4. f
5. j
6. d
7. a
8. i
9. e

Basic Exercises

1. a. increase; right; decrease
   b. decrease; left; increase

Self-Tests for Understanding

Test A

1. b
2. d
3. d
4. c
5. b
6. b
7. c
8. b
9. d
10. c
11. c
12. d
13. b
14. b

15. b

16. a, c

17. a

18. a

19. a, d

20. b

Test B

1. T

2. F

3. F

4. F

5. F

6. F

7. F

8. T

9. T

10. T

Supplementary Exercises

1. a. $Y = 9,200$; $C = 6,050$; $I = 1,600$; $G = 1,500$; X-IM = -150

    b. Y increases to 9,400; C= 6,250; $I = 1,800$; $G = 1,600$; X-IM = -150

    c. In this model, equilibrium in the income-expenditure diagram depends on the rate of interest. The expenditure schedule is as follows:

    $C + I + G + (X - IM)$

    $= 1,550 + 0.6(5/6) \ Y + 2,000 - 50R + 1,500 - 150$

    $= 4,900 - 50R + .5Y$

    The 45-degree line is $C + I + G + (X - IM) = Y$. Solving these two equations for one expression in Y and R yields

    $Y = 9.800 - 100R$

    Setting the demand for bank reserves equal to supply of bank reserves yields a second expression in Y and R.

    $Y = 50OMO + 250R.$

Once the Fed determines OMO this equation along with the expenditure schedule can be used to find Y and R. When $OMO =$ 140, $R = 8$; $Y = 9,000$

    d. Now R is treated as known, $R = 4$, and one can use the two equations to solve for OMO and Y. OMO=168; Y = 9,400.

2. a. $1,500; $600

    b. $1,220.80; $698.87

Chapter 14

Chapter Review

(1) GDP; money

(2) nominal GDP; M; V; P, Y

(3) money; does not; nominal GDP; 200

(4) should not; increase; decrease

(5) velocity

(6) decline; increase; increase

(7) higher; increase; higher

(8) monetary; fiscal

(9) higher; higher; left; right

(10)   output; prices; steep; short; long

(11)   does not

Important Terms and Concepts Quiz

1. e

2. c

3. d

4. b

Basic Exercises

1. a. V_1: 6.50; 7.09; 7.72; 8.07; 8.35; 8.88; 8.93; 8.75; 8.77; 8.83

    V_2: 2.07; 2;10; 2;12; 2.08; 2.05; 2.05; 1.95; 1.87; 1.86; 1.88

    b. Estimates based on V_1: 7,166.4; 7,623.8; 8,369.1; 8,954.7; 9,234.2; 10,062.4; 10,705.6; 10,986.3; 11,643.5
    Estimates based on V_2: 7,728.6; 8,226.2; 8,904.4; 9,388.3; 9,831.3; 10,636.2; 10,968.8; 11,060.0; 11,564.0

    c. Errors are highest when velocity changes. The greater variation in V_1 leads to larger prediction errors based on M_1.

2. Each speaker is arguing that the demand for money has shifted to the right. In both cases the shift

is consistent with the reported increase in *M* and *r*.

Speaker A is arguing that the shift in the demand for money derives from an autonomous shift in the aggregate demand curve to the right. According to A, it is the increase in nominal GDP that has shifted the demand for money schedule. A shift of the money supply curve to the left, i.e., an open market sale, would increase interest rates even further, inducing an offsetting shift of the aggregate demand curve to the left. With a bit of luck, the policy induced shift of the aggregate demand curve to the left would offset the autonomous shift in the aggregate demand curve to the right, and there would be no inflation.

Speaker B is arguing that there has been an autonomous increase in the demand for money, that is an increase that is unrelated to any change in nominal GDP. If there is no offsetting increase in the supply of money schedule, the rise in interest rates will cause a decline in interest sensitive spending and a shift of the aggregate demand curve to the left increasing unemployment. In this case the appropriate action would be to shift the money supply curve to the right and hold interest rates constant to avoid inducing a shift in the aggregate demand curve.

The appropriate policy response, whether to focus on M or r, depends upon the origins of the shift in the demand for money.

Self-Tests for Understanding

Test A

1. c
2. b
3. a, b, c, d
4. a, b, d
5. c
6. a

7. d
8. d
9. b
10. c
11. d
12. c
13. a, b, c, d
14. b
15. b
16. a, b
17. a
18. b
19. d
20. c

Test B

1. T
2. F
3. F
4. T
5. T
6. T
7. F
8. T
9. T
10. F

Supplementary Exercise

NBER identifies a total of 9 recessions between 1950 and 2004. Based on the graph, you most likely found more than nine downturns in the stock market.

Chapter 15

Chapter Review

(1) spending; revenue; revenue; spending; deficit; surplus

(2) down; left; decline; decline; deficit; increase; decrease; accentuate

(3) will; will not

(4) increase; reduction

(5) monetized; greater

(6) foreigners; investment

(7) recession; war; crowding in; crowding out; high; out

(8) right; restrictive; deficit; higher; lower; more slowly

Important Terms and Concepts Quiz

1. d
2. a
3. h
4. c
5. f
6. g
7. e

Basic Exercises

1. a. Total spending: 10,200; 10,250; 10,300; 10,350; 10, 400; 10,450; 10,500; 10,550; 10, 600; equilibrium = 10,400

   b. Budget is balanced

   c. Surplus; 75

   d. Total spending: 10,100; 10,150; 10,200; 10,250; 10, 300; 10,350; 10,400; 10,450; 10, 500; equilibrium = 10,200; actual deficit increases to 50; structural surplus is unchanged at 75

   e. Total spending: 10,050; 10,100; 10,150; 10, 200; 10,250; 10,300; 10,350; 10, 400; 10, 450; equilibrium = 10,100; the reduction in government spending reduces GDP which reduces tax receipts; deficit declines but not to zero because the decline in GDP reduces taxes.

2. a. An open market sale would reduce bank reserves, increase interest rates, reduce investment spending and shift the aggregate demand curve to the left, offsetting the shift to the right from the reduction in taxes.

    b. Under option B the reduction in taxes will mean more consumption spending, while higher interest rates will reduce private investment spending. As a result, option B is likely to be associated with lower rates of economic growth.

Self-Tests for Understanding

Test A

1. d
2. d
3. a
4. c
5. c
6. a
7. a
8. c
9. b, c
10. b, c
11. d
12. c
13. d
14. c
15. a, b, c, d, e, f It all depends on why the deficit increased
16. d
17. d
18. b
19. a, b
20. d

Test B

1. F
2. F
3. F
4. T
5. T
6. F
7. F
8. T
9. T
10. T

Supplementary Exercises

1. It is important to distinguish between deficits during periods of recession and deficits from deliberate increases in G or reductions in T. All of the examples come from periods when the economy was falling into recession.

2. Repudiating the national debt would almost certainly make it more difficult to issue securities to finance deficit spending in the future. Once a nation defaults on its debt, investors are not likely to trust that it will keep its promise to make interest payments on debt in the future. As a result a country will need to pay higher interest rates to attract willing investors in the future.

Chapter 16

Chapter Review

(1) higher; lower; negatively; Phillips; negative

(2) incorrect

(3) inflationary; natural (or full-employment); vertical

(4) smaller; larger; higher; steeper

(5) vertical

(6) indexing

(7) increase; more

Important Terms and Concepts Quiz

1. a

2. g
3. c
4. b
5. e
6. f

Basic Exercise

1. purchase; decrease; increase; increase

2. 103

3. The aggregate supply curve will continue to shift up as long as output exceeds the full-employment level of output.

4. a. expansionary; 109

    b. restrictive; 10,167

Self-Tests for Understanding

Test A

1. d
2. d
3. a
4. d
5. c
6. a
7. a
8. c
9. a
10. c
11. d
12. a, c
13. d
14. b
15. d
16. c
17. d
18. a
19. c
20. d

Test B

1. F
2. F
3. T
4. T
5. T

6. F

7. T

8. F

9. F

10. F

Chapter 17

Chapter Review

(1) scale

(2) comparative

(3) A; B; 100,000; wheat

(4) 80,000; 70,000; cars; wheat

(5) tariffs; quotas; subsidies; price; quantity

(6) government

(7) low; do not; can

(8) adjustment

(9) defense; infant

(10) both; comparative

Important Terms and Concept Quiz

1. j

2. d

3. g

4. m

5. i

6. n

7. f

8. a

9. l

10. h

11. k

12. b

13. e

Basic Exercise

1. Japan; Japan

2. 1.25; 1.5; Canada; Japan; Canada; Japan

3. Calculators: 1,500,000; 3,000,000; 4,500,000

Backpacks: 1,200,000; 2,000,000; 3,200,000

4. 600,000; 480,000

5. 1,200,000 hours; 600,000 calculators; 400,000 backpacks

6. increase; 80,000

7. Calculators: 900,000; 3,675,000; 4,575,000

Backpacks: 1,680,000; 1,550,000; 3,230,000

The output of both calculators and backpacks has increased as compared to the initial situation in Question c.

8. Canadian backpack output would fall to 720,000. Japan would need to reallocate 1,440,000 labor hours. Total calculator output would fall to 4,380,000. This reallocation is not in line with the principle of comparative advantage.

9. There will be no change in total world output. Neither country has a comparative advantage. The opportunity cost of increased calculator or backpack production is the same in both countries.

Self-Tests for Understanding

Test A

1. b

2. d

3. b

4. d

5. a

6. b

7. d

8. d

9. a

10. a

11. c

12. a

13. a

14. b

15. c

16. c

17. d

18. c

19. b, d

20. c

Test B

1. F

2. F

3. T

4. T

5. F

6. F

7. T

8. F

9. F

10. F

Appendix

1. India: $10; 1,000 United States: $40; 800

2. $20; India: 800; 1,200: 400; 0

United States: 1,000; 600; 0; 400

3. India: 15; 900; 1,100; 200; 0

United States: 30; 900; 700; 0; 200

United States; India; United States; India

4. $15

Supplementary Exercises

1. a. Baulmovia: 8,100; Bilandia: 17,150

b. 12; Baulmovia; Bilandia; 100

c. Baulmovia: price = 10;

Bilandia: price = 14.5;

Trade = 50.

d. 50

Tariff revenues accrue to the government. Tariffs do not protect high-cost foreign producers.

2. a. Arcadia

b. Ricardia

c. Arcadia should increase the production of computers and export computers to Ricardia which should increase the production of cheese and export cheese to Arcadia. For example

Change in Production

	Computers	Cheese
Arcadia	+ 4	− 2
Ricardia	− 2	+ 4
World	+ 2	+ 2

Following the changes in production, both countries will be able to consume outside their PPF. If Arcadia exports up 3 computers for 3,000 pounds of cheese while Ricardia imports 3 computers for 3,000 pounds of cheese, both countries end up with 1 more computer and an additional 1000 pounds of cheese as compared to their pre-trade situation. Try locating these points of production and consumption to illustrate that adjustments of production in line with the law of comparative advantage allows both countries to consume outside their production possibilities frontier.

3. Production of 14.4 million bolts of cloth and 10.8 million barrels of wine allows Cimonoce to choose from the outermost consumption possibilities line. Note that to be on the outermost consumption possibilities line Cimonoce must choose to produce at the point where the slope of the production possibilities frontier equals the ratio of world prices.

Chapter 18

Chapter Review

(1) exchange; appreciated; fewer; depreciated

(2) demand; supply; exports; physical; financial; supply

(3) demand; increase; appreciation; supply; depreciation;

(4) purchasing power parity; depreciate; depreciation; appreciation; appreciating

(5) Bretton

(6) deficit; demand; supply; surplus;

(7) surplus; exchange rate

(8) buy; increasing

(9) deficit; increase; decrease; contraction; reduction

(10) speculators

(11) euro

Important Terms and Concepts Quiz

1. b
2. n
3. a
4. k
5. d
6. c
7. q
8. o
9. h
10. p
11. l
12. i
13. m
14. e
15. j
16. f

Basic Exercises

1. a. $14.40. Sales of French wine would increase. Sales of California wines would decrease. The U.S. balance of payments would show a deficit.

   b. $1.30; appreciation; depreciation

   c. United States (30 percent vs. 20 percent)

   d. deficit

   e. depreciate

2. Col. 1: $28,000,000; £10,000,000

   Col. 2: $28,000,000; £10,769,231

   Col. 3: $28,000,000; £11,666,667

   If there is no devaluation, you are out only the transactions costs. If the pound is devalued, you stand to make a handsome profit. As the prospect of devaluation increases, there is a greater incentive to sell your pounds before their price falls. Your efforts to sell pounds, along with similar actions by others, will only increase the pressure for devaluation.

   On November 18, 1967, the pound was devalued from $2.80 to $2.40.

3. a. left; right; depreciation; deficit

   b. right: no shift; appreciation; surplus

   c. left; no shift; deprecation; deficit

   d. left; right; depreciation; deficit

   e. no shift; right; depreciation; deficit.

Self-Tests for Understanding

Test A

1. b
2. c
3. c
4. b, c
5. a, c
6. c
7. b
8. b, d, f
9. f
10. b
11. c, possibly d
12. d
13. b
14. a

15. b

16. a

17. c, d

18. a, c, d

19. c

20. b

Test B

1. F

2. F

3. T

4. T

5. T

6. T

7. F

8. F

9. T

10. F

Supplementary Exercise

According to data from the IMF, world trade has grown more rapidly than world GDP since 1970, a period dominated by floating exchange rates among the worlds leading industrial countries. Since 1970, world output had grown at an annual rate of 3.7% while world trade has grown at an annual rate of 5.9%.

Chapter 19

Chapter Review

(1) closed; open

(2) decrease; are

(3) less; increase; decrease; decrease; increase; decrease; increase

(4) shift in; down; left

(5) less; downward; more; upward

(6) increase; appreciation

(7) decrease; up; right; appreciation; left; down; offset; lower; increase; offset

(8) appreciation; enhance

(9) decreased; increased

(10)   exports; lower

Important Terms and Concepts Quiz

1. d

2. f

3. c

4. a

5. e

Basic Exercises

1.   Appreciation: Exports decrease; Imports increase; Net exports decrease; Expenditure Schedule shifts down; Aggregate Demand Curve shifts to the left; Aggregate Supply Curve shifts down; Real GDP decreases; Price level decreases.

Depreciation: Exports increase; Imports decrease; Net exports increase; Expenditure Schedule shifts up; Aggregate Demand Curve shifts to the right; Aggregate Supply Curve shifts up; Real GDP increases; Price level increases.

2.   Decrease in G: Interest rate decreases; Exchange rate depreciates; GDP and price level up, which work to offset the initial impact of the decrease in G.

Decrease in Taxes: Interest rate increases; Exchange rate appreciates; GDP and price level down, which work to offset the initial impact of the increase in G.

Open Market Sale: Interest rate increases; Exchange rate appreciates; GDP and price level down, which work to enhance the initial impact of the open market sale.

Open Market Purchase: Interest rate decreases; Exchange rate depreciates; GDP and price level increase, which work to enhance the initial impact of the open market purchase.

3.   The impact of monetary policy is enhanced. The impact of fiscal policy is diminished.

Self-Tests for Understanding

Test A

1. c

2. b

3. b

4. a

5. a

6. c

7. c

8. d

9. a

10. b, d

11. b

12. c

13. c

14. b

15. a

16. c

17. b

18. a, c

19. c

20. b, c

Test B

1. F

2. F

3. F

4. T

5. T

6. T

7. F

8. F

9. F

10. F